125

45504

Rebirth of a Culture

REBIRTH OF A CULTURE

*Jewish Identity and Jewish Writing
in Germany and Austria Today*

Edited by

Hillary Hope Herzog,
Todd Herzog & Benjamin Lapp

Berghahn Books
New York • Oxford

First published in 2008 by

Berghahn Books
www.berghahnbooks.com

©2008 Hillary Hope Herzog, Todd Herzog, and Benjamin Lapp

Library of Congress Cataloging-in-Publication Data

Rebirth of a culture : Jewish identity and Jewish writing in Germany and Austria today / edited by
Hillary Hope Herzog, Todd Herzog & Benjamin Lapp.
    p. cm.
Includes index.
ISBN 978-1-84545-511-8 (hardback : alk. paper)
    1. German literature—Jewish authors—History and criticism.   2. German literature—21st
century—History and criticism.   3. Jews—Identity.   4. Jewish authors—Germany.   5. Jewish
authors—Austria.   I. Herzog, Hillary Hope.   II. Herzog, Todd.   III. Lapp, Benjamin, 1958–

PT169.R38 2008
830.9'3529240905--dc22   2008017384

British Library Cataloguing in Publication Data
A catalogue record for this book is available from the British Library

Printed in the United States on acid-free paper.

ISBN: 978-1-84545-511-8 hardback

CONTENTS

INTRODUCTION

Dagmar C. G. Lorenz

The collection of articles *Rebirth of a Culture: Jewish Identity and Jewish Writing in Germany and Austria Today* features Germanophone Jewish writing at the turn of the millennium and examines works by authors of different generations as well as larger cultural topics. Prominent survivors of the Nazi era such as Stefan Heym, George Tabori, Marcel Reich-Ranicki, and Ruth Kluger are discussed throughout the volume and in individual articles, as are major representatives of the post-Shoah generation including Lea Fleischmann, Ruth Beckermann, Barbara Honigmann, Esther Dischereit, Henryk Broder, Robert Schindel, Robert Menasse, and Rafael Seligmann and also authors born in the 1960s and 1970s, such as Maxim Biller and Doron Rabinovici. The volume explores cultural phenomena, individual texts, and the conditions from which specifically Jewish points of view and textual strategies emerged. Of particular interest are issues affecting late twentieth- and early twenty-first-century Germanophone Jewish writing, namely, transatlantic and global cross-fertilization as well as conflicts, intellectual debates that reach beyond the boundaries of German-speaking countries, and the position and status of Germanophone Jewish literature within and outside Germany and Austria.

The project *Rebirth of a Culture* had its beginnings in the four-week Summer Seminar *Boundaries Crossing Boundaries. Jewish Identity and Jewish Writing in German after 1980* at the Einstein Forum in Potsdam in July 2002, arranged through the Humanities Lab at the University of Illinois at Chicago and the German Academic Exchange Service (DAAD). Sander L. Gilman inspired, initiated, and organized the seminar, which I designed and taught. The seminar participants and contributors to the volume are bilingual and bicultural experts in Jewish cultural studies. They are affiliated with colleges and universities in the United States, Canada, and Great Britain, and bring to the topic a unique "transatlantic" perspective that informs their diverse critical approaches to post-Shoah culture and the "new" Germanophone Jewish culture within a larger international context. Original texts by literary authors who read from their works and gave presentations at the seminar are included in the volume as well. They provide the important dimension of the literary author and reveal that, in the field of German-Jewish literature and culture, an especially close connection exists between authors and critics and between literary and scholarly writing. Contemporary Jewish writers tend to participate in more than one genre. They respond to public debates with essays and polemics, write novels, short narrative prose, poetry, and dramas, and are active as filmmakers and critics.

Since 1945, Jewish writing in German has neither been possible nor imaginable without references to the Shoah. Only in the 1980s, after a period of mourning, silence, and processing the trauma, did a new Jewish literature evolve in Germany and Austria (Gilman and Remmler 1994). Even though the leading voices were those of children of survivors and exiles, representatives of previous generations took a major part in the new Jewish culture. Authors such as Hilde Spiel, Elias Canetti, and Friedrich Torberg kept the legacy of the interwar period alive and provided an intellectual continuity for younger authors, whom they inspired and mentored. Shoah survivors and exiles, whose careers began after the Holocaust, made important contributions to German and Austrian literature as well. Jakov Lind, Edgar Hilsenrath, and Erich Fried, to mention just a few representatives of this group, wrote about the Shoah for German and Austrian audiences hesitant to confront the past. They provided alternative and oppositional versions of the interwar period, the Shoah, and the Second World War, versions that question mainstream memory and historiography. In the 1960s, exile authors, who like the celebrated poet Hilde Domin, returned to the country of their youth, wrote about their experience. Domin revealed how her initial euphoria of seeing the places she once knew turned into disillusionment when she encountered anti-Semitism and the rise of rightwing extremism. In *Das zweite Paradies*, she documents the hostile public climate with excerpts from current newspapers. In her book, she revises the optimistic West German historical narrative about denazification and reconstruction. In a similar vein, the narratives of the Shoah generation revisited, as did Jurek Becker's *Jakob der Lügner* (Jacob the Liar, 1969), sites and events of the Shoah constructing a specifically Jewish point of view. Becker's later novels *Der Boxer* (The Boxer, 1976) and *Bronsteins Kinder* (Bronstein's Children, 1986) tell stories from Berlin during the postwar era and the Ulbricht era in the GDR from a critical Jewish perspective with a focus on the repression of Jewish culture in the socialist state.

The 1980s was a decade when the lingering controversies and debates about the legacy of the Nazi era, anti-Semitism, and Jewish identity came to a head. The relationship between children of Holocaust survivors and exiles and those of former Nazis and Nazi collaborators was at the core of the new culture of polemics and activism; the Second post-Shoah generation had come of age. These new debates set the stage for the conflicts at the beginning of the twenty-first century. In the 1980s, for the first time after the Shoah, Holocaust denial and anti-Semitic sentiments were openly expressed in public forums in Germany and Austria—and not only there. In German-speaking countries, Jewish intellectuals moved to the forefront of oppositional and anti-fascist writing and filmmaking to express their protest and continued to respond vigorously to the offensive discourse and misrepresentations of Jewish concerns. Against revisionist attempts to "normalize" the past and trivialize the genocide, they set their own views of history and society. Jewish oppositional voices articulated themselves in the interview projects undertaken by Henryk Broder, Michel Lang, and Peter Sichrovsky, and in autobiography and fiction chronicling the Jewish experience in Germany and Austria. They provided alternative perspectives to the mainstream narratives by following the example of earlier dissenters such as Hilsenrath and Lind. Likewise in the 1980s, Jewish writing became increasingly "gendered." Jewish women authors juxtaposed the male visions of the earlier decades with specifically female representations of the Shoah (Gerty Spies), of growing up Jewish in Germany and Austria (Ruth Beckermann), and of forging a Jewish woman's identity in and through the German language and culture (Barbara Honigmann).

In the 1990s, the focus of Jewish writing shifted toward exploring the mentality of the perpetrators and their attitudes after the Shoah. Authors such as Schindel and Rabinovici contrasted the experience of the German and Austrian mainstream with the Jewish experience. Ruth Beckermann's documentary film *Jenseits des Krieges* (East of War, 1997) is paradigmatic of the way post-Shoah Jewish intellectuals challenged the call of the non-Jewish public to let bygones be bygones by confronting members of the Nazi generations directly and personally. Beckermann conducted interviews with former members of the Nazi military at the controversial exhibit *Vernichtungskrieg. Verbrechen der Wehrmacht 1941–1944* (War of Elimination—Crimes of the Germany Military 1941–1944) and documented the denial on the part of veterans, their refusal to face the past, and the spreading of the attitudes of former Nazis to the following generations. At the turn of the millennium, Jewish writing shows an even broader, more comprehensive outlook. Some authors such as Barbara Honigmann and Robert Menasse include the Sephardic tradition in their writing. Others explore relationships between Jews and other minorities, for example Doron Rabinovici, or they situate the Jewish experience within a global context, as is the case in the works of Anna Mitgutsch, Vladimir Vertlib, Maxim Biller, Irina Liebmann, and Robert Menasse.

Immediately after the Holocaust, German Jewish writing still resounded with the ambiences and themes of earlier German literature, including the Enlightenment and Romanticism. It was not at all uncommon to call for a rational approach to the Shoah, even for reconciliation with the perpetrators. Reverence for the classical German heritage and the Humanistic tradition was common among older German and Austrian Jewish writers and scholars. Continuities between the emotional fervor of the Romantics, Expressionists, and the style of early post-Shoah literature can be observed as well. In order to come to terms with the horrific situation after 1945, some Jewish authors resorted to the familiar ideas and imagery of nineteenth- and early twentieth-century German and Austrian literature. Others tried to establish links with the Jewish tradition that had emerged in the late nineteenth century or in the fight against anti-Semitism and National Socialism to articulate specifically Jewish positions and forms of expression. Within societies that discouraged an open confrontation with the Nazi past, including information and discussions about the Holocaust and the destroyed Jewish culture, establishing a post-Shoah Jewish identity was a difficult proposition. Critics, publishers, and the mainstream readership resisted attempts on the part of Jewish authors to reveal and discuss the past in their writings and to commemorate the Holocaust. Edgar Hilsenrath's novel *Nacht*, for example, was repressed by its publisher (Moeller 1994). In a hostile climate, it was easy for Jewish writers initially intent on telling their stories to become discouraged. Some stopped publishing altogether, turned to different topics, or wrote only indirectly about the Shoah.

In the 1980s, younger Jewish authors issued harsh criticism of German and Austrian post-Shoah reality, for example, Lea Fleischmann in her account of leaving the Federal Republic, *Dies ist nicht mein Land* (This is not my Country), and Henryk Broder in the introduction to her book. The feature film *Kieselsteine* (Pebbles) by the Czech-Austrian filmmaker Nadja Seelich explored relationships between Jews and Austrians in Vienna and recorded the shocking naiveté with which non-Jews perpetuate anti-Semitic and racist stereotypes and cling to the residues of Nazi ideology. The public debates of the decade included the Bitburg controversy occasioned by US President Reagan's visit at a German military and SS-cemetery, and the scandal involving the planned staging of Rainer Werner Fassbinder's play *Der Müll, die Stadt und der Tod* (Garbage, the City, and Death), both in 1985. The latter involved charges of anti-Semitism and the defamation of Ignatz Bubis, a leading figure in the *Zentralrat* of Jews in Germany. This controversy was followed in 1986 by the Austrian Waldheim scandal over the election of former UN Secretary Kurt Waldheim to the office of president despite revelations about his membership in special Nazi units on the Balkans. The year 1987 marked the Historian's Debate stirred by historical revisionism on the part of conservative historians such as Ernst Nolte. In Germany, the debates reached their apex with the unification in 1989 and they continued into the 1990s. In 1996,

Daniel Goldhagen's study, *Hitler's Willing Executioners: Ordinary Germans and the Holocaust*, about atrocities committed by the *Wehrmacht*, the regular German military, and Goldhagen's concept of German eliminationist anti-Semitism motivated an international debate questioning German claims that the Nazi crimes had been condoned by only a small part of the population and that the perpetrators were the exception: radicals and party operatives. In 1998, the Walser-Bubis debate followed, sparked by a speech of the prominent writer Martin Walser, who trivialized the significance of the Holocaust and termed the recurring reminders of the Nazi past an assault on German integrity. Likewise in the 1990s, Austria's political right wing party, the so-called Freedom Party, celebrated unprecedented successes, and oppositional activities increased proportionately. Prominent Jewish and Jewish-identified authors such as Doron Rabinovici and Elfriede Jelinek played a key role in the anti-racist activities and publications in Austria. The coalition government of the conservatives and the Freedom Party formed in 2000 elicited widespread protest. It is obvious that in the last decades of the twentieth century, Germanophone Jewish literature has become increasingly political and activist, responding to domestic and international political and social issues. These included the Gulf wars, the political struggle in Sri Lanka, and Arab-Israeli relations. Jewish writing has furthermore thematized the "memorialization" of the Holocaust exemplified by the Jewish museums in Berlin and Vienna, Holocaust memorials, and the nostalgic revival of pre-Shoah Eastern European culture in German-speaking countries. It has addressed the German, Israeli, and American Jewish dialogue and other global aspects of contemporary Jewish culture, taken up gender issues, and explored the topic of crime and the criminal, including terrorism and international spy networks before the background of the state-sanctioned crimes of the Nazi era. German- and Austrian-Jewish writing at the turn of the millennium is local and global, aware of the interconnectedness of Jewish concerns and world history.

The public debates and the responses of Jewish intellectuals at the turn of the millennium reveal that the Shoah and the Nazi past continue to influence the sense of Jewish and non-Jewish identity in German-speaking countries. There is still a perception of separate histories, Jewish and "German," as analyzed by Dan Diner in "Negative Symbiosis." The struggles as to how the past is to be remembered, who is to record German and Austrian history, and in which way, have not been laid to rest, as historical reassessments such as Rabinovici's *Instanzen der Ohnmacht* (Agencies of Powerlessness) reveal. The Shoah and the National Socialist past are highly sensitive issues that involve memory, identity, and history as well as legal issues, property rights, and claims for restitution, not only for the second post-Shoah generation, but for the third and fourth generations as well.

Looking at the beginning of a new millennium as a cultural and literary caesura may seem arbitrary. However, as far as Jewish culture, identity, and writing in German-speaking countries are concerned, such a division makes sense. More than half a century has passed since the Shoah, the "destruction of the European Jews," was compellingly analyzed by Raul Hilberg and other scholars. The generations of the Holocaust survivors and exiles have become almost extinct, and the children of survivors and exiles who in the 1980s began new Jewish cultural and literary initiatives are being challenged by younger intellectuals and by writers and critics from different cultural spheres, not excluding the powerful Hollywood film industry and international media as well as the worldwide web. After German unification and the restructuring of the Eastern Block countries, Jews took advantage of the new opportunities available to them and left Eastern Europe, most notably the former Soviet Union. They moved not only to Israel and the United States, but also to Germany and Austria where they have a major impact on Jewish life and culture. In 2003, the United Press International reported that Germany was the nation with the fastest growing Jewish community in the world. According to the report, as the result of this accelerating migration, the Jewish population in Germany increased from 15,000 at the end of the Second World War to 33,000 in 1990, the year of German unification, and to 100,000 in 2004 (Netto 2003). A point has been reached where the German government is beginning to consider measures to stop the influx of Jewish migrants, most of whom are coming from the "lower socio-economic rungs" (Lamb 2004). Many immigrants do not join the established congregations in Germany and Austria, but consider themselves culturally Jewish. Because of Austria's political situation—growing conservatism and restrictive immigration politics—Ariel Muzicant, the President of the Vienna Jewish community (IKG), expressed concern about the shrinking of the contemporary Austrian-Jewish community (Axelrod 2002). The vast majority of Austrian Jews live in Vienna. In 2002, the community estimated that between 7,000 and 8,000 members lived in Austria, consisting primarily of Holocaust survivors and their descendents, returning Austrian expatriates, and immigrants from Eastern Europe and Iran. Clearly, the conditions under which Germanophone Jewish authors live, write, and produce are changing, and the beginning of a new millennium is bringing new concerns and perspectives.

The sense of transition is reflected in the topical and contemporary emphasis of *Rebirth of a Culture*. The four sections of the volume draw attention to important aspects of Jewish literary and cultural expression. "German-Jewish Writing and Culture Today" is devoted to continuities, new beginnings, and reevaluations of texts and authors; "The Case of Austria" appropriately singles out Austria because of the recent controversies as well as the impressive range of the Jewish literary and critical production; "Transatlantic Relationships" explores the interrelationship between Germanophone Jewish writing and international events and literary movements and initiatives; while, finally, the interviews and original texts in "Jewish Writers in Germany and Austria" introduce important contemporary authors in their own words.

Within all of the sections, historical perspectives arise. This is the case in Cathy S. Gelbin's chapter exploring the use of the Golem myth in contemporary Jewish writing, "The Monster Returns: Golem Figures in the Writings of Benjamin Stein, Esther Dischereit, and Doron Rabinovici." Gelbin examines the function of the Cabbala-inspired literary trope of the artificial human in the works of Stein, Dischereit, and Rabinovici before the background of Christian and Jewish traditions. The Golem and the associated figures of Rabbi Loew and Emperor Rudolf captured the imagination of Christian and Jewish authors. Gelbin reviews different configurations of the Golem motif prior to the Shoah, noting that in the German tradition it assumed anti-Semitic meaning as a trope of Otherness, as for example in Wegener's silent film. The Golem's popularity during transitional periods suggests that contemporary Jewish writers also use the trope to characterize their era as a time of change. Gelbin maintains that for them, the Golem denotes both a critical reassessment of the pre-Shoah tradition and a proclamation of cultural continuity, of having survived. With reference to the devaluation of Jewish culture on the historic territory of the Shoah in the United States and Israel, Gelbin concludes that the Golem character in German-Jewish texts signifies a utopian vision of healing and unity of the Jewish people across the globe.

Petra Fachinger's chapter, "Hybridity, Intermarriage, and the (Negative) German-Jewish Symbiosis," analyses the representation of relationships between Jews and Germans. Fachinger focuses on Austrian-Jewish and German-Jewish publications by four writers born after World War II, Peter Henisch's *Steins Paranoia* (Stone's Paranoia), Lena Kugler's *Wie viele Züge* (How Many Trains), Anna Mitgutsch's *Abschied von Jerusalem* (Lover, Traitor), and Lothar Schöne's *Das Jüdische Begräbnis* (Jewish Funeral). Traditionally, marriage and intimate encounters between Jews and non-Jews were used by authors such as Schnitzler, Torberg, and Feuchtwanger as a commentary on the relationship between the dominant culture and the Jewish minority. Fachinger reveals that in contemporary Jewish writing, this is still the case. However, for non-Jewish authors this theme is of relatively small significance, she writes. This is why she includes two exceptional texts by non-Jewish authors in her analysis: Zafer Şenocak's *Gefährliche Verwandtschaft* (Dangerous Relatives) and Anja Tuckermann's *Die Haut retten* (Saving One's Skin).

With an eye on Dan Diner's concept of the negative German-Jewish symbiosis, Fachinger concludes that in the last two decades of the twentieth century, the representation of cross-cultural relationships has undergone decisive changes. She reads the Austrian-Jewish texts as rather optimistic—they imply that eventually it will be possible to overcome the rift between Austrian Gentiles and Jews. Even the more ambivalent Austrian texts do not suggest a national trend, Fachinger writes, because they show intimate relationships between Jews and non-Jews that have the potential to succeed. According to Fachinger, the increasingly transnational perspectives and contacts have a transformative effect on the German/Austrian-Jewish condition. A "cultural third" represented by the United States, Israel, Eastern Europe or Turkey provides the necessary impetus to disrupt the polarity of the "negative symbiosis." Hybridity, Fachinger maintains, seems to create a new dynamic that calls for a sense of self-definition beyond ethnicity and nationality in German-speaking countries and makes it possible to think in terms of multiple identity.

"A Political Tevye? Yiddish Literature and the Novels of Stefan Heym," by Richard Bodek, provides a much needed reassessment of one of the most important German-Jewish authors whose career began in the pre-Shoah era. On the basis of painstaking historical research, Bodek argues that Heym's reputation as a Socialist ideologue and the resulting negative memory was confirmed in disparaging but incorrect evaluations and obituaries. Bodek uses as his most striking example the obituary in *The New York Times* that seems to aim at "Heym's demonization." He identifies oblique insults, half truths, and allusions that turned Heym into "that most despicable of figures, the hypocritical, high-living, communist." As a corrective, Bodek traces Heym's career and analyzes his works in the context of the historical situation at the time of their publication. He convincingly shows that Heym was an anti-fascist ill-disposed toward authoritarianism, and later ranked among the GDR's foremost critical intellectuals. While in exile in the United States, Heym exposed Nazi depravity and brutality, and he discussed the psychological pressure brought to bear upon opponents of the Nazi regime. Bodek also discusses Heym's critical attitude toward the victorious Western Allies in the early phase of the occupation of Germany. He convincingly argues that Heym's skepticism eventually included Eastern Bloc politics and the GDR regime. He concludes that throughout his career, Heym was "deeply committed to humanity." In that respect, he terms him a "Scholem Aleichem for the twentieth century." Bodek's fundamental reassessment of an important leftist intellectual associated with the GDR points toward a task for the future: to review Socialist authors and intellectual life and achievement within the repressive GDR system.

Roland Dollinger's chapter, "Anti-Semitism *because of* Auschwitz: An Introduction to the Works of Henryk M. Broder," examines the contributions of one of Germany's most insightful and controversial critics, the filmmaker, journalist, and author Henryk Broder. With a focus on the legacy of the Shoah and aspects of Jewish intellectual life in contemporary Germany, Broder, who is known for tackling highly sensitive issues, is notorious for evoking passionate reactions in the German public. Dollinger traces Broder's career from the much debated early essay, "Why I would rather not be a Jew, and if absolutely necessary then preferably not in Germany," to his later publications, including *Der ewige Antisemit* (The Eternal Anti-Semite) and *Ich liebe Karstadt und andere Lobreden* (I Love Karstadt and Other Eulogies), and *Die Irren von Zion* (The Idiots of Zion). Broder's personal and intellectual development reveals the identity conflicts of a

German-speaking secular Jew. For Broder, who in the 1980s had left the Federal Republic to live in Israel, the Israeli/Palestinian conflict and religious fundamentalism became increasingly problematic. He came to describe his position as that of "a cultural outsider, who keeps his distance to both the German and Jewish establishment." Dollinger argues that this position apart from the German as well as the Israeli mainstream enabled Broder to recognize the absurdities of either sphere, including the lucrative "Shoah" business and the politics of memory in Germany and the United States.

Dollinger documents the correlation between Broder's work on the anti-Semitic "anti-Zionism" proclaimed by seemingly divergent "progressive" movements such as the New Left and the Peace Movement, and the author's critical assessment of the symbolic resistance to National Socialism by Germans born after the Shoah. Clearly, Germans of different political orientation instrumentalize the memory of the murdered Jews to justify attacks on the Jewish State and pro-Israeli sympathizers. In his discussion of Martin Walser's polemic novel *Tod eines Kritikers* (Death of a Critic), Dollinger argues that anti-Semitism continues to be a powerful force in Germany. He credits Broder for convincingly recording and astutely analyzing anti-Semitic sentiments and incidents in Germany that occurred since the 1970s as a larger international phenomenon.

Margy Gerber begins her examination one of the most thought-provoking novels of recent years in "'What once was, will always be possible': The Echoes of History in Robert Menasse's *Die Vertreibung aus der Hölle*," with a question of genre and classification. Indeed, Menasse's monumental suprahistorical novel calls to mind the great works of Thomas Mann, Heimito von Doderer, and Robert Musil, and it is intriguing to speculate whether his literary tour de force through the centuries is primarily a historical discourse, a modern or a postmodern novel, or something entirely different. Gerber correctly surmises that Menasse wants to have it both ways: like a postmodern, he rejects the notion of telos, but he also opposes postmodern relativism. The two life stories in *Vertreibung aus der Hölle* (The Expulsion from Hell) and the lack of an authorial voice call for multiple interpretations and constructions of the past, Gerber argues. Yet, she concedes, the historian Menasse also looks for patterns and meaning in history.

According to Gerber, Menasse deviates from traditional models of history, including Hegel's idealistic *Geschichtsphilosophie* and Marx's Dialectical Materialism. Rather, Menasse introduces a notion of the regressiveness of history that corresponds to the critical revision of the dialectic model by Horkheimer and Adorno. Having his novel begin at the time of the Spanish Inquisition—seen as the catalyst of Enlightenment—and having it end in his own era, Menasse encases, so to speak, Enlightenment history, its beginnings, its apex, and its decline. Within this framework he focuses on Jewish characters, notably Manasseh and Spinoza, who survived the horrors of the Inquisition and "yearned for a societal system based on reason and rationality." The end point of Menasse's novel is marked by the bankruptcy of the Enlightenment under National Socialism, which is constructed as "a repeat of the Spanish Inquisition with greater technical sophistication." However, Gerber argues, Menasse sees no new Enlightenment after the horrors of the Nazi era. Instead, the novel culminates in the complete discrediting of reason and rationality after the Shoah.

"The Global and the Local in Ruth Beckermann's Films and Writings" is an astute analysis by Hillary Hope Herzog of the works of the prominent critic and filmmaker Ruth Beckermann. In the Austrian context, Herzog writes, city writing plays a greater role than in Germany, especially among Jewish writers. This is not surprising in view of the fact that Vienna is Austria's major urban center and the former capital of the Austro-Hungarian Empire to which Jews came from all parts of the multi-national monarchy. Indeed, for most Jewish writers of the post-Shoah generation, Vienna serves as a more powerful referent than Austria, and their sense of identity is derived primarily from Vienna as a traditionally Jewish site. In her analysis of Beckermann's essay *Unzugehörig* (Not Belonging) and the film *Die papierene Brücke* (The Paper Bridge), Herzog shows how intimately Beckermann's representation of the Jewish postwar experience is linked to the larger framework of central European Jewish history.

Referring to a paradigmatic statement by Beckermann that reveals the filmmaker's attachment to her native city, Herzog discusses the profound attachment of Viennese Jews for "their" city. Yet she cautions that in the imagination of Beckermann and other Austrian Jewish authors, Vienna figures as a tenuous space intimately linked to the Jewish past. Moreover, she suggests that the attachment Beckermann and other authors (Hilde Spiel and Ilse Aichinger could be mentioned as well) have expressly involves Vienna, its streets, buildings, and its geographical setting rather than the people of Vienna. This makes for an uneasy experience, which, Herzog explains, is captured in the image of a Viennese café patronized by the filmmaker and other Jewish authors in Beckermann's film *Die papierene Brücke*. The windows of the café look out at a statue of Karl Lueger, who became mayor of Vienna on a populist anti-Semitic platform. Rather than avoiding this site, Herzog notes, Austrian-Jewish writers "have carved a place for themselves alongside it, where it stands as a reminder they seem to welcome, *unheimlich heimisch* in their Vienna."

Beckermann's recent highly personal film *homemad(e)* focuses on the filmmaker's own Viennese neighborhood. The Jewish and liberal intellectuals featured in the film experience the familiar environment with a sense of alienation because they cannot feel a part of the broader community where every third Austrian and every fourth Viennese voted for Haider. The election results and the protest movement against the right-of-center coalition government are major concerns in the discussions captured in the film. Herzog emphasizes the sense of vulnerability that permeates the home environment of the residents of Beckermann's street and the traditional Jewish Salzgries neighborhood. In contrast to the situation of German writers, Herzog argues, the sense of being threatened is especially acute for Austrian-Jewish authors such as Beckermann, Rabinovici, Schindel, and Menasse, because they consider Vienna their home and make it the focus of their work.

"The Holocaust Survivor as *Germanist*: Marcel Reich-Ranicki and Ruth Kluger," by Benjamin Lapp, takes up an intriguing topic: the fact that Jewish survivors placed German culture and literature at the center of their professional lives. In addition to the prominent personalities Lapp discusses, others come to mind as well: Hans Weigel and Hermann Hakel, who were mentors to countless postwar writers, Theodor W. Adorno and Hans Mayer, who returned from exile to Germany, Oskar Seidlin, Egon Schwarz, Dorrit Cohn, Guy Stern, and many other *Germanists* in the United States. The fact that Jewish German authors and intellectuals such as Elias Canetti, Ernst Waldinger, and Berthold Viertel felt a responsibility toward the German language and the future of German culture, despite the experience of being persecuted and expelled, indeed deserves attention. Lapp focuses on two important memoirs, those of Kluger and Reich-Ranicki, two members of the "second generation" of German-speaking Jews. He writes that Reich-Ranicki's *Mein Leben* (The Author Himself) and Kluger's *weiter leben* (Still Alive) reflect upon the end of the German-Jewish *Bildungsbürgertum*, the educated middle class, and the Holocaust, which marked the end of that tradition. Both survivors come from this social group and seek, according to Lapp, "some sort of dialogue with the Germans," perhaps even with the Germans representing what is left of their parents' class of academics and professionals, many of whom ended up supporting National Socialism. Even though an unproblematic identification with German culture and *Bildung* are impossible for any Holocaust survivor, the language and concepts of the Humanistic tradition continued to resonate with the Jewish survivors, because they identified with the values of the German and Austrian middle class. Observing the critic and philosopher Jean Améry (Hanns Maier) and his complete break with the history of assimilation, Lapp shows that the issue of German-Jewish identity is a highly personal and complex one. Similar to Hans Weigel and his positive statements about Austria, Reich-Ranicki expressed in his memoir a passion for German literature and culture. More cautious than Reich-Ranicki, Kluger also reestablished connections with German culture. However, she did so in Germany rather than in her native Austria, thereby retaining the sense of distance that Austrians feel toward Germany and the Germans.

Lapp problematizes Kluger's and Reich-Ranicki's relationship with Germany by referring to Geoffrey Hartman, who asserted that despite the cultural destruction wrought by the Nazis, Germany's contributions to art suggest "the possibility of hope." Lapp believes that the participation of the two authors in contemporary German culture reveals an interest on their part to "preserve and redeem the humanistic elements of the German cultural tradition." At the same time, he observes a difference in the two authors' engagement with Germanophone culture. Reich-Ranicki takes an ongoing and highly visible part in the German media, while Kluger participates from a distance, retaining California as her base. Neither Kluger's nor Reich-Ranicki's involvement with contemporary German culture is based on a false sense of harmony. Mindful of the National Socialist past and the genocide, both intellectuals refrain from calling Germany or Austria their "homeland." They make no attempt to assimilate themselves into the dominant culture, but seek to create opportunities for debate and discussion.

Iris Bruce's chapter, "Transatlantic Solitudes: Canadian-Jewish and German-Jewish Writers in Dialogue with Kafka," opens new perspectives on the past and across the Atlantic through a gendered analysis of images of Jews in Germany and Canada. Bruce begins by examining the legacy of Kafka among Canadian- and German-Jewish authors. She reveals connections deriving from the common reception of this path-breaking Jewish author by Anglophone and Germanophone authors. With a focus on Montréal, Bruce explores the conditions from which Canadian-Jewish writing emerged, namely, within a multi-cultural urban French and Anglophone setting. Among the writers under discussion are the pre-Shoah author A.M. Klein, and younger authors such as Leonard Cohen, Régine Robin, Irena Eisler, and Gabrielle Goliger. In the case of poet, singer, and songwriter Cohen, the relationship is quite mutual: Cohen visited Vienna frequently and poets such as Ilse Aichinger refer to him. It is impossible to overestimate the impact of Kafka on European postwar literature. Bruce observes that Kafka also played an important role in the process of identity construction in the second and third generations, for example, in Rabinovici's novel *Suche nach M.* (The Search for M.) Reestablishing a post-Shoah Jewish identity is also a major issue in *The Second Scroll* by the Canadian novelist A.M. Klein. Bruce maintains that Klein constructs Jewish male identity in rather traditional terms. In contrast, Cohen's approach is postmodern and questions dominant cultural and gender constructs and proposes images of the "New Jew," "the founder of Magic Canada, Magic French Québec, and Magic Canada . . . queer, militant, invisible, part of a possible new tribe." Contrary to him, Bruce holds, German male authors lack ironic distance, particularly when regarding the Jewish male. She juxtaposes male Jewish authors with Canadian women writers who functionalize Kafka's solitude as emblematic of their own situation. Whether they seek "admittance to the Castle on the hill," reconciliation after the Shoah, or attempt to construct a new identity, their works have, according to Bruce, the closest affinity to Germanophone Jewish writing, notably authors such as Rabinovici.

Todd Herzog explores another transatlantic relationship—that between German and US authors—in "A German-Jewish-American Dialogue? Literary Encounters between German Jews and Americans in the 1990s." He opens with a critique of Rothschild's review of Rabinovici's *Ohnehin* (Nonetheless), a novel thematizing memory after the Shoah. The reemerging memory of a Nazi perpetrator and the possibility he might disclose in his old age what he kept silent throughout the previous decades presents Rabinovici's protagonists with a host of problems—some of them want disclosures to be made, others want to avoid them. Herzog dismisses Rothschild's assumption that Rabinovici and other German-Jewish authors are attributed an undeserved importance at American universities. Rather, he argues, their topics are of intrinsic interest to readers in the United States. He then proceeds to problematize the reemergence of Germanophone Jewish literary culture in Central Europe, aptly pointing out that the strongest creative impulses for these authors came from the United States, rather than from pre-Shoah German-Jewish writing. Hence, the space and the concept of America have come to play a central role in their works. In this context, Herzog discusses Ganzfried's *Der Absender* (The Sender), Barbara Honigmann's *Eine Liebe aus nichts* (A Love Made Out of Nothing) as well as Dische's and Biller's short prose, which moves "fluidly between American and German locations and even identities." He also examines the attempts of the protagonist in Seligmann's *Der Milchmann* (The Milkman) to get an American audience interested in a film project he wishes to undertake. In these and other works, Herzog writes, the importance of American Jewish literature for German-Jewish writing is obvious.

Yet, Herzog reveals, the position of German-Jewish authors in the US and in Germany is problematic. American critics and authors viewed Germany and Austria as inauthentic spaces for post-Shoah Jewish life. German critics, on the other hand, consider the United States a space of inauthenticity as well, but for different reasons. They criticize Germanophone Jewish authors for failing to establish continuity with the Jewish pre-Shoah tradition and authors such as Heine and Kafka. Discounting the most extreme views, Herzog notes that the reception of contemporary German-Jewish literature in America is limited. However, he sees signs of a beginning transatlantic interest. Because Americans have been suspicious of German-Jewish writing and therefore kept a distance from it, there is now much room for romanticization. For German-Jewish writers, America still represents a space of unlimited possibilities, while, in turn, German-Jewish culture for American audiences has assumed an aura of cosmopolitanism.

The last four contributions introduce the authors Barbara Honigmann, Esther Dischereit, Jeannette Lander, and Doron Rabinovici in their own words. Bettina Brandt interviewed Barbara Honigmann in "'Attempts to Read the World': An Interview with Writer Barbara Honigmann"; Esther Dischereit provides her perceptions of living as a Jew among German non-Jews in an original literary text "Behind the Tränenpalast"; Jeannette Lander, in "Germans Are Least Willing to Forgive Those Who Forgive Them: A Case Study of Myself," discusses representative works of her oeuvre as she surveys her career as a Germanophone author born in the United States; and Doron Rabinovici, in "Mischmasch and Mélange," reflects upon his development as an Israeli-born writer and public intellectual in Austria.

Each of the contributions touches upon recurrent themes in the biographies and writings of Jewish writers in Germany and Austria, including issues of multiple identity, memory, and the tenuous relationships with the dominant culture, which is far from casual or normal. Most striking, however, are the widely varying solutions and the ways in which these writers position themselves within today's German and Austrian intellectual culture.

Honigmann moved from the German Democratic Republic to France, leaving the world of East German theater to live as a member of the Jewish community in Strasbourg. Living in France with the goal of establishing for herself a Jewish way of life, Honigmann nonetheless continued writing in German for Germanophone audiences. She expresses her sense of identity with great clarity when she states: "Well, I am quite simply not French. I am German, German without a doubt, and there is nothing to be done about that either. I am *profondément* not a French woman." At the same time, she admits that her knowledge about Germany is limited, probably because "her" Germany was the GDR, and she allows a certain nostalgia to surface when writing about East German culture. Honigmann's statements about modesty, her learning about the Jewish tradition and studying Scripture, and the description of her circle of friends reveal that she embarked deliberately on a project of shaping and changing herself. However, she is aware that the transformation is ultimately incomplete: within her community she is "not at all the writer," because the writer would be of no interest in that context. Yet, she is a writer, a prominent Jewish-German writer, who decided to explore her Jewish identity and in the process had to negotiate multiple identities. Honigmann is aware of the divergence between secular literature, especially German literature, and religious Judaism. However, she also senses that her preoccupation with texts, religious and secular, may ultimately help her to overcome the rift between the different aspects of her existence.

Esther Dischereit's short narrative "Behind the Tränenpalast" evokes certain Berlin locations—Berlin is the city with which the author is identified. The mother-daughter story reveals the ever present presence of the past in a post-Shoah setting. The motif of the star, in this text connected with Israel, calls to mind the Jewish Star of the Nazi era as well as the star as a Zionist symbol. Both signify aspects of Jewish identity, one calling to mind the Shoah and Jewish victimhood, the other associated with Jewish resistance and victory. Dischereit is uncomfortable with both. She sketches situations that go to the core of German-Jewish identity and evoke dissonant feelings and carry different associations for the Jewish and the non-Jewish characters. When the non-Jewish Ann gives her son a Jewish name, wears a T-shirt with a Star of David, which she brought from a trip to Israel, and gives identical shirts to the Jewish speaker and her daughter, she seemingly does so naively and with the best intentions. However, the Jewish narrator and her child are incapable of wearing these shirts. For the narrator, choosing a name for her daughter was a highly complicated matter in Germany.

The text reveals furthermore that the German language itself is laden with anti-Semitic expressions. Anti-Semitism is already deliberately expressed among schoolchildren and affects the speaker and her child profoundly.

The use of the words "Jude" (Jew) or "jüdisch" (Jewish) throughout the text is striking. It calls attention to the anxiety the word evokes in the Jewish speaker and to the fact that these words, which were taboo in the postwar era, are also emotionally charged for non-Jews. In addition, there are other terms alluding to events and locations that call to mind Jewish history and the genocide: "Scheune" (barn) evokes the Scheunenviertel, the Berlin Jewish immigrant quarter and site of a pogrom in 1923. The German Shepherd dog by the entrance of a theater calls to mind the dogs of the SS used to torment Jewish prisoners. Dischereit's narrator is mortified when she sees the animal. Throughout the text, there is no indication of a merging of Jewish and non-Jewish points of view. The members of the minority are expected to keep their memories and feelings to themselves and repress any misgivings the insensitivity and insults on the part of the non-Jews may evoke. Members of the dominant culture do not seem to find it necessary to examine their words and actions, according to the text, and expect minorities to accommodate them in every way.

Jeannette Lander's "Germans Are Least Willing to Forgive Those who Forgive Them: A Case Study of Myself" surveys the author's life and writing since she came to Berlin as a young American Jewish wife to join her German husband. The innocence and optimism Lander brought to Germany were lost as she was drawn into the German language and culture. This process is illustrated by her writing, which began with multilingual texts—English, German, and Black English in *Ein Sommer in der Woche der Itke K* (A Summer in the Week of Itke K.)—and ended with masterpieces of German high culture—*Jahrhundert der Herren* (Century of the Masters). In spite of her growing disillusionment with post-Shoah Germany, Lander refuses to take a victim role. She emphasizes that her special position of detachment allows her to keep her mind open and her spirit free, and that it enables her to cross borders and boundaries "completely without luggage." Indeed, not being born in the lands of the Holocaust, Lander's presentation reveals, helped her to live in Germany among Germans. She also credits her background and experience for making her aware of problems associated with American culture, especially at the time of the Vietnam War when the image of the United States had reached a low point. However, toward the end of her essay, she discloses that the Shoah and issues of guilt and responsibility have become increasingly important to her—even a Jewish daughter of a nation of liberators had to ask herself upon meeting individual Germans, "how the person in question had acted under Hitler, how he had stood then and how he stood now regarding the extermination of the Jews." Conversely, she asks of the Jews, who in her mind went to the slaughter virtually without resistance, "What kind of people are we that we could do this? . . . I want to know why we marched into the gas chambers." For Lander, the world is not divided into categories of good and evil, but rather consists of a complex, hard-to-assess reality that defies solutions and unequivocal answers.

Doron Rabinovici's "Mischmasch and Mélange" is set in Vienna, the cradle of modern anti-Semitism and Zionism, and heir to unresolved issues and an unresolved history. Reviewing a class photo, Rabinovici's narrator becomes aware of the difference he always sensed between himself and his fellow Austrian students. He recalls that he went through a period of adjustment after leaving Israel and coming to Austria. He remembers his disappointment over the peculiar mentality of his new classmates. Learning German and establishing a relationship with the new language as a tool of orientation were essential processes helping him to cope with the unfamiliar environment. Rabinovici reveals that the necessity of expressing his Jewish experience caused him to develop a multiple identity, Jewish, Israeli, and Austrian, a speaker of German and Ivrit.

Introducing new and reexamining already recognized authors, embarking upon new discussions and identifying new areas of inquiry, *Jewish Identity and Jewish Writing in Germany and Austria Today* opens new vistas and charts new territory in the field of Jewish cultural studies. Reaching beyond familiar boundaries into transnational contexts, this collection of articles makes a scholarly contribution to debates introducing a new phase of Germanophone Jewish writing and culture.

Works Cited

Beckermann, Ruth. Dir. *Jenseits des Krieges*. Wien: filmladen 1997. Also: *Jenseits des Krieges*. Wien: Döcker Verlag, 1998.

———. *Unzugehörig*. Wien: Lücker, 1989.

Becker, Jurek. *Jakob der Lügner*. Frankfurt: Suhrkamp, 1969.

———. *Der Boxer*. Frankfurt: Suhrkamp, 1976.

———. *Bronsteins Kinder*. Frankfurt: Suhrkamp, 1986.

Broder, Henryk and Michel Lang, eds. *Fremd im eigenen Land*. Frankfurt: Fischer, 1979.

Bunzl, Matti. "Counter Memory and Modes of Resistance: The Uses of Fin-de-Siecle Vienna for Present-Day Austrian Jews." *Transforming the Center, Eroding the Margins. Essays on Ethnic and Cultural Boundaries in German-Speaking Countries*. Eds. Dagmar C. G. Lorenz and Renate S. Posthofen. Columbia: Camden House, 1998. 169–184.

Diner, Dan. "Negative Symbiosis: Germans and Jews after Auschwitz." *Reworking the Past: Hitler, the Holocaust, and the Historians' Debate*. Ed. Peter Baldwin. Boston: Beacon Press, 1990. 251–61.

Domin, Hilde. *Das zweite Paradies. Ein Roman in Segmenten*. Munich: Piper, 1968.

Fassbinder, Rainer Werner. *Der Müll, die Stadt und der Tod*. Frankfurt: Verlag der Autoren, 1981.

Fleischmann, Lea. *Dies ist nicht mein Land: eine Jüdin verläßt die Bundesrepublik*. Hamburg: Hoffman und Campe, 1980.

Gilman, Sander L. and Jack David Zipes, eds. *Yale Companion to Jewish Writing and Thought in German Culture*. New Haven: Yale University Press, 1997.

———. *Jews in Today's German Culture*. Bloomington: Indiana University Press, 1995.

Gilman, Sander L., Jack David Zipes, and Karen Remmler, eds. *Reemerging Jewish Culture in German Life and Literature since 1989*. New York: New York University Press, 1994.

Goldhagen, Daniel. *Hitler's Willing Executioners. Ordinary Germans and the Holocaust*. New York: Knopf, 1996.

Hilberg, Raul. *The Destruction of the European Jews*. Chicago: Quadrangle Books, 1961.

Hilsenrath, Edgar. *Der Nazi und der Friseur*. Cologne: Literarischer Verlag Braun, 1977.

———. *Nacht*. Frankfurt: Fischer, 1980. [Munich: Kindler, 1964.]

Honigmann, Barbara. *Roman von einem Kinde*. Darmstadt: Luchterhand, 1986.

Huyssen, Andreas. *Twilight Memories: Marking Time in a Culture of Amnesia*. New York: Routledge, 1995.

Lind, Jakov. *Eine Seele aus Holz*. Neuwied: Luchterhand, 1962.

Mayer, Hans. *Der Turm von Babel. Erinnerung an eine Deutsche Demokratische Republik*. Frankfurt: Suhrkamp, 1991.

Moeller, Susann. "Politics to Pulp a Novel: The Fate of the First Edition of Edgar Hilsenrath's *Nacht*." *Insiders and Outsiders. Jewish and Gentile Culture in Germany and Austria*. Eds. Dagmar C.G. Lorenz and Gabriele Weinberger. Detroit: Wayne State University Press, 1994. 224–234.

Morris, Leslie and Karen Remmler. *Contemporary Jewish Writing in Germany. An Anthology*. Lincoln: University of Nebraska Press, 2002.

Rabinovici, Doron. *Instanzen der Ohnmacht. Wien 1938–1945. Der Weg zum Judenrat*. Frankfurt am Main: Jüdischer Vlg., 2000.

———. *Suche nach M*. Frankfurt: Suhrkamp, 1997.

Rapaport, Lynn. *Jews in Germany after the Holocaust: Memory, Identity, and Jewish-German Relations*. Cambridge: Cambridge UP, 1997.

Schedel, Angelika. "Nachwort." In *Der Fund*. Munich: Hanser, 2001. 309–324.

Schindel, Robert. *Gebürtig*. Frankfurt am Main: Suhrkamp, 1992.

Seelich, Nadja script; Stepanik, Lukas dir. *Kieselsteine*. Wien: cinéart, Filmverleih Hans Peter Hofmann, 1982.

Seghers, Anna. *Der Ausflug der toten Mädchen*. New York: Aurora, 1946.

———. *Die Toten bleiben jung*. Berlin: Luchterhand, 1962.

Sichvorsky, Peter, ed. *Wir wissen nicht, was morgen wird, wir wissen wohl was gestern war. Junge Juden in Deutschland und Österreich*. Köln: Kiepenheuer & Witsch, 1985.

Spies, Gerty. *Drei Jahre Theresienstadt*. Munich: Kaiser, 1984.

Thalberg, Hans. *Von der Kunst, Österreicher zu sein*. Vienna: Böhlau, 1984.

Weigel, Hans. *Man kann nicht ruhig darüber reden: Umkreisung eines fatalen Themas*. Graz: Styria, 1986.

Part I

GERMAN-JEWISH WRITING AND CULTURE TODAY

THE MONSTER RETURNS

Golem Figures in the Writings of Benjamin Stein,
Esther Dischereit, and Doron Rabinovici

Cathy S. Gelbin

For two centuries, the Golem, a literary trope inspired by the Cabbalah that in turn took its cues from the Hebrew Bible and the Talmud, has enjoyed heightened popularity during periods of major historical junctures and shifting social constellations. Its recent revival in the work of young Jewish writers signifies the second generation's step into the cultural limelight and, indeed, a wider Jewish renewal occurring alongside the shifting political, economic, and cultural constellations in post–1989 Europe.

A figure from Jewish tradition seized upon by Christian German writers and subsequently adopted by their Jewish counterparts, the Golem has long embodied the ambivalent in- and outside perspectives on Jews in the German-speaking lands. Reports of a Polish-Jewish folk tale featuring an ever-growing Golem first reached a German-speaking audience in 1714 with Johann Jacob Schudt's book *Jüdische Merkwürdigkeiten* (Jewish Oddities) (Goodman-Thau 1999: 105f.). Schudt's version was adopted by Jakob Grimm (1869) in 1808, followed by Achim von Arnim's (1997) version in 1812, and E.T.A. Hoffmann's (1996) literary renditions, first published in 1822. The emergence of the Golem as a literary trope representing the 'Otherness' of the Jew indicates the contemporaneous anxiety about Jewish emancipation when Prussian Jews briefly won citizenship rights in 1812.

By the early twentieth century, the Golem had metamorphosed into a figure of haunted memory. These associations were shaped largely by Annette von Droste-Hülshoff's poem "Die Golems" (The Golems, 1976; first published in 1844) and culminated in Gustav Meyrink's surrealist novel *Der Golem* (The Golem, Meyrink, 2000; first published in 1915). The historical and discursive junctures of the early twentieth century, with its clashing of Jewish assimilation and growing anti-Semitism, spawned a number of Golem renditions and related figures (Demetz 1994), including Max Brod's *Tycho Brahes Weg zu Gott* (Brahes Path to God, 1915), Paul Wegener's film *Der Golem, wie er in die Welt kam* (The Golem: How He Came Into the World, 1920), and Fritz Lang's *Metropolis* (1927).

Jewish writers during the first two decades after the Shoah adopted the Golem's association with haunted memory, a tradition shaped by non-Jewish authors Droste-Hülshoff and Meyrink. As Dagmar Lorenz (1998) has shown, Leo Perutz (2000; first published in 1953), Frank Zwillinger (1973), and Friedrich Torberg (1977; first published in 1968) seized upon the tropes of the Golem and its creator, the Maharal (Rabbi Löw), in order to commemorate the destroyed pre-war Jewish life and the Shoah itself.

The multiple signification of the Golem as a Jewish figure of ethics and resistance, and a Christian image of the uncanny Jew, infuse the rewriting of this trope by second generation authors such as Benjamin Stein (1998), Esther Dischereit (1996), and Doron Rabinovici (1999). In their writings, the Golem returns as a figure of rupture, memory, and renewal, representing both the crimes of the Shoah and the powerful reemergence of German-speaking Jewish culture since the 1980s.

Benjamin Stein, *Das Alphabet des Juda Liva*

Benjamin Stein's novel *Das Alphabet des Juda Liva* (The Alphabet of Juda Liva, 1998), first published in 1995, employs the Golem to portray the disenchantment of the second East German-Jewish generation, with its parents' communist ideals from the 1980s onward. Stein rewrites the historical figures of the false seventeenth century Messiah Shabbatai Zvi and his prophet Nathan of Gaza into the hilarious tale of young Alexander Rottenstein and the mysterious Jacoby alias Nathan ben Gazi. Based on the recordings of the latter, the novel's narrator charts Rottenstein's mystical transformation from young East Berlin "Goi" to Shabbatai Zvi *Beth* (Number Two) via Berlin, Prague, Budapest, Jerusalem, and back. The narrator's presentation of his story in the shape of a mosaic mirrors Rottenstein's genealogical technique piecemeal and forces the reader to 'repair' the disjointed narrative, translating the Jewish imperative of *tikkun* into the acts of storytelling and reading.

Gershom Scholem has described the mystical experience as essentially uncertain and inarticulate (Scholem 1973: 19), characteristics that also mark the Cabbalistic Golem. The Golem is neither human, animal, nor dead matter. It silently hovers in between life and death, for only the first letter of the Hebrew word inscribed on its amulet, *emeth* (truth), separates it from the word *met* (death). These mystical meanings of the Golem set in motion Rottenstein's spiritual transformation through his encounters with the Golem in the Prague of in 1987 and 1991.

The protagonist's surreal awakening as the Messiah, set in Prague and propelled by the threshold figure of the Golem, invokes and inverts the animal symbolism of Kafka's "*Die Verwandlung*" (The Metamorphosis, 1995b). Where, as Ritchie Robertson argues, Kafka's 'hybrid' beetle represents the individual disintegration of the assimilating Western Jew (Robertson 1885: 189f.), Stein's Golem signifies the protagonist's disavowal of assimilation and his reassertion of a traditional Jewish identity. In the Golem, Rottenstein perceives his *Gestalt* in the Cabbalistic sense, reflecting both his base self in the material world and his mystical potential. Stein's construction of the Golem as an adolescent, at age twelve on the cusp of a boy's religious initiation into Judaism through the Bar Mitzvah, reflects Rottenstein's yet unevolved ethical and spiritual self as conditioned by assimilation.

The figure twelve also symbolizes the abandonment of Judaism by Rottenstein's great-great grandfather Salomon in the novel's second book, entitled "*Die zwölf Einfachen oder Vom Bruch der Gefäße*" (The Twelve Basics or The Crack in the Vessels) and the turn of the following three generations of his family to communism. Drawing on the Cabbalistic belief that twelve letters of the Hebrew alphabet symbolize base human preoccupations, such as sex, anger, and sleep, Stein configures assimilation as a false ideal ultimately leading to the fires of the Shoah. However, capitalism does not seem to pose any alternatives, as the consumerism brought to post-socialist Prague by fun-seeking Western youths merely appears as the last manifestation of the 'real' world. It is this realm of the 'real' that Rottenstein must overcome to bring on *tikkun*, the messianic repair of the broken vessels of divine light.

The threshold aspect of the android signifies the political transitions occurring between Rottenstein's two encounters with the Golem, but also signifies his schism as "the most Jewish goy the world had ever seen" (Stein 1995: 249). Rottenstein's ruptured Jewish genealogy causes his disregard as a "German goy" (Stein 1995: 249) by Jacoby, and indeed by rabbinic law, yet plays an important part in the novel's mystical scheme of redemption. Cabbalism placed great emphasis on the flawed origins of the Messiah, believing either that the Messiah would be reincarnated from the sinner Adam through David to his current manifestation, or even appear as a new soul not circulated through previous Jewish generations (Scholem 1977: 211 and 201).

While challenging the prevailing insistence on ethnic and religious homogeneity in traditional Jewish communities, Stein's construction of a 'hybrid' Messiah falls back on the negative inscription of ethnic, cultural, and religious boundary crossings often associated with the Golem. Where Arnim's female Golem is created in the image of the Dutch 'Gypsy' Isabella to destroy the latter's liaison with a virtuous Christian, Hoffmann's *Die Geheimnisse* (The Secrets) casts a cunning, button-animated Cabbalist and his android remake of a Greek-German Baron as the negative aspects of a hybridized 'Orient.' Meyrink's Golem reflects the physical, moral, and sexual corruption of the former Jewish quarter's mixed population, while Wegener's film Golem poses the destructive potential of Christian-Jewish sexual and cultural encounters (Gelbin 2003).

In line with the frequent association of 'racial hybridity' with sexual transgression (Braun 1995), the Golem also betrays Rottenstein's sexual misdemeanors. Although Scholem rejects this connotation (Scholem 1973: 212), the term Golem has been translated as "embryo," perhaps owing to its original meaning as "shapeless mass" (Gesenius 1962: 142). By embodying both Alex's sinful wasting of his seed twelve years ago and the aborted child he unknowingly fathered as an adult, the Golem stands for the novel's construction of unrestrained masculinity as a sign of flawed human nature. For in the 'real' world, the text's men abuse and forsake the women who love them, a chain of betrayals leading to the violent destruction of Rottenstein and his male predecessors.

In contrast, the novel's major female characters, the Angel of Death and the Fire Angels Miriam, Lydia, and Eva, figure as the earthly manifestation of a higher symbolic. At the same time, the female principle is absent from the male-dominated world above, a construction reminding of traditional Judaism's casting of female figures as mediators between the male God and the sons of Israel. The Cabbalistic book of the *Sohar* thus imagined the Torah as a woman wooing the mystic before disappearing to her hiding place. However, Stein's supernatural female figures, with their sublime and destructive implications, also reiterate the notion of the both benevolent and punishing *Shekhinah*, God's female aspect that followed the Jews into exile.

Stein's gendered representation of the worlds below and above conveys the traditional Jewish elevation of the masculine to the higher symbolic, which the feminine merely mediates or represents in its negative aspects. Female figures operating on the realm of the symbolic are destructive or catalyze the transformation of Rottenstein's unethical male nature, without themselves entering the realm of the divine. The Golem ultimately represents the overcoming of the female principle of exile that alienates the sons of Israel from their male God, with the fires of the Shoah—symbolized in the Angel of Death's garden of ash—problematically configured as the divine punishment for the vice of assimilation.

Esther Dischereit, *Als mir mein Golem öffnete*

In contrast to Stein, Dischereit's rewriting of the Golem tradition emphasizes the irrevocable disruption of genealogies and cultural traditions through the Shoah. Her volume of poetry, *Als mir mein Golem öffnete* (When My Golem Opened Itself to Me, 1996), throws into relief the question of Jewish existence after the Shoah along the lines of Gershom Scholem's observation that the Golem signifies the collective experience of the Jewish people (Scholem 1973: 259). At the same time, Dischereit employs this figure to postulate the particularities of female Jewish identity (see also Shedletzky 1998).

Since its arrival in the literary arena, the Golem has repeatedly symbolized the interplay between gendered and Jewish subjectivities, beginning with its first literary appearance in Arnim's *Isabella von Ägypten*. Dischereit's volume contributes to a body of texts produced mainly by women authors working in the North American and British contexts, such as Marge Piercy's *He, She and It* (1991), Ellen Galford's *The Dyke and the Dybbuk* (1993), and Cynthia Ozick's 1997 *Puttermesser Papers* (2000). These novels equally invoke the Golem tradition to portray the shifting constellations of Jewish, gender, and sexual identities during the late twentieth century. The heterogeneous figure of the Golem enables these writers to negotiate multiple alterities within a Jewish collective that takes its central signifiers from the European-Jewish experience.

While Dischereit insists on the particularities of female Jewish subjectivities, she also points out the limitations of gender discourses in the face of the Shoah, which targeted the Jewish people in its entirety:

> The genocide against the Jews should have been spoken of as the murder of millions of *Jewesses* and Jews. Although we were all women, we Jewesses could not free ourselves from this linguistic correctness because in the face of Nazi racial politics any distinction between the genders was razed. It was of no concern for the killers whether one was a man or a woman. . . . We were Jews, had always been Jews as those before us had also always been Jews. It seemed to us as if the tenuous bond that connected us to our parents and grandparents and the unknown others would be broken to serve another purpose. (Dischereit 1999: 240–41)

Dischereit's insistence on the absence of gender distinctions during the Shoah must be read as a strategic rejection of feminist attempts to gender the Nazis' victims. Joan Ringelheim in particular (1992) has argued that while the Shoah targeted European Jewry in its entirety for death, the exploitation of young Jewish men as slave laborers enabled the latter to survive longer. In contrast, Jewish women—especially those with young children—were usually sent to the gas chambers immediately upon their arrival at extermination camps. A member of the tiny remnant of Jews in postwar Germany, Dischereit confronts the notion that gender mattered during the Shoah. Through the Golem, she instead foregrounds the collective Jewish experience of persecution and annihilation in order to construct a fragile bond both with the generations lost in the Shoah and the surviving remainder.

While Dischereit's poetry rejects the possibility of reappropriating prewar Jewish traditions, the Golem as a symbol of destruction allows her to position her own writing within a ruptured tradition of Jewish poetry in the German language. As her work insists, writing in the language of the genocide requires a mode of discourse that exposes the irrevocable ruptures caused by the Shoah. The second generation may practice Jewish ritual as a form of cultural resistance against the continuing fear of annihilation: "Übe das Tales tragen / [. . .] / schütze dich vor der Hand, die über die Buchstaben streicht" (Dischereit 1996: 10), yet these gestures remain hollow, for "Niemand kann sich den G'tt / wie ein Bonbonglas kaufen" (Id.).

In the first poem, the lyrical narrator encounters the Golem as the embodied memory of the Shoah: "Ich saß / vor deiner Tür / als mir mein Golem / öffnete" (Dischereit 1996: 5). In the second line, however, the lyrical narrator obviously changes into the perspective of this Golem, who is destroyed by an anonymous other: "führte mich / abseits / und strich / mir die Zeile / aus" (Dischereit 1996: 5). This seems to refer to the lyrical addressee who sweeps dust—obviously the remains of the Golem—at the end of the poem. Dischereit's production of grammatical uncertainties and the many line breaks of her poems leading to heterogeneous significations reflect the rupture of language and meaning through the Golem's destruction as a metaphor for the Shoah.

The ambiguous signification of the Golem as the source of destruction and its victim suggests an annihilation from within, paralleling the rise of the genocide from the very culture in which German-speaking Jews partook. The lyrical addressee thus represents the German's betrayal of the prewar Jewish dream of the "German-Jewish symbiosis" and, in her radical disappearance from the second line of the poem, the impossibility of dialogue across the divides of the genocide. Dischereit's imagery in this poem cites the rich and diverse associations of the literary Golem tropes, such as with Droste-Hülshoff's and Meyrink's construction of the Golem as an uncanny *doppelgänger* of memory.

However, Dischereit also evokes the Jewish icons of poetry after the Shoah that continue to shape the German imagination of Jewish culture. In Nelly Sachs's poem "Golem Tod" (Golem Death), first published in her 1949 volume *Sternverdunkelung*, the Golem represents the Jews' adversary, as well as the indestructibility and sanctity of the Jewish people. Sachs's Golem ultimately serves to integrate adversary—the skeleton that opens its arms "mit falschem Segen"— and victim—God's lost bride of Israel—into a scheme of divine redemption, for "nicht kann Geschaffenes ganz zugrunde gehn– / Und alle entgleisten Sterne /

finden mit ihrem tiefsten Fall / immer zurück in das ewige Haus" (Sachs 1996: 118–19).

Paul Celan's poetry similarly unfolds the Jewish hope for redemption in the face of slaughter, albeit by throwing Messianism itself into question. In his Rabbi-Löw poem "EINEM, DER VOR DER TÜR STAND" (One Who Stood Before the Door, 1975: 242–43), first published in 1963 in *Die Niemandsrose* (The No One's Rose), Celan plays on the Golem tradition. The anonymous one standing outside the door one evening might be the Golem who, according to the folktale tradition, unleashed its orgy of destruction on the eve of Shabbat (Neumann 1990: 44–51), or even the Prophet Eliyahu announcing the Messiah's arrival (Derrida 1994: 62).

Neumann points out the poem's "messianic polarity" between utmost strife and the stifled cry for redemption (1990: 48), a duality also found in Kafka's evocation of the Golem in *"Das Stadtwappen"* (The City Coat of Arms, 1995a; see also Goodman-Thau 1999: 114). Celan's rupture of his poem's last word, "Ra- –", suggests the terrible clashing of Jews' messianic hope with their annihilation, conceived by the Nazis as a spiritual and physical purification of the German people. The arriving one's messianic implications and his association with the adversary, "dem / im kotigen Stiefel des Kriegsknechts / geborenen Bruder" (Celan 1978: 242), indeed seem to echo in the polarity of Dischereit's Golem figure.

Dischereit invokes these canonic Jewish poets of the Shoah in order to expose their fetishism and reconciliatory uses in postwar German culture. Furthermore, her *Golem* volume proclaims the reappropriation of the poetic medium by Jewish poets, a tradition that, as Hans Magnus Enzensberger asserted, would expire with Sachs as "the last poet of Judaism in the German language" (Sparr 2000: 503). While drawing on this canon, however, Dischereit rejects the continuation of poetic modes of discourse that hold the promise of redemption attributed to Sachs[1] or those of dialogue associated with Paul Celan and Rose Ausländer.

Itta Shedletzky has described Dischereit's position as a Jewish author in postwar Germany with the notion of living in a *"Mutterland Wort"* (Motherland Word, Shedletzky 1998: 201). Not incidentally, the phrase was coined by Rose Ausländer in her 1978 poem *"Mutterland"* (Motherland) to claim a linguistic and gendered space uncorrupted by the genocide: ""Mein Vaterland ist tot / sie haben es begraben / im Feuer / Ich lebe / in meinem Mutterland / Wort" (Ausländer 2001: 94). In contrast, the linguistic distortions in Dischereit's poetic language discard the possibility both of such an untainted linguistic space, and of returning to prewar poetic and cultural traditions altogether.

In the second poem of Dischereit's volume, the Golem returns in the form of the lyrical narrator; however, now as *a* golem rather than *the* Golem: "Ich wurd / als golem / euch geboren / noch fünfzig Jahr / und später" (Dischereit 1996: 6). The lowercase spelling of the word golem signifies the diminishment of Jewish communities through the Shoah and the postwar perception of Jews as an anonymous mass of victims, a guilt returning to haunt Germans after the genocide. At the same, the collation of Arabic, German, and Yiddish words in phrases such as "Chabibi / mein waibele" (Dischereit 1996: 13) resists the forging of coherent linguistic and cultural identities from the Jewish experience.

This linguistic strategy points to the alienated and jumbled nature of Jewish identity and culture after the Shoah, parodying the attempted appropriation of Jewish traditions and culture by postwar Jews and non-Jewish Germans. Such phrases not only ridicule the farcical German fascination with Klezmer music in the 1990s, but also parody young Jews' construction of an 'authentic' identity by resorting to the annihilated Eastern European Jewish culture. "Chabibi" (Arabic for "my beloved") casts young Jews' flirtation with Jewish tradition as a dance with a dibbuk, like the Golem an undead figure associated with the magical traditions of a mythologized Jewish past: "tanzen chassiden / in dein Herz / keine Mesuse / an deiner Tür / Mespochen / schneiden / dein Haar / daß es mit dem dibbuk / tanze" (Dischereit 1996: 13).

Through the missing *mezuzah* and the flawed genealogy indicated by the inaccurate transliteration of the Yiddish word for family, *mishpokhe*, Dischereit insists on the inherently partial and distorting nature of such appropriations. As her poetry suggests, fragmentation marks both the postwar Jewish experience at large, and female Jewish subjectivity in particular. Through a problematic appropriation of the Arab 'Other' in the Jewish-Arab constellation, "Chabibi" thus claims the outsider position of Jewish women within non-Jewish German and Jewish culture.

In contrast, Dischereit rejects the appropriation of the 'Other' subject position within the German-Jewish and male-female encounters in poems such as "*Deutsches Lied*" (German Song) and "*Ich esse meinen Namen*" (I Eat My Name), the latter closing the volume (Dischereit 1996: 16, 53). Dischereit's gendering of the German-Jewish encounter exposes the obscene features of postwar Jewish culture in Germany, and indeed of Dischereit's own work. As she observes elsewhere, "To write in Jewish in front of a German-German audience has a slatternly prostituting air about it—like a woman getting undressed in front of the eyes of men, I know. But I see no alternative" (Dischereit 1994: 281).

Young Jews' attempts to reclaim fragments of Jewish tradition, to want "a little bit of Aleph" (Dischereit 1996: 9)—referring to the meanings of life and death implied in the Golem's amulet—merely testify to the death of the culture that sustained the physical presence of Jews. While this construction overtly fixates Jews in a victim position, other writings by Dischereit (1994: 281) pose self-conscious fragmentation as a form of political agency to resist new cultural and political hegemonies, such as the policies of exclusion, displacement, and physical violence perpetrated by Israeli Jews on the Palestinians.

Doron Rabinovici, *Suche nach M.*

Similarly to Benjamin Stein and Esther Dischereit, Doron Rabinovici's allusions to the Golem figure negotiate young Jews' quest for an identity encompassing the memory and continuity of Jewish life. In contrast to Dischereit, however, Rabinovici also insists on the second generation's need for a self-referential Jewish identity signifying beyond the genocide. His 1997 novel *Suche nach M.* (The Search for M.) draws on the rich secular tradition of literary writings about the Golem as a figure of doubling, haunted memory, and return.

The novel's title invokes Fritz Lang's 1931 M—*Eine Stadt sucht einen Mörder* (M—A City Searches for a Murderer), a film questioning the adequacy of the judicial system versus personal revenge in confronting a serial killer. However, Rabinovici's M. also bears some resemblance with Meyrink's *Golem* novel, whose *doppelgänger* theme equally melds the crime genre with the Golem tradition. The narrative structure of Rabinovici's collage of seemingly unrelated stories gradually forming into a novel also parallels that of Leo Perutz's 1953 *Nachts unter der steinernen Brücke* (By Night under the Stone Bridge, 2000), a novel employing the Maharal (Rabbi Löw) tradition to commemorate the annihilated European-Jewish culture (Lorenz 1998).

In Rabinovici's M., a serial killer and his double, the uncanny Mullemann, stalk postwar Vienna. Not only are Mullemann's tall stature and his "Siberian" appearance (Rabinovici 1999: 159) reminiscent of the Asiatic, i.e., "Mongolian" features of Meyrink's Golem (2000: 48), like the latter, Mullemann is alluded to variously as a phantom, a puppet or a human being in disguise. Rabinovici's cloaked and silent mummy, communicating frantically in Morse code, ultimately is revealed as Dani Morgenthau, the son of survivor parents. Similarly to the Golem, whose body bears the Hebrew word *emeth*, Dani's pursuit of justice has literally inscribed itself on his body. He has become the gauze covered mummy Mullemann, because his body responds to the hidden crimes of his environment by developing a debilitating rash as the sign of truth.

As in Dischereit, the Golem configures the return of a guilt that haunts postwar society through the visible sign of the second Jewish generation. However, Rabinovici also postulates the limits of the second generation's identification with the wounds inflicted on the parent generation, which stunts the subjectivity of survivors' children. Dani's emotional ties to his parents oblige him to embody the memory of those murdered, "as a reincarnation of various relatives, as a recurrence in multiple forms, as triumph and restitution for that which had been destroyed and killed. . . . Dani Morgenthau was supposed to be a reincarnation of the Jews, their beliefs, thoughts, and dignity" (Rabinovici 1999: 71).

In order to protect his parents from further grief, Dani abdicates all rebellion. Occupying the emotional space in between the living and the dead, Dani's emergence as the gauze covered Mullemann expresses his symbolic ingestion of his parents' pain. As a child, Dani would lie on his father's belly listening to stories about his family's decimation while the threads of his father's shirt gathered in his mouth (Rabinovici 1999: 24ff. and 104f.). However, Mullemann's larvae-like body postulates this state as transitory. It can be overcome and the second generation is released from the historic wounds of the Jewish people only if the guilty are brought to justice. Rabinovici, too, thus rejects the possibility of wholesale reconciliation between the generations of the victims and perpetrators of the Shoah.

Rabinovici constructs the postwar Jewish body as a relic both preserving memory and transcending death, for the cloaked Mullemann reminds Dani's friend Arieh of Egyptian mummies, those fossils bearing the encryptions of the past (Rabinovici 1999: 213). In an attempt to understand Mullemann, Arieh wraps a piece of gauze around his own head, reflecting on how he laid *tefillin* during his father's memorial service. The *tefillin*, inscribing God's three-letter name *Shadday* on his body similar to the Golem's three-letter amulet, had left markings on Arieh's skin.

As the corresponding acts of wrapping gauze and laying *tefillin* indicate, Shoah commemoration has supplanted Jewish religious culture. In contrast to Jewish tradition, however, commemorating the genocide represents an involuntary, i.e., external inscription on the body of the postwar Jewish generation: "We, our entire generation, we were all born with a blue number on our arm! All of us! It may be invisible, but it has been tattooed into us, under our skin" (Rabinovici 1999: 219). The textual allusions to the Golem tradition convey the ways in which the second generation is locked into a deadly past, bearing living testimony to the wounds inflicted on the parent generation, but lacking its own identity. Again, as in Stein's novel, the female principle functions as the redeeming symbolic, when Dani's non-Jewish lover successfully tends his rash, enabling him to discard his cloak of gauze.

Conclusion

For Stein, Dischereit, and Rabinovici, the Golem motif signifies the inscriptions of the deadly past on the body of the postwar Jewish generation. Rabinovici's text, however, insists that the utopian healing of these historic wounds can only occur within the Jewish-Gentile dyad, a resolution that both Stein and Dischereit resist.

The recent revival of the Golem trope signifies the cultural, political, and geographical reference points of second- and third-generation Jews in German-speaking countries within the expanded area of the European Union. Jewish communities in Germany currently represent the only growing Jewish population worldwide, owing to large scale immigration from the countries of the former Soviet Union. However, the renaissance of Jewish life reverberates across Eastern and Western Europe, even while the Jewish community in Vienna, for example, is threatened with the prospect of closure after the cut of state funds.

The emergence of a scene of young Jewish artists attests to this trend, which is documented in new European-wide journals like the Berlin-based *Golem* or *Jewish Renaissance*, published in London. In particular, Diana Pinto's "Diaspora Manifest" in the trilingual magazine *Golem. European-Jewish Magazine*, the mouthpiece of the Berlin-based new group of Jewish artists *Meshulash* (triangle), formulates a new European-Jewish identity arising from a shared history beyond national confines: "From an historic point of view, we do not belong to a specific European country. . . . We are all descendants of the survivors of the Shoah yet we find our context in today's living Jewry. . . . We define ourselves as the third column of Jewry alongside Israel and the USA" (Pinto 2002: 96).

It is precisely because of the shared history of the Golem tradition that this trope lends itself to the negotiation of European-Jewish identity on the cusp of a new millennium and political era. The Golem serves young Jewish artists as a means to postulate the resistance, continuity, and revival of Jewish culture in Europe after the genocide and the Cold War ideological divides. Furthermore, the Biblical, Talmudic, and Cabbalistic origins of this trope enable them to stress the shared heritage of Ashkenazi, Sephardi, and Middle-Eastern Jewish cultures. The Golem figure thus serves young Jewish artists to proclaim both the continuity of Diaspora culture on the historic territory of the Shoah, often devalued by Jews in the US and Israel after the war, and the utopian unity of the Jewish people across the globe.

Note

1. Annette Bühler-Dietrich (2003) shows how non-Jewish critics appropriated Sachs in particular for a discourse of reconciliation even though her work resists the pacification of the genocide.

Works Cited

von Arnim, Achim. *Isabella von Ägypten, Kaiser Karl des Fünften erste Jugendliebe*. Stuttgart: Reclam, 1997.

Ausländer, Rose. *Sanduhrschritt*. Frankfurt A.M.: S. Fischer Verlag, 2001.

Bühler-Dietrich, Annette. *Auf dem Weg zum Theater. Else Lasker-Schüler, Marieluise Fleißer, Nelly Sachs, Gerlind Reinshagen, Elfriede Jelinek*. Würzburg: Königshausen & Neumann, 2003.

von Braun, Christina. "*Blutschande*: From the Incest Taboo to the Nuremberg Racial Laws." In *Encountering the Other(s). Studies in Literature, History, and Culture*. Ed. Gisela Brinkler-Gabler. Albany, NY: SUNY Press, 1995. 127–48.

Brod, Max. *Tycho Brahes Weg zu Gott*. Leipzig / Wien: K. Wolff, 1915.

Celan, Paul. *Gedichte in zwei Bänden*. Frankfurt A.M.: Suhrkamp, 1975.

Demetz, Peter. "Die Legende vom magischen Prag." In *Transit. Europäische Revue* 7/1994. 142–61.

Derrida, Jacques. "Shibboleth. For Paul Celan." In *Word Traces. Readings of Paul Celan*. Ed. Aris Fioretos. Baltimore / London: Johns Hopkins UP, 1994. 3–72.

Dischereit, Esther. *als mir mein golem öffnete. gedichte*. Passau Stutz: 1996.

———. "Der kubistische Blick. Wer schreibt eigentlich, wenn ich schreibe?" In *AufBrüche. Kulturelle Produktionen von Migrantinnen, Schwarzen und jüdischen Frauen in Deutschland*. Ed. Cathy Gelbin, et al. Königstein / Ts.: Ulrike Helmer Verlag, 1999. 237–52.

———. "No Exit from This Jewry." In *Reemerging Jewish Culture in Germany, Life and Literature Since 1989*. Ed. Sander L. Gilman and Karen Remmler. New York: NYU Press, 1994. 266–81.

von Droste-Hülshoff, Anette. "Die Golems." *Werke und Briefe*. Ed. Manfred Häckel. Leipzig: Insel Verlag, 1976. Vol. I: *Lyrik: Epische Dichtungen*, 639–41.

Galford, Ellen. *The Dyke & the Dybbuk*. London: Virago Press, 1993.

Gelbin, Cathy S. "Narratives of Transgression, from Jewish Folktales to German Cinema: Paul Wegener's *Der Golem, wie er in die Welt kam* (*The Golem: How He Came into the World*, 1920)." In *Kinoeye. New Perspectives on European Film*, vol 3 / 11 2003, 1–10.

Gesenius, Wilhelm. *Hebräisches und aramäisches Handwörterbuch über das Alte Testament*. Berlin / Göttingen / Heidelberg: Springer, 1962.

Goodman-Thau, Eveline. "Golem, Adam oder Antichrist—Kabbalistische Hintergründe der Golemlegende in der jüdischen und deutschen Literatur des 19. Jahrhunderts." In *Kabbala und die Literatur der Romantik*. Ed. Eveline Goodman-Thau, Gert Mattenklott, and Christoph Schulte. Tübingen: Niemeyer, 1999. 81–134.

Graham, Elaine. *Representations of the post/human. Monsters, Aliens and Others in Popular Culture*. New Brunswick: Rutgers UP, 2002.

Grimm, Jakob. *Kleinere Schriften*. Berlin: Dümmler, 1869. Vol. IV, 22.

Hoffmann, E.T.A. *Die Geheimnisse*. Frankfurt a.M. / Leipzig: Fischer, 1996.

Kafka, Franz. "Das Stadtwappen." In *Sämtliche Erzählungen*. Frankfurt a.M.: Fischer Taschenbuch Verlag, 1995. 306–7.

———. "Die Verwandlung." In *Sämtliche Erzählungen*. Frankfurt a.M.: Fischer Taschenbuch Verlag, 1995. 56–799.

Lang, Fritz. *Metropolis*. Germany: 1927.

———. *M.—Eine Stadt sucht einen Mörder*. Germany: 1931.

Lorenz, Dagmar. "Transcending the Boundaries of Space and Culture: The Figures of the Maharal and the Golem after the Shoah—Friedrich Torberg's *Golems Wiederkehr*, Leo Perutz's *Nachts unter der steinernen Brücke*, Frank Zwillinger's *Maharal*, and Nelly Sachs's *Eli. Ein Mysterienspiel vom Leiden Israels*." In *Transforming the Center, Eroding the Margins. Essays on Ethnic and Cultural Boundaries in German-Speaking Countries*. Columbia, SC: Camden House, 1998. 285–302.

Malchow, Howard L. *Gothic Images of Race in Nineteenth-Century Britain*. Stanford, CA: Stanford UP, 1996.

Meyrink, Gustav. *Der Golem*. Berlin: Ullstein, 2000.

Neumann, Peter Horst. *Zur Lyrik Paul Celans. Eine Einführung*. Göttingen: Vandenhoeck & Ruprecht, 1990.

Ozick, Cynthia. *The Puttermesser Papers*. London / Sydney / Auckland / Endulini: Knopf, 2000.

Perutz, Leo. *Nachts unter der steinernen Brücke*. Wien: Zsolnay, 2000.

Piercy, Marge. *He, She and It*. New York: Knopf, 1993.

Pinto, Diana. "Diaspora Manifest." In *Golem. European-Jewish Magazine* 3/2002. 96.

Rabinovici, Doron. *Suche nach M*. Frankfurt A.M.: Suhrkamp, 1999.

Ringelheim, Joan. "Verschleppung, Tod und Überleben. Nationalsozialistische Ghetto-Politik gegen jüdische Frauen und Männer im besetzten Polen." In *Nach Osten. Verdeckte Spuren nationalsozialistischer Verbrechen*. Ed. Theresa Wobbe. Frankfurt a.M.: Neue Kritik, 1992. 135–60.

Robertson, Ritchie. *Kafka: Judaism, Politics, and Literature*. Oxford / New York / Toronto: Oxford UP, 1985.

Sachs, Nelly. *Das Leiden Israels. Eli. In den Wohnungen des Todes. Sternverdunkelung*. Frankfurt A.M.: Suhrkamp, 1996.

Scholem, Gershom. *Von der mystischen Gestalt der Gottheit. Studien zu Grundbegriffen der Kabbala*. Frankfurt a.M.: Suhrkamp, 1977.

———. *Zur Kabbala und ihrer Symbolik*. Frankfurt A.M: Suhrkamp, 1973.

Shedletzky, Itta. "Eine deutsch-jüdische Stimme sucht Gehör–Zu Esther Dischereits Romanen, Hörspielen und Gedichten." In *In der Sprache der Täter. Neue Lektüren deutschsprachiger Nachkriegs- und Gegenwartsliteratur*. Ed. Stephan Braese. Opladen / Wiesbaden: Westdeutscher Verlag, 1998. 199–225.

Shelley, Mary. *Frankenstein*. London / New York: Oxford UP, 1994.

Sparr, Thomas. "Sachs, Nelly." In *Metzler Lexikon der deutsch-jüdischen Literatur. Jüdische Autorinnen und Autoren deutscher Sprache von der Aufklärung bis zur Gegenwart*. Ed. Andreas B. Kilcher. Stuttgart / Weimar: Metzler 2000. 502–4.

Stein, Benjamin. *Das Alphabet des Juda Liva*. München: dtv, 1998.

Torberg, Friedrich. "Golems Wiederkehr." *Golems Wiederkehr und andere Erzählungen*. Frankfurt A.M.: Fischer, 1968. 137–85.

Wegener, Paul. *Der Golem, wie er in die Welt kam*. Germany: 1920.

Zwillinger, Frank. "Maharal. Schauspiel in 5 Akten." *Geist und Macht. Vier Dramen. Österreichische Dramatiker der Gegenwart*. Ed. Friedrich Geyer. Wien: Österreichische Verlagsanstalt, 1973.

2

Hybridity, Intermarriage, and the (Negative) German-Jewish Symbiosis

Petra Fachinger

As Leslie Morris and Jack Zipes observe in their introduction to *Unlikely History: The Changing German-Jewish Symbiosis, 1945–2000*, "it seems that Dan Diner's declaration of negative symbiosis between Germans and Jews that may have been true during the first 30 years following the Holocaust may no longer be true. Certainly, the relations between Jews and Germans since 1945 keep undergoing major shifts" (Morris and Zipes 2002: xii). In much of the Austrian-Jewish and German-Jewish fiction of the 1980s and 1990s, and particularly in texts by writers born after World War II, the relationship between Jews and non-Jews is one of the central themes. The term Austrian/German-Jewish fiction refers to a body of texts written by self-identified Jewish writers dealing with the experience on the part of the narrator or the protagonist of being a Jew. Dan Diner, who reintroduced[1] the term "negative symbiosis" to the discourse on German and Jewish identities in the early 1980s, claims that for both Jews and Germans, "the aftermath of mass murder has been the starting point for self-understanding—a kind of communality of opposites" (Diner 2002: 251). Although Diner addresses the German, not the Austrian, situation, this chapter will discuss Austrian and German Jewish fiction in tandem. While both Austrian and German Jews are exposed to anti-Semitism and are marginalized in various ways in their respective societies, the historical, political, and cultural contexts in which the non-Jewish/Jewish dialogue takes place differs in these two countries. The myth of

Austria as Hitler's first victim enabled successive governments after the war to avoid serious confrontation with the past. Ironically, Austria's alleged innocence made it easier for Jews born after the war to integrate themselves into Austrian society. Matti Bunzl observes that while Austria's seemingly unproblematic relationship to the Nazi past in the pre-Waldheim era "allowed 'ordinary' Austrians to effectively externalize the Nazi past as an episode of German, not Austrian, history, it also invited Jews to imagine the country as a genuinely anti-Fascist state that had overcome anti-Semitic prejudice and welcomed its Jewish citizens into the symbolic fold of the nation" (Bunzl 1999: 351). Jews growing up in the Federal Republic of Germany have never been integrated into German society to the same extent as their Austrian counterparts were prior to the Kurt Waldheim scandal. Yet despite these historical and cultural differences, Austrian-Jewish and German-Jewish texts share a number of themes, narrative strategies, and literary tropes that justify discussing them together.

This article argues that cross-cultural romance/intermarriage between Jews and non-Jews is the most prominent literary trope for representing the (negative) symbiosis in contemporary Austrian-Jewish and German-Jewish fiction. In this writing, the conflicts that arise out of the burdened and complex relationships are usually played out in the private sphere, that is, within the family and between lovers, rather than in public. The success or failure of marriages and romantic relationships between Austrian/German Jews and their non-Jewish counterparts mirrors belief in or doubt about the possibility of a constructive dialogue between Jews and non-Jews. Although many Austrian and German-Jewish novels and short stories written during the 1980s and 1990s could serve to illustrate this point, the discussion will focus on four texts that have not yet received much critical attention: Peter Henisch's Steins Paranoia (Stone's Paranoia, 1988), Lena Kugler's Wie viele Züge (How Many Trains, 2001), Anna Mitgutsch's Abschied von Jerusalem (Lover, Traitor: A Jerusalem Story, 1997), and Lothar Schöne's Das jüdische Begräbnis (The Jewish Burial, 1996). While the discussion of personal relationships between Jews and non-Jews, as representative of the (negative) symbiosis, is so central to contemporary Jewish writing both in Austria and Germany, few non-Jewish writers have dealt with this issue in their fiction. Two interesting exceptions are Zafer Şenocak's Gefährliche Verwandtschaft (Dangerous Affinities, 1998) and Anja Tuckermann's Die Haut retten (Saving One's Skin, 2002).

In all of these texts, a "third," usually presented as yet another cultural context or an intermediary figure from another culture, disrupts the symbiosis and dismantles the duality. This "disruption" is an indication that the (negative) German-Jewish symbiosis, and by extension the (negative) Austrian-Jewish symbiosis, can no longer be viewed as self-contained. Karen Remmler quite rightly wonders if we can "even confine German-Jewish studies to these borders [of Germany], when other global contingencies influence the relation between Germans and others on a larger scale?" (Remmler 2002: 16). In the age of transnationalism, cultural and national borders have become too permeable to justify notions of fixed identity. "Hybridity," like "symbiosis," a term borrowed from biology to refer to cultural and sociological phenomena, is often invoked to signify a disruptive, resistant, and subversive "third" or "third space." First applied to the postcolonial context to describe the creation of "new transcultural forms within the contact zone produced by colonization" (Ashcroft 1998: 118), the term has, over the last decade, been most strongly associated with the work of Homi Bhabha, especially *The Location of Culture* (1994). Yet Bhabha's notion of hybridity is not easily identifiable with the transcultural concept of creolization, *métissage* or *mestizaje* developed by Caribbean and Latin American writers and critics. Creolization is the creation of a new form through the fusion of cultures that can be set against the old form from which it evolved. Bhabha's notion of hybridity, on the other hand, is much more radical in that he claims that cultural identity always emerges in a contradictory and ambivalent interstitial space where no new form is produced, but which is characterized by heterogeneity, discontinuity, and the permanent revolution of forms. Cultural critics today, drawing on both models, often view hybridity as having the potential to destabilize power relations; that is, challenge and resist a dominant cultural power. As I will show, the texts that I discuss associate hybridity with the future and portray it as capable of subverting the *status quo*.

It is this counter-hegemonic and counter-discursive potential that has for some time preoccupied postcolonial and ethnic minority theories. Chicana writer and critic Gloria Anzaldúa, for example, envisages the space between cultures, "borderland" as she refers to it, in the following way: "[A borderland] is in a constant state of transition. The prohibited and forbidden are its inhabitants. *Los atravesados* live here: the squint-eyed, the perverse, the queer, the troublesome, the mongrel, the mulato, the half-breed, the half dead; in short, those who cross over, pass over, or go through the confines of the 'normal'" (Anzaldúa 1987: 3). In Anzaldúa's provocative list of terms, some of which refer to nature and some to culture, the inherent dilemma of the term "hybrid" as it is applied today becomes obvious. As part of his comprehensive critique of the current understanding of hybridity in postcolonial theory, Robert J. C. Young has drawn attention to the dangers of employing a term so rooted in nineteenth-century thinking about race and intermarriage.

In "Hybrids and *Mischlinge*: Translating Anglo-American Cultural Theory into German," Todd Herzog discusses the challenges that this resignification poses within the context of contemporary Austrian and German-Jewish literature. This context is particularly vulnerable to the dangers to which Young refers because of the Nazis' racial laws and the Holocaust. In his discussion of texts by Maxim Biller, Irene Dische, Esther Dischereit, and Barbara Honigmann, Herzog comes to the conclusion that "the contemporary hybrid is continually read—unwittingly and at all levels, from authors' self-assessments, to publishers' blurbs, to newspaper reviews, to academic criticism in Germany and the United States—in terms of the century-old model of the *Mischling*" (Herzog 1997: 15). The model to which Herzog refers is that of the *Mischling*, as theorized in racial science of the late nineteenth and early twentieth centuries as a pathological character, a psychologically unbalanced hysteric lacking a stable identity and therefore ultimately unable to tell a coherent story. Herzog points to passages in the texts by the above authors in which "notions of hybridity are fouled by the historical model of the *Mischling*—the Jew can 'pass' as a German for a while, but s/he will ultimately reveal his/her Semitic markings" (Herzog 1997: 5).

Although I agree with Herzog that one needs to tread carefully when applying the notion of postcolonial hybridity to the Austrian and German-Jewish context, I believe that the concept can still be used constructively in light of the increasing permeability of national and cultural borders, the globalization of Holocaust memory, and its implications for Jewish and non-Jewish identity politics. The texts under consideration all deal with relationships between Jews and non-Jews and with the identity crises that the children of such unions suffer. Although not all protagonists may succeed in reconciling Austrianness/Germanness and Jewishness, the texts suggest that defining identity exclusively within the parameters of the (negative) German-Jewish symbiosis is no longer constructive or even possible. By introducing a disruptive cultural "third," the texts undermine the notion of biological hybridity inherent in the model of the *Mischling*.

Dvorah, the protagonist of Anna Mitgutsch's *Abschied von Jerusalem*, who had a Jewish maternal grandmother, decided in her early twenties to adopt Judaism although her grandmother, who raised her, never practiced it. In Jerusalem, she conceals her mixed heritage from her Israeli friends, who think of her as a fellow Jew. Dvorah, who lives in New York, visits Israel regularly to come to terms with her dual identity: her non-Jewishness, which the text equates with her Austrianness and which implicates her in the collective guilt of the Nazi crimes, as well as with her Jewishness, which she is attempting to reclaim.

One of the text's major strategies is the disruption of the victim-perpetrator dichotomy. While some of Dvorah's family members are identified as perpetrators, others are portrayed as victims, who, to save their lives, had to position themselves with those in power. Dvorah's paternal uncle was a member of the Nazi party, and other family members on the paternal side are depicted as anti-Semites. One of her maternal aunts, on the other hand, had an affair with an influential Nazi in order to secure for herself the certificate of Aryan ancestry, which she needed to keep her government job. The fact that the narrative takes place in Jerusalem in the late 1980s during the first Intifada adds the Arab perspective and, so to speak, a third party to the conflict between non-Jewish Austrians/Germans and their Jewish counterparts. In addition to granting Dvorah's Palestinian lover a voice in condemning Israeli aggression and portraying Jews as perpetrators and Arabs as their victims, the text also aligns non-Jewish

German/Austrian characters with the Arabs against the Jews and particularly against Israeli Jews. A young East German tourist couple, for example, complains about the arrogance and greed of the Israeli Jews, while they are full of praise for the Arabs whom they have encountered. As well, Dvorah's Austrian ex-husband told her on a previous trip to Israel that he hates Israelis and makes it clear that he is on the Arab side of the conflict. At the end of the novel, Dvorah feels that, by having had a love affair with a Palestinian terrorist and by unwittingly having become an accomplice in the preparations for a terrorist attack, she has betrayed the citizens of Jerusalem as well as her Jewish identity.

In Dvorah's case, one could argue that it is not the Jew "who will out" (as Herzog puts it in a different context, see Herzog 1997: 5), but the Austrian. That she is ultimately unable to hide her Austrianness is corroborated by the fact that the alleged terrorists are upset when they discover that Dvorah holds an Austrian, rather than an American, passport. Involving an American in the planned attack would better serve the group's purposes. Dvorah fails to reconcile her Austrian and her Jewish identities, not only because of Austria's complicity in the Holocaust and the anti-Semitism in her own family, but also because of the Israeli/Arab conflict in which she becomes directly involved.

The only character in the text that feels comfortable with her multiple identities is the daughter of Jewish immigrants from Iran, Dvorah's friend Nurit. She explains to Dvorah that she does not think of herself as a Jew, but as *Orientalin*, a term comprising both Arabs and Sephardic Jews. As a "celebration of hybridity" is impossible in the multicultural Jerusalem, Nurit decides to move to India. Neither Dvorah nor Jerusalem shares Nurit's philosophy of believing in various truths simultaneously, even if they seem to contradict one another. Jerusalem, where multiple identities may be common but where such hybridity is dangerous, if not life threatening, does not tolerate ambiguity.

As in *Abschied von Jerusalem*, non-Jewish Austrianness and Jewish Austrianness seem irreconcilable in Peter Henisch's novel *Steins Paranoia*. The protagonist Max Stein is the son of Jewish parents who escaped the Holocaust by fleeing to France and later to Canada, where Stein was born. While Stein's mother refuses to live in Austria, Stein and his son return to Vienna in 1950 when Max is five years old. At the beginning of the novel, Stein is married to a non-Jewish Austrian, with whom he has a daughter. Not only is he indifferent to his Jewish roots, but he also married his wife against the wishes of his father, who subsequently disowned him. Stein is drawn abruptly out of the comfort and security of assimilation when he overhears an anti-Semitic remark, the content of which is not revealed, made by an Austrian man of the generation of perpetrators and bystanders. For the remainder of the novel, Stein is more distressed about his failure to confront the man than about the slur itself. Significantly, it upsets the "Jew" in Stein, rather than the Austrian citizen who would also be expected to be appalled by this open show of anti-Semitism. One could therefore argue that the message of *Steins Paranoia* is that Jews are both forced and obligated to "out" themselves, rather than that they "ultimately reveal [their] Semitic markings" inadvertently or even against their own volition.

The novel is set in 1987, a year after the Waldheim affair, which coincidentally is also the year of the beginning of the first Intifada. Once this anti-Semitic remark comes to change his life, Stein perceives signs of growing anti-Semitism everywhere around him. Forced by the political circumstances to separate his Jewishness from his Austrianness, he leaves his wife and moves into an apartment that happens to be located next to a former synagogue. While Stein's "Jewish awakening" is triggered by anti-Semitism, his grandfather, who died in a concentration camp, appears in magic realist fashion to "educate" his grandson in things Jewish and to show him the importance of the knowledge of the past for the present. At the same time, Stein meets the Jewish-American Clarissa, who is in Vienna to report on the recurrence of anti-Semitism in Austria. Clarissa, who knows much more about the city than Stein does, particularly its Jewish history, reveals Vienna to him, a place in which he has been living oblivious of its Jewish past for thirty-seven years. When asked why Clarissa approached him of all people when she was conducting interviews in the street, she replies that she recognized him as "their own" (Henisch 1988: 31). Stein is reluctant to believe in what he refers to as a myth: "blood without soil" (Henisch 1988: 32). But Clarissa insists that their meeting was no coincidence. When Clarissa returns to New York, Stein, after a failed attempt to emigrate, decides to stay in Vienna where he belongs, as he is advised to do by an old Jewish émigré.

Like *Abschied von Jerusalem*, *Steins Paranoia* ends ambiguously and does not indicate whether or not Stein made the right decision. In an apocalyptic dream at the end of the novel, Stein has a vision of Vienna submerged by water. While he is struggling not to drown in the flood, his daughter has no difficulty keeping afloat. When her father asks her how she manages to do so, she explains that the key strategy is to stay calm and to swim against the current. Stein, however, is unable to do so. His inability to keep afloat seems to indicate that the generation of Jews born right after World War II, of which both Stein and Henisch as well as Anna Mitgutsch represent, faces the greatest challenges dealing with the aftermath of the Holocaust and reconciling multiple identities. Yet the intermediary figure from another culture in *Steins Paranoia*, the Jewish-American Clarissa, who is of Stein's generation, has no identity problems. The confidence and ease with which Clarissa expresses her Jewishness contrasts with Stein's struggle to reconcile his Austrianness with his Jewishness. Not only is Clarissa unburdened by the implications of the (negative) Austrian/German-Jewish symbiosis, she is also a more "authentic" Jew than the Austrian Jews. The positive description of American Jewishness in *Steins Paranoia* contrasts with the image of American Jewry in some more recent Jewish writing in German. Sander L. Gilman, for example, demonstrates that Daniel Ganzfried's *Der Absender* (The Sender,

1995), Doron Rabinovici's *Papirnik* (1994), and Benjamin Stein's *Das Alphabet des Juda Liva* (The Alphabet of Juda Liva, 1995) all represent the United States as an "inauthentic space," where American Jews are shallow and superficial, and Jewish-American culture is indistinguishable from mainstream culture. By contrast, Clarissa, a political activist, is concerned about the rise of anti-Semitism in Austria, a place that is geographically removed from her own life; she believes in Jewish solidarity; and, last but not least, she knows much about Jewish history. Clarissa's expectation, however, that Stein join her in New York and Stein's inability to follow her, indicate the challenge, if not the impossibility, of transposing the experience of American Jewishness to Austria and vice versa.

While political events, the first Intifada and Kurt Waldheim's election, as well as the setting, Jerusalem and Vienna respectively, play a major role in the two texts discussed above, *Das jüdische Begräbnis* takes place in Frankfurt in 1993, the location associated with the controversy over Rainer Werner Fassbinder's play *Der Müll, die Stadt und der Tod* (Garbage, the City, and Death) in 1985. Jewish protestors objected to the anti-Semitic content of the play and decided to hinder its staging—a protest that represents an important act of building budding Jewish self-confidence in postwar Germany. The fact that *Das jüdische Begräbnis* (The Jewish Burial) takes place after the fall of the Berlin Wall in 1989 is also significant. Along with the Fassbinder affair, the Bitburg scandal, and the Historians' Debate, the fall of the Wall and the subsequent unification of the two Germanies are key events for Jews in Germany, in the wake of which they have become increasingly more visible and have succeeded in making their voices heard.

Lothar Schöne's book deals with the wish of a deceased Jewish woman to be buried next to her Christian husband with a Jewish burial ceremony. The narrator, the woman's son, who is married to a non-Jewish German, is left with the challenge of finding a rabbi willing to perform a Jewish ritual in a Christian cemetery. *Das jüdische Begräbnis*, unlike *Abschied von Jerusalem* and *Steins Paranoia*, focuses on the trauma inherited by the children of survivors. As the only child of a mother whose five siblings were murdered in the Holocaust and who suffers from clinical depression, the narrator was expected to be a happy child who would enable his parents to forget the past. As his mother wanted to protect him from anti-Semitism, she raised him as a Protestant. His parents' suffering and the imposed silence about the Holocaust traumatize the narrator during his childhood and adolescent years. A recurring nightmare, in which he sees himself fall into a crevice, still haunts him in his forties. His cousin Fred, a survivor himself, who lives in Israel and thinks of himself as an atheist, helps the narrator to come to terms with his identity.

While the narrator's search for a rabbi willing to perform a Jewish ritual on Christian soil remains unsuccessful, a Protestant minister agrees to give his mother a Jewish burial. The fact that the Protestant minister is portrayed as more open-minded and willing to bend the rules than the rabbi, does not pass judgment on the two religions. Rather, by making reference to Martin Luther's anti-Semitism, the text represents the minister's decision as a gesture of reconciliation. The minister's compassion as well as his cousin's good-humored opposition to any inhumane adherence to rules, enables the narrator to recite the Kaddish at his mother's burial, although he previously had refused to do so. This symbolic marriage of Judaism and Christianity at the end of the text does not gloss over the hardships of a mixed marriage that took place in 1929, just four years before the *Arierparagraph* was released. Almost immediately after 1933, the Nazi regime bribed and threatened "Aryans" to divorce their Jewish spouses, intermarriages resulted in ostracism and impoverishment, and mixed couples faced tremendous social pressure. Yet, ironically, Hitler's race politics saved the couple's lives. As the wife of a Christian, the narrator's mother was taken to Sakrau rather than to Auschwitz, and his father, who, as a soldier, participated in the invasion of Poland, was later dismissed because the Nazis wanted to avoid having to pay pensions to Jewish widows of those killed in action.

Like his parents, the narrator has a successful marriage. Here *Das Jüdische Begräbnis* differs from both *Abschied von Jerusalem* and *Steins Paranoia*, in which mixed marriages and cross-cultural romance are doomed to fail. But as the child of a mixed marriage, the narrator is both exposed to anti-Semitism in the larger society and is discriminated against by German Jews. When, for example, he reveals his family background to a Jewish acquaintance, the man's response, "Then you are only a half-Jew!" (Schöne 1999: 19) upsets the narrator. He explains that he would have forgiven his acquaintance the word "half," but not the word "only." The narrator's cousin Fred, on the other hand, who is a child survivor, refuses to accept any notions of fixed identity. Like Clarissa in *Steins Paranoia*, Fred functions as the narrator's guide and as a representative from a country that serves as an antithesis to Austria/Germany with regard to Jewish experience. Apparently living a contented life in Israel, although he is critical of ultra-Orthodox Judaism, Fred still refers to Germany as his *Heimat* and to himself as a German Jew. Aware of the fact that having lived in Israel for several decades has contributed to shaping his identity, the narrator and Fred jokingly suggest introducing a third cultural category for him. The text reads: "'I am trying to find out whether you possess an Ethiopian-Egyptian skull or a Caucasian skull.' 'I can tell you precisely what kind of skull I possess. It is a Schlesian skull that has over the years hardened into a thick Israeli skull.' 'Then we have to introduce a third category'" (Schöne 1999: 58). Unlike the narrator at the beginning of the novel, Fred has managed to reconcile his Germanness and his Jewishness.

While Israel functions as a hypothetical counter-world to Austria/Germany in a number of recent Austrian and German Jewish novels, the return journey to Eastern Europe—a quest for ethnic roots, for family history, for Jewish community, and self-discovery—is also a common motif in this fiction. However, more often than not, this journey fails to fulfill its initial promise. In *Wie viele*

Züge, Jula, the daughter of a Jewish-Hungarian father and a non-Jewish German mother, travels to a small town at the border of Hungary and Slovakia to find the house in which her father was born. This quest is motivated by her father's recent death as well as by Jula's attempt to come to terms with her Jewishness. The life of Jula's father is cloaked in secrecy, her mother being unwilling to share with her daughter what she knows about the early years of her husband's life. Furthermore, Jula's mother avoids telling her own father that her husband is Jewish. Despite the imposed silence, Jula knows that her father is a survivor while his mother, as well as his first wife and their daughter, perished in the camps. Her father also tells her that he grew up in a blue villa, surrounded by vineyards, and that, as a member of the Red Army, he fought against the Nazis. Yet Jula learns from letters and photographs she discovers after his death that her father was telling her only half the truth.

Not only is Jula frustrated by not being able to learn the whole truth about her father's life, but during his lifetime she also suffers from her parents' unwilling-ness to live together in the same house. Consequently, the teenaged Jula has to commute between her mother's home in Germany and her father's on the other side of the Swiss-German border. The fact that her family consists literally of two halves that are separated by a national border serves as a metaphor for Jula being the child of a mixed marriage. The narrator in Barbara Honigmann's *Eine Liebe aus nichts* (A Love Out of Nothing, 1991) imagines that if she had a child with a non-Jewish German, this child would not be able to live: "I saw the child in nightmares, how it was only loosely constructed from individual pieces that did not hold together and that separated and broke and could not remain upright" (Honigmann 1991: 46). Metaphorically speaking, the impossibility of reconcil-ing Jewishness and Germanness marks the child's body. Although Jula is far from decomposing into fragments, the pieces of her father's life refuse to stay together to form a coherent story. She needs to discover more about him to be able to come to terms with her own Jewishness. Yet she *is* marked by some kind of differ-ence. Her fellow German classmates, who, like Jula, are spending a semester in Ukraine to learn Russian, make it clear to her that she is not like them. Unlike her colleagues, Jula has been ignored by Ukrainian students seeking relation-ships with the German women. When her lack of attraction for the Ukrainians becomes a topic at the dinner table, Jula wonders if she is not pretty enough. One of the students disagrees and suggests that Jula stop parading her Jewishness. She explains to Jula that the young Ukrainians want to go to Germany rather than be shot in the desert, a comment that Jula counters by pointing out that the synagogue and the Israeli army are not the same thing. Although, in the eyes of her non-Jewish classmates, Jula has revealed her cultural rather than biological/genetic "Semitic markings," she does not become a victim or lose her agency. She is no helpless hysteric, but an independent and resourceful young woman. Being cast as the "Other" makes her more determined to find her father's villa.

Jula seeks the help of her friend Ilya, whom she met in the small Jewish community of S., and who like her father was born in 1919, to reclaim the latter's estate. As a painter who used to specialize in portraying the victories of the Red Army, Ilya, inspired by Jewish mysticism, now attempts to capture Jewish spirituality in his paintings. Despite his return to his roots, as he refers to it, Ilya dons his Soviet uniform when he goes to the synagogue on the high holidays. Roguishly practicing cultural hybridity, he takes on the role of Jula's confidante and guide. His grandson Venja, a mafia boss, locates the village where Jula's father was born and gives her the money to travel there. But instead of the villa, Jula finds a dilapidated shack in what used to be the Jewish ghetto. Recalling her father's words "they took everything from me, the villa, the vineyard, everything," Jula realizes that the villa had been her father's metaphor for the better life he had dreamed of when he was a boy. The novel concludes with a trip to Israel that Jula and Venja take two years later to visit Venja's great uncle. When asked by Venja's relative where she was originally from, Jula replies "from Odessa" (Kugler 2001: 122). This is reminiscent of her father, who used to suggest jokingly: "Aren't we all from Odessa?" (Kugler 2001: 10). The novel's conclusion, in keeping with the implications of the rhetorical question, suggests that personal myths are no less valid than historical truths. Why Odessa? One possible reason would be that through the nineteenth century and into the twentieth century, Odessa was thought to be a land of opportunity. However, this image of Odessa as the "Russian El Dorado" (Weinberg 1993: 12) often conflicted with the harsh reality of life in the city. Because of its rise as a commercial and financial center, Odessa attracted a population that was ethnically and nationally heterogeneous to a much larger extent than either St. Petersburg or Moscow (Weinberg 1993: 12). As a meeting point of different cultures, a frontier and borderland, Odessa embodies cultural hybridity to a higher degree than most other Eastern European cities. To Russian Jews, Odessa's second major ethnic group, the city "offered an environment in which the traditional values and norms of Jewish society and culture enjoyed less influence" (Weinberg 1993: 10). As Robert Weinberg observes, resettlement in Odessa was an attractive alternative to emigration to Western Europe or the United States. The newness of the Jewish community in Odessa and its liberal and cosmopolitan atmosphere transformed the city into one of the major centers of Jewish Enlightenment (Weinberg 1993: 10).

Wie viele Züge, with its "Russian" component, also seems to be making a gesture to the thousands of Jews from the former Soviet Union who have made Germany their new home since the fall of the Wall. For many Russian, Ukrainian, and Baltic Jews who did not want to emigrate to war-threatened Israel and who were unable to obtain immigrant visas to the United States, Germany was the next best alternative. According to Michael Brenner, "in most smaller places the 'Russians' constitute the vast majority of Jews" (Brenner 2002: 56). In Berlin, more than fifty percent of the members of the Jewish community are of a

"Russian" background. Their numbers, as well as the fact that "they usually do not know what it means to be Jewish" (Brenner 2002: 55), have changed the face of the Jewish community in Germany and have caused a major shift in the relationship between non-Jewish Germans and their Jewish counterparts. Has Berlin, where Lena Kugler lived when she was writing this book, in some ways become the Odessa of the twentieth century?

While intermarriage and mixed heritage are discussed from a Jewish perspective in the four texts that have been analyzed so far, Anja Tuckermann's *Die Haut retten* presents these issues from a non-Jewish German angle. As noted above, very few recent texts written in German by non-Jewish authors address Jewish themes, let alone cross-cultural romance and intermarriage. One may wonder why this is the case. An easy answer would be that the smaller a minority is, the greater the need for members of that minority to marry out. Lynn Rapaport identifies six reasons for German-Jewish "persistence of interethnic intimacy": limited opportunity structures; the incest taboo and the lack of personal attraction to Jews; the forbidden fruit syndrome and a special erotic attraction to Germans; interethnic intimacy as rebellion against parents and the *Gemeinde*; interethnic dating that allows a Jew to have casual sex without obligation; and the perception that etiquette rules violate a sense of democratic individualism (Rapaport 1997: 224). On the other hand, proportionally few non-Jewish Germans enter into mixed marriages. Demographic facts, however, are not the only answer. One could also argue that this apparent disinterest is yet another manifestation of the lack of reciprocity that has always characterized the (negative) German-Jewish symbiosis. Yet I believe that what accounts most significantly for the small number of non-Jewish texts dealing with this topic is the legacy of the Holocaust and Nazi racial laws. *Die Haut retten* is a problematic text that demonstrates how difficult it is to deal with mixed marriages between Jews and non-Jews from a non-Jewish perspective. In *Die Haut retten*, a Jewish musician from New York and a non-Jewish German woman, the narrator, are having a sexual relationship and are even contemplating marriage and having a child together. Karla already has a son from a previous relationship with a Turkish German, from whom she is separated. The novel is set in post-unification Berlin and succeeds in capturing the spirit of a city in transition and under reconstruction. By focusing on the homeless, the displaced, and other outsiders in her description of Berlin's inhabitants, the narrator creates the kind of "urban realism" that characterizes many recent Berlin novels. The narrator and her friends, of whom most are of ethnic backgrounds other than German, live in constant fear of neo-Nazi attacks. Insecurity and fear serve as the political and emotional backdrop against which Karla's and Joschi's relationship develops.

The narrative is told in retrospect with flashbacks to earlier stages of the relationship. Joschi has gone to visit his parents in New York, and upon his return, Karla expects him to make a decision with regard to their future. Karla is upset because Joschi has neglected to phone her. From the beginning, the relationship is burdened by the implications of the (negative) German-Jewish symbiosis. Apart from the fact that Joschi has a successful career in Germany, the text explains neither why Joschi originally chose Germany over any other European country, nor why he has stayed for five years even though living in Germany makes him uncomfortable. When Karla asks him if he would feel more at ease in Holland or Belgium, he replies that as soon as he leaves German territory, he can breathe more freely. To add to his unease, Joschi's parents want him to return to the US, as they believe that Germany is no place for Jews; they would be shocked if they knew he was living with a German woman. This response echoes Lynn Rapaport's findings. She identifies eight factors that deter Jews from entering into a relationship with non-Jewish Germans: etiquette rules in Jewish-German relationships; lack of guidelines when these rules are broken; opposition to the relationship by a third party; the lack of social attraction; the prototype of the German as a murderer; personal guilt from violating one's internalized norms concerning endogamy; perceived difficulties for intermarried couples in raising a family; and difficulties in accepting a familial alliance with a German family (Rapaport 1997: 210).

Die Haut retten constructs Karla as a likeable character. She genuinely loves Joschi, she is a good mother, and her behavior is "politically correct." The fact that she has a child with a Turkish German, who not only was given a Turkish first name, but also bears his father's surname, characterizes her as open-minded and as embracing difference. She also is sensitive to social injustice, and she makes an effort to learn as much as possible about Judaism. Joschi, on the other hand, who is characterized as emotionally immature, inflexible, and prejudiced, continues to remind Karla that she is the offspring of a nation of murderers. At best, he comes across as confused and overwhelmed by his attraction to a non-Jewish German. He tells Karla that he is relieved that she is not blond, and encourages her to search her family tree for any potential Jewish ancestors. When she discovers a few gaps in the *Ariernachweis*, her first reaction is one of joy. However, overwhelmed by shame, she decides that even if she had had a Jewish great-grandmother, she would not tell Joschi about it. She regrets having followed his suggestion to check for Jewish ancestry at all. Here, as in other places, the text creates an inappropriate reversal of the roles of victim and perpetrator, Jew and German, by casting Karla, who suffers because Joschi continuously "others" her, as the victim and Joschi as a proponent of racist essentialism.

Die Haut retten concludes with Joschi suddenly changing his mind about a long term commitment to Karla. Although, upon returning from New York, he tells Karla that he is unable to continue living with her, he eventually offers to marry her. When Karla reminds him of his parents' disapproval of their union, he explains that what is important to them is Joschi's happiness. Karla, however, unwilling to tolerate this emotional up and down, discloses to him that her grandfather was a member of the German National Socialist Party. While the reader knows that there is no evidence for this claim, Joschi does not. Karla seems to be either testing his love for her in the hope that it will be strong enough to overcome even this obstacle, or she realizes that he will not be able to live with this revelation and uses it to "punish" him for his undecidedness. The message of *Die Haut retten* is that the (negative) German-Jewish symbiosis makes it impossible for Jews and Germans to have a satisfying life together.

However, while in other texts that reach a similar conclusion the lovers themselves are not at fault, in *Die Haut retten*, the reader gets the impression that what keeps this couple from living happily ever after is their personalities rather than the historical and moral legacy of the Holocaust. A comparison of this novel with Barbara Honigmann's *Eine Liebe aus nichts* and Rafael Seligmann's *Rubinsteins Versteigerung* (Rubenstein's Auction, 1989), texts that Tuckermann uses as models, lends support to this observation. While the narrator in Honigmann's novel realizes that she has no future with her non-Jewish German lover because he is too "German," her relationship with an American Jew also fails. The latter, like Joschi, was raised to think of Germany as no place for Jews. In order to be able to live with him, the narrator would have to suppress her Germanness, which he finds irreconcilable with Jewishness. The similarities between *Die Haut retten* and *Rubinsteins Versteigerung* are even more conspicuous. The Jewish protagonist's non-Jewish German girlfriend ends their relationship because her father was a member of the SS. Although, or rather because, she truly loves him, she realizes that he would never be able to live with this information and remain on speaking terms with his mother.

Tuckermann's novel also enters into a textual dialogue with *Gefährliche Verwandtschaft*, the final text to be discussed in this essay. Like *Gefährliche Verwandtschaft*, *Die Haut retten* establishes a linkage between "things Jewish" and "things Turkish." The constellation of characters in Tuckermann's text suggests two cultural "thirds" that disrupt the (negative) German-Jewish symbiosis: the Jewish American and the Turkish German. Yet unlike the Jewish-American Clarissa in *Stein's Paranoia*, Joschi struggles with questions of Jewish identity. The differences between the two characters' sense of self can be explained first of all by the fact that Clarissa is only a tourist in Vienna while Joschi considers permanent residency in Germany. But more importantly, Joschi, by having an intimate relationship with a non-Jewish German, is forced to confront his Jewish heritage in a unique way. Contemplating marriage to Karla also fuels his fear of becoming a potential target of neo-Nazi assaults, a fear that he shares with Adem's father and Karla's Turkish friends. This shared experience of Jews and Turks, which links the Holocaust with the assaults on Turks and other "foreigners" in postwar Germany, represents a structural moment in *Die Haut retten* to which Leslie Adelson in her analysis of post-unification Turkish-German literature refers as "touching." Adelson states: "Narratives in which victimized Turks make contact with victimized

Jews are 'touching' tales of Turks, Germans, and Jews, in part, because they evoke a culturally residual, referentially non-specific sense of guilt, blame, and danger" (Adelson 2000: 102). In her essay, Adelson asks what untold story can be related when Turkish and Jewish figures meet in German fiction, and more specifically, how Turkish Germans have intervened "meaningfully in the narrative of postwar German history" (Adelson 2000: 96). While in *Die Haut retten* the outcome of the (negative) German-Jewish symbiosis is predictable—the novel confirms that because of the Holocaust, Jews and Germans cannot come together happily in marriage—the Turkish story reiterates a common trope in German literature: the Turk who does not speak. Not only is Adem's father, along with other Turks, absent from the text, but Adem, who looks "German," bears no physical resemblance to his father. While the "proximity" (Adelson) of Jews, Turks, and Germans is configured differently and less predictably in *Gefährliche Verwandtschaft*, its conclusion holds little if any greater promise than that of *Die Haut retten*.

Like the other texts discussed in this essay, Zafer Şenocak's *Gefährliche Verwandtschaft* deals with the unhappy romantic relationship between a woman and a man of differing ethnic backgrounds. The text actually represents three generations of failed cross-cultural romances. In the narrative present, the narrator Sascha Muhteschem, who is the son of a German-Jewish mother and a Turkish father, and Marie, a non-Jewish German, fall in love in a small college town in the American Midwest and return to Berlin together. As in the other texts—with the exception of *Das Jüdische Begräbnis*—cross-cultural relationships are not successful in *Gefährliche Verwandtschaft*: the love affair of Sascha's Turkish grandfather with an Armenian woman in 1915–16 ends with his suicide in 1936, Sascha's late parents separated, and Sascha leaves Marie at the end of the novel. Şenocak uses these three private relationships as tropes for the cultural and political relations between Turks and Armenians, Turks and Jews, Germans and Jews, and Germans and Turks during three interrelated historical periods: World War I, World War II, and the time after the fall of the Berlin Wall. By making a connection between the Armenian massacres, the Holocaust, and the neo-Nazi assaults in the wake of unification, Şenocak disrupts the duality of the (negative) German-Jewish symbiosis and dismantles the victim-perpetrator dichotomy. With Sascha, Şenocak creates a character who, like Dvorah in Anna Mitgutsch's *Abschied von Jerusalem*, is the grandchild of both victims and perpetrators. Whereas most of his Jewish relatives perished in the Holocaust, Sascha discovers that his Turkish grandfather was involved in the Armenian massacres.

Sascha's Jewish grandparents left Germany for Turkey in 1934 and returned to Munich after the war. They originally chose Turkey as the place of exile because Sascha's grandfather fought as a soldier in a German regiment that together with Mustapha Kemal Pasha's troops defeated the Allies in a decisive battle in 1916. His parents joined his grandparents in 1954 because Sascha's mother wanted to give birth to her son in Germany to make a true "German" of him. In light of the fact that most of her relatives were killed by the Nazis, her intention to raise her son "German" prompts the question of how "German" identity can be constructed from different cultural and historical perspectives. Is Sascha, who has a German passport and speaks very little Turkish, German? As a Turkish German, is he "less German" than Marie whose father is of Huguenot background and whose mother is an ethnic German from Silesia? How does his Jewishness fit into the equation? In the eyes of the Germans, is Sascha Turkish German or German Jewish? Are the Turks the Jews of today? Or are the Turks, as one of Sascha's interviewees puts it, "the Germans of tomorrow" (Şenocak 1998: 96)? By giving Sascha multiple identities, each of which has a problematic relationship with each of the other two, Şenocak not only disrupts the above dichotomies, but also deconstructs biological essentialism. Being blond and blue-eyed, Sascha does not fit the stereotype of either Jew or Turk. In other words, he could easily pass as "German" if it were not for his Turkish surname. As far as the "ultimate marker" of male Jewishness goes, Sascha chooses not to answer a German colleague's question if he is circumcised. But then, most Turkish men are circumcised too. While Sascha identifies with his Turkish background in his journalistic work—a portrayal of young Turks in Germany based on interviews—he avoids Turkish subject matter in his creative writing and refuses to sell himself as a "Turkish" writer to the German readership.

Although Sascha takes a definite position vis-à-vis his Turkishness, he eschews confrontation with his Jewishness. Wondering if his refusal to adopt a specific ethnic identity is responsible for his lack of success as a creative writer, he concludes that, although his mother was a German Jew, he is not entitled to identify himself as a Jew with a direct line to the Holocaust: "I could have been a Jew, with a direct lineage to the Holocaust. But that is not entirely correct—even if my mother was a German Jew" (Şenocak 1998: 127). I agree with Roland Dollinger that Sascha's refusal to acknowledge his Jewishness is a result of trauma not yet worked through. When a philo-Semitic neighbor, for whom a neo-Nazi assault on Turks in Germany is reminiscent of *Kristallnacht*, offers protection to any tenants who might be Jewish, Sascha decides to not out himself: "I consider whether I should out myself in order to get to know him, but then I just let it be" (Şenocak 1998: 122). The neighbor's analogy between Jewish persecution in the Third Reich and neo-Nazi assaults on Turks in contemporary Germany, an analogy that has been drawn repeatedly in German public and political discourse, demonstrates that Sascha will not be able to separate his Turkish from his Jewish identity. In a rather utopian passage in the text, the narrator suggests that dismantling the German-Jewish dichotomy could free both groups from their traumatic experiences. This healing process could be initiated by embracing a third party: the Turks. Turks in Germany, in turn, would have to treat German Jews not only as part of German history, but as partners. Without the Jews, on the other hand, Turks in Germany are doomed to live in a negative symbiosis with the Germans. But Jews in Germany can come to terms with their German-ness only by identifying with the Turks (Şenocak 1998: 89–90). Unfortunately, Sascha is not able to apply this theory to his own life.

If Sascha is not able to "triangulate," neither is Marie. Although she has no problem acknowledging his Turkishness, she fails to acknowledge Sascha's Jewishness. Marie, who works on a documentary film about Talaat Pasha, one of the leading forces among the Young Turk leaders responsible for the Armenian massacre, argues with Sascha about the appropriate approach to making this film. When Sascha suggests that she needs to overcome her Western biases to be able to portray Talaat objectively, she asks him if he expects her to be sympathetic to this mass murderer, although it would be regarded as inappropriate if she attempted to "understand" Hitler's motives: "Should I sympathize with a mass murderer? I am not permitted to love Hitler" (Şenocak 1998: 15). When Sascha questions the validity of the analogy between the Armenian massacre and the Holocaust and blames her for adopting a one-sided perspective, Marie accuses him of speaking like a Turkish politician. She offers the following advice: "You have to get rid of torture if you wish to become European" (Şenocak 1998: 16). With this illogical response, Marie makes two things clear: she thinks of Sascha as a Turk, not as a German, and she refuses to see Turkey as a modern/European nation.

The text describes Marie as intolerant and self-righteous. She breaks off contact with her parents because they support the Christian Democrats rather than the Green Party of which she is a member. She is also a great admirer of Leni Riefenstahl, whose collaboration with the Nazi regime she defends by pointing out that many artists had to make compromises at the time. In "Negative Symbiosis," Dan Diner, who argues that "a critical mass of [collective] guilt remains" in Germany as a "result of the abstract, depersonalized, and collective division of labor through which the extermination of the Jews was carried out" (Diner 1990: 253), identifies three major reactions to a sense of collective guilt: appropriating victim status; an "archaic feeling of immanent punishment;" and the projective comparisons of degrees of guilt by drawing attention to other genocides. While Karla in Anja Tuckermann's *Die Haut retten* adopts victim status, Marie seems to be unconsciously dealing with feelings of guilt by focusing on the Armenian genocide in her work. The return of the repressed is after all one of the novel's major themes. As the narrator observes: "One never forgets, one represses" (Şenocak 1998: 129). *Gefährliche Verwandtschaft* successfully demonstrates how the repressed continues to return throughout history, thus operating as a subversive "third." Yet the subversive "third" is not only the main subject of a text that suggests the "triangulation" of Germans, Jews, and Turks, but also its structural principle. By crossing the borders of fact and fiction and those of various literary genres, the text itself is a hybrid construct. True to its vision of a "trialogue" among Germans, Jews, and Turks, it engages in intertextual relations with various contemporary texts written by Turkish Germans, by German Jews, and by non-Jewish Germans, thus creating new hybrid relations among texts. Texts that come to mind are Feridun Zaimoglu's *Kanak Sprak* (1995) and *Abschaum* (Vermin, 1997), Edgar Hilsenrath's *Das Märchen vom letzten Gedanken* (The Tale of the Last Thought, 1989), Barbara Honigmann's *Eine Liebe aus nichts*, and Anna Mitgutsch's *Abschied von Jerusalem*, to name only a few. Lessing's *Nathan der Weise* (Nathan the Wise, 1779) and Goethe's *Die Wahlverwandtschaften* (Elective Affinities, 1809) are obviously also major intertexts.

This analysis has attempted to show that the (negative) German-Jewish symbiosis as it is reflected in cross-cultural relationships has undergone major transformations over the last two decades. Compared to the two Austrian-Jewish texts, *Abschied von Jerusalem* and *Steins Paranoia*, the two German-Jewish texts, *Das Jüdische Begräbnis* and *Wie viele Züge*, are more optimistic about the possibility of reconciling Jewish and non-Jewish Austrianness/Germanness. Yet the skeptical, or at least ambivalent, attitude in the Austrian texts is not indicative of a national trend. Robert Schindel's *Gebürtig* (Born, 1994) and Doron Rabinovici's *Suche nach M.* (The Search for M., 1997), for example, both demonstrate that personal relationships between Jewish and non-Jewish Austrians, and by implication those between non-Jewish Austrians/Germans and their Jewish counterparts in general, have the potential to succeed. In all texts considered here, the (negative) German-Jewish symbiosis is disrupted by a cultural third. The United States, Israel, Eastern Europe, and Turkey are introduced as cultural and political spaces from which Jewish and non-Jewish Austrians/Germans can no longer separate themselves in defining their mutual relationship. The answer to what it means to be Jewish in Austria/Germany today is in constant flux. Furthermore, each of the texts expresses a belief in the positive power of cultural hybridity as personified by one of its characters: Nurit in *Abschied von Jerusalem*, Stein's daughter in *Steins Paranoia*, Fred in *Das Jüdische Begräbnis*, Ilya in *Wie viele Züge*, and Karla's son Adem in *Die Haut retten*. Although *Gefährliche Verwandtschaft* is the text that most strongly advocates hybridity to subvert the *status quo*, Sascha fails to reconcile his triple identity in the Germany of the mid-1990s. As long as "hybrid" and "German" are perceived as mutually exclusive, the German-Jewish symbiosis will have to be defined as "negative."

Notes

1. According to Katja Behrens, the term "negative symbiosis" was first used by Hannah Arendt in a letter to Karl Jaspers in 1946, at a time when Arendt still believed that non-Jewish Germans would never be able to dissociate themselves from the Holocaust (Behrens 2002: 32). Yet the term is most often associated with Gershom Scholem's dismissal of the "German-Jewish symbiosis" as a fantasy on the part of the Jews in pre-Nazi Germany. Jews sought dialogue with the Germans, but the attempt was not mutual.

Works Cited

Adelson, Leslie A. "Touching Tales of Turks, Germans, and Jews: Cultural Alterity, Historical Narrative, and Literary Riddles for the 1990s." *New German Critique* 80 (2000): 93–124.

Ashcroft, Bill, Gareth Griffiths, and Helen Tiffin. *Key Concepts in Post-Colonial Studies*. London: Routledge, 1998.

Anzaldúa, Gloria. *Borderlands/La Frontera: The New Mestiza*. San Francisco: spinsters/aunt lute, 1987.

Behrens, Katja. "The Rift and Not the Symbiosis." *Unlikely History: The Changing German-Jewish Symbiosis, 1945–2000*. Ed. Leslie Morris and Jack Zipes. New York: Palgrave, 2002. 31–45.

Brenner, Michael. "The Transformation of the German-Jewish Community." *Unlikely History: The Changing German-Jewish Symbiosis, 1945–2000*. Ed. Leslie Morris and Jack Zipes. New York: Palgrave, 2002. 49–61.

Bunzl, Matti. "From Kreisky to Waldheim: Another Jewish Youth in Vienna." *Contemporary Jewish Writing in Austria*. Ed. Dagmar C.G. Lorenz. Lincoln, NE: U of Nebraska Press, 1999. 349–58.

Diner, Dan. "Negative Symbiosis: Germans and Jews after Auschwitz." *Reworking the Past: Hitler, the Holocaust, and the Historians' Debate*. Ed. Peter Baldwin. Boston: Beacon Press, 1990. 251–61.

Dollinger, Roland. "Hybride Identitäten: Zafer Şenocaks Roman *Gefährliche Verwandtschaft*." *Seminar* 38.1 (2002): 59–73.

Gilman, Sander L. "America and the Newest Jewish Writing in German." *The German Quarterly*. 73.2 (2000): 151–62.

Henisch, Peter. *Steins Paranoia*. Salzburg: Residenz, 1988.

Honigmann, Barbara. *Eine Liebe aus nichts*. Reinbek: Rowohlt, 1993.

Herzog, Todd. "Hybrids and *Mischlinge*: Translating Anglo-American Cultural Theory into German." *The German Quarterly*. 70.1 (1997): 1–17.

Kugler, Lena. *Wie viele Züge*. Frankfurt/Main: Fischer, 2001.

Mitgutsch, Anna. *Abschied von Jerusalem*. Reinbek: Rowohlt, 1997.

Morris, Leslie, and Jack Zipes. "Preface: German and Jewish Obsession." *Unlikely History: The Changing German-Jewish Symbiosis, 1945–2000*. Ed. Leslie Morris and Jack Zipes. New York: Palgrave, 2002. xi–xvi.

Rapaport, Lynn. *Jews in Germany after the Holocaust: Memory, Identity, and Jewish-German Relations*. Cambridge: Cambridge UP, 1997.

Remmler, Karen. "Encounters Across the Void: Rethinking Approaches to German-Jewish Symbioses." *Unlikely History: The Changing German-Jewish Symbiosis, 1945–2000*. Ed. Leslie Morris and Jack Zipes. New York: Palgrave, 2002. 3–29.

Schöne, Lothar. *Das jüdische Begräbnis*. Munich: DTV, 1999.

Şenocak, Zafer. *Gefährliche Verwandtschaft*. Munich: Babel, 1998.

Tuckermann, Anja. *Die Haut retten*. Leipzig: Reclam, 2002.

Weinberg, Robert. *The Revolution of 1905 in Odessa: Blood on the Steps*. Bloomington: Indiana UP, 1993.

Young, Robert J.C. *Colonial Desire: Hybridity in Theory, Culture and Race*. London: Routledge, 1995.

3

A POLITICAL TEVYE?

Yiddish Literature and the Novels of Stefan Heym

Richard Bodek

Memory is not history. Neither is history memory. Intertwined, mutually re-inforcing, yet at times contradictory, they represent the past in different ways. Obituaries straddle the line between the two. Not fully objective, yet relying on facts to frame their narrative, obituaries frequently become hagiographies. This makes *The New York Times'* obituary of Stefan Heym especially surprising (Binder 2001). The piece seems to have Heym's demonization as its central con-cern. Employing a host of vaguely insulting phrases, half truths, and non sequi-tors, Stefan Heym appears as that most despicable of figures, the hypocritical, high-living, communist.

Heym himself claimed that he began to think about presenting the story of his life when Alden Whitman, a journalist from *The New York Times*, visited him in the early 1970s to gather information for his obituary (Heym 1988: 842–44). In the course of their conversation, Heym asked when he could see the piece, to which Whitman answered, 'never.' Heym concluded with the claim that every time he met a reporter from *The Times*, he would ask to see a copy of the piece, to which the reporter would respond, 'As you know, Mr. H. . . .' Thus, he wrote *Nachruf* (an 844 page autobiography/riposte) to get the first crack at the story. Much that was black in *The Times* is white in *Nachruf*. As one critic comments, "If the abiding interest in *Nachruf* lies in the fact that it chronicles events in the odyssey of a German Jew who chanced to be born in 1913, it is perhaps fitting that its title should relate to the style and direction of an obituary tribute . . ." (Pender 1991: 73).

Rather than throw up our hands in desperation, or try to discern the 'truth' about Heym and his career, we can seek a different approach to Stefan Heym's concerns. We will begin by rehearsing *The New York Times'* assessment of Heym's career, comparing it to that of *The Guardian*, which published a critical, yet altogether more positive piece. Finally, we will construct our own intellectual biography of Heym, one based on the evolution of his novels from the 1940s through the 1980s, focusing on the moral center that is always key to his work. Furthermore, we will question the nature of that moral center. In the process of that questioning, we will see how certain motifs and structures from turn-of-the-century Yiddish literature have direct echoes in Heym's oeuvre.

If David Binder, *The Times'* obituarist, is to be believed, Stefan Heym was a "lifelong Marxist-Leninist" (Binder 2001). Precisely what this is meant to convey is unclear, although in the context of the piece it is not a positive description. Binder refers to Heym as "an intellectual nomad," a storyteller rather than a "transcendent writer." Although Heym saw the German Democratic Republic (GDR), his postwar home, as "a blank spot in literature for me to fill in," Binder's omniscient authorial voice counters that, "East Germany produced a number of greatly talented *homegrown* (italics added) novelists and poets whose works filled in virtually all of that blank spot." Mr. Binder emphasized what he termed Heym's "rootlessness." Heym's exile in America undoubtedly had an effect on his literary style. *The Times* emphasizes this with the following: "Klaus Korn, a retired university professor in Berlin, said of Mr. Heym: 'We saw him as somebody from over there, from America. His novels were more in the American style, Sinclair Lewis or Norman Mailer, than German.'" Who Professor Korn is, from what department he retired, or whom "we" represents is never indicated. *The Times* then points up Heym's own multifaceted personal identity: part Jew, part German, often American. The obituary calls to mind the Wandering Jew, a stereotypically anti-Semitic portrait: superficially talented, rootless, dishonest, and fundamentally untrustworthy. As we will see, Heym himself was quite interested in this legendary figure, but changed the moral signposts to make him heroic. *The Times* continues its denigration of Heym in its discussion of his self-imposed exile from the United States in 1951. What Heym referred to as a protest against the Korean War, *The Times* cast as a 'fear' of HUAC (which the obituary seems to have confused with Joseph McCarthy's Senate Committee). He is then said to have participated in "anti-American propaganda campaigns." In short, Heym appears as an abject Stalinist apologist who somehow fell into disfavor with the Party, but who was able to afford "a comfortable house in the lakeside borough of Grnau and [who] drove a Lancia Roadster." Nonetheless, the obituary claims that Heym had nothing but contempt for the East German uprising in 1953 or for the East German interest in Western consumer goods after the fall of the Wall in 1989.

It is profitable to contrast this portrayal with the obituary in *The Guardian* (Tate 2001). In brief, *The Guardian's* Dennis Tate sympathetically portrays Heym as a lifelong, outspoken dissident who refused to bow before any authority that Heym considered illegitimate. Thus, we face two radically different, self-styled authoritative memories. The American inscription damning, the British sympathetic. What holds these two assessments together is their focus on Heym's socialism, real or hypocritical, which both thought to infuse his writing. Certainly, this assessment also runs through the critical literature on Heym.

We will explore this assessment by looking at a representative sample of Stefan Heym's work. This includes two novels from the 1940s—*Hostages* and *The Crusaders: A Novel of Only Yesterday*. Both of these were written in the United States, the second when he was a citizen. We will then consider two later works—*The King David Report* and *The Wandering Jew*. These both date to his GDR career.

The secondary literature on these works is in keeping with the mainstream of Heym scholarship. Commenting on one of the first two novels mentioned, Reinhard Zachau argues that Heym uses stick figures to represent good and bad in *Hostages* and *The Crusaders*. He assumes that Heym chose this mode of representation to appeal to an American readership (Zachau 1982: 22, 35). Marc Temme sees *The Wandering Jew* as a story designed to come to grips with the GDR's power structure (Temme 2000: 7). Indeed, as he states, "GDR institutions and Party cadres are constantly attacked and laid bare in *Ahasver*" (Temme 2000: 102).

Two recent examples of Heym scholarship emphasize Heym's concern with socialism, even when dealing with Jewish subjects. Meg Tait comments that the western media sees *The King David Report* as a critique of the Stalinist state. (Tait 2001: 97) For Malcolm Pender, the Israel of *The King David Report* functions as a parallel of the GDR. (Pender 1991: 68) Furthermore, Pender claims that, "*Ahasver*, which takes place at four levels—out with the normal framework of time, at the time of Christ, in the sixteenth century at the time of the reformation and in contemporary East Berlin and Jerusalem—presents the widest-ranging examination in Heym's writing of the forces of movement and inertia, order and disorder in the body politic." (Pender 1991: 71) Even that scholarship which deals with Heym's Judaism tends to emphasize its relationship to socialist politics. (Frei 1992 and Fox 2003)

In this piece, I would like to take a different path, using the four above-mentioned novels to compare the heroes in Heym's works to two of Scholem Aleichem's most famous characters, Tevye the Milkman and Menachem Mendl. These figures evince habits, characteristics, and a quiet heroism that recur in Heym's work from the 1940s through the 1980s. They also face many of the same types of problems that confront characters in Heym's work. Central among Heym's concerns is the question of how good, outwardly ordinary, men can conduct themselves in a world that might render them powerless or incapable of action. Related to this is Heym's interest in the insidious nature of illegitimate authority: its perverting effect on those who wield it, and opportunities that might exist to challenge it. Certainly Heym's sojourn in the United States had an impact on his political thought and actions. This impact, however, was not necessarily direct. When, in 1937, he sought to alert the American public to the growing Nazi threat, and 'strengthen the president's backbone' to fight it, Heym lit upon the figure of Karl Schurz. Schurz, a figure from the failed German Revolution of 1848, confronted President Lincoln with the necessity to free the slaves. Heym, a Jewish exile from Germany, felt that his painfully acquired knowledge would help in this new fight (Heym 1988: 158–59). The knowledge was acquired in Germany; the moral fiber to interpret and implement it came from the Jewish past.

Brutality and brutal characters appear in the work of both Scholem Aleichem and Heym. Opportunities to oppose them could be open and dramatic or small and personal. Responses might be political or spiritual. I will begin by looking at Menachem Mendl and Tevye as moral figures. Then I will turn to the question of Yiddish literature in the Weimar Republic.

Menachem Mendl, who appears in a number of epistolary stories, has both outsized virtues and faults (Aleichem 1921b and 2002). Avuncular yet roundabout in conversation, moral, yet not obviously meant to be taken seriously, possessing a strong sense of community and able to make grand themes local, he is an outsized portrait of the *Ostjude*. Scholem Aleichem presents him as a human being, flawed certainly, but with dignity and a strong sense that events in the world matter and that the personal and local are often tragic. The very name, Menachem Mendl, has come to evoke a specific Eastern European type; the 'Luftmensch' who although often well intentioned, barely makes ends meet, yet always follows one or another chimerical possibility.

In 1913, Menachem Mendl ponders the state of the world. Seeing the possibility of war among the great powers, he is quite concerned about ways in which it can be averted (Aleichem 2002: 8). He equates the impending disaster with the mundane problem of dealing with bad neighbors and other local problems (Aleichem 2002: 18, 20). As we will see, this attitude is also strongly evinced by Janoshik, the pub worker/Czech underground fighter in Stefan Heym's *Hostages*. When faced with the delicate problem of a German army officer who has mysteriously vanished, Janoshik can relate the issue to a certain Otto Krupatschka, whose wife, "very good at making meatballs, meatballs and a special sauce with lots of pepper in it," also vanished. Although she vanished with her lover, a medical student (Heym 1943: 11–12), Janoshik knows what would befall innocent Czechs if German officers disappear. He also has a sense of the tragedies of everyday life. This will catch up with him, as the Nazis sweep him up in a hostage-taking action in retribution for the German officer's disappearance.

Like Janoshik, Menachem Mendl frequently finds himself at odds with the police authorities of an authoritarian state, in his case Czarist Russia. Indeed, a recurring issue for him is not having the proper residency papers to reside in certain Russian cities (Aleichem 2002: 50–51). Although Sheyne-Sheyndl, Menachem Mendl's wife, finds his thoughts too abstract, she agrees with his moral compass. Extolling the virtues of a simple life, she is greatly disturbed by the suicide of an acquaintance and its moral ramifications. "What can I tell you, Mendl, whoever was not at that funeral will live twenty years longer. It was a funeral never to be forgotten! It was like Tisha B'Av, I tell you, the Destruction of the Temple! To this day I can see Berl-Isaac in my mind, with his poor worried face and glazed eyes, a person who has lost everything" (Aleichem 2002: 57). She reminds her husband to say Kaddish, as it is both right and proper to remember the dead (Aleichem 2002: 10). In short, she is both concerned and practical.

Tevye the Milkman, probably Aleichem's most famous character in English-speaking countries (due to the popularity of *Fiddler on the Roof*) is similarly concerned with the order of the world. Although he does not understand high finance, he would be perfectly happy to become rich (Aleichem 1921a: 39–40). Nonetheless, he knows that work is more important than wealth (Aleichem 1921a: 53–54). He is willing to help strangers in the forest and to reject bullying as an acceptable kind of behavior (Aleichem 1921a: 14–15). Although he does not fully understand his daughter Hodl's attraction to a man whom Tevye thinks must be a thief, her story is written in such a way as to show Tevye's admiration and fondness for Pfefferl, her revolutionary husband (whom the author also paints in a positive light) (Aleichem 1921a: 87–109). Tevye's life is a series of tragedies—often having to do with anti-Semitism or his encounters with the wealthy—which he is able to face because of his humanity and strong sense of justice. In short, over the course of several linked short stories, Scholem Aleichem paints the portrait of a man battered by economic and reactionary forces who nevertheless never loses his ability to act morally and with a social conscience. He expects no less from others. As one critic put it, "Like man, God is expected to act like a *mentsh*, and should He refuse, Tevye has every right to complain" (Pinsker 1991: 32). None of this should be surprising. Scholem Aleichem was a Socialist Zionist (Gittelman 1974: 57). As such, he equated wealth with the loss of humanity, and understood that the *shtetl* was squalid, but its inhabitants, as is common in the description of workers in much leftist literature, were strong (Gittelman 1974: 56, 58, 59). If, as Mikhail Krutikov claims, "[the] structural principle [of the Menakhem-Mendl and Tevye stories] is the recurrent pattern of expectation, derived pleasure (real or imagined) and inevitable failure" (2001: 55), we will see how the work of Stefan Heym takes these characters to victory.

First, we must consider our own knowledge of this literature. As is well known, Yiddish, and the Eastern European *shtetl* world in which it had its home, traditionally held little regard among German Jews. In the nineteenth century, the reputation of these Kaftan Jews was one of backwardness and provincialism. This was "the rag-bag man, dirty, ignorant, living on the fringes of proper society. . . .

The Haskala, the Jewish Enlightenment, set out to destroy the image of the Jew as isolated from what it considered the main body of Western experience. To accomplish this, the image of the hard-working, unemotional intellectual Jew was created" (Gilman 1979: 339). Yiddish itself, as a language, had a reputation for barbarism. Much ink was spilled by German-Jewish writers in their quest to civilize their benighted cousins, to drag them into the modern world. "Schiller in Barnow" exemplifies this attitude, telling the story of the enlightening effect of a work of Schiller's in a small *shtetl* (Franzos 1876).

This widespread, nineteenth-century phenomenon began to change markedly during World War One and the Weimar Republic. In this era, defined by the radicalization of German politics, rising anti-Semitism, and the questioning of the once seemingly solid German-Jewish symbiosis, Eastern European Jewish culture came to symbolize an authenticity that German Judaism had seemingly lost (Brenner 1996; Meyer 1998). As Kurt Blumenfeld wrote in his memoirs, among the Jews,

> from the East who left Russia after the Revolution there were numerous personalities who were very soon admired as 'complete Jews' by the German Jews who were insecure in their Jewishness. The upbringing, knowledge and Jewish consciousness of the Eastern Jews stood in marked contrast to the situation of the German Zionists who drew their strength solely from their cultural conflict. (quoted in Gilman 1979: 360)

Martin Buber valorized the Hasidim in his work, *Tales of the Hasidim*. Much thought was given to the value of Yiddish as an important literary language. As early as 1901, *Ost und West*—a journal dedicated to bringing Yiddish literature to German readers—opened up the world of Yiddish thought (Grossman 2000: 215).

Certainly, Stefan Heym had none of the widespread German-Jewish prejudice against 'Tevyes.' As early as the sixth page of his autobiography, Heym invokes the image of Tevye in his description of his father, who had seven sisters for whom he was responsible, as Heym's grandfather died during his father's youth (Heym 1988: 7). With bitter irony, Heym describes his family's move from the town of Schrimm to Chemnitz:

> Schrimm lay in the province of Posen. Posen was Prussian; therefore its Jews were German Jews. But the Russian border was very close, so close that the shadow of class free-fall hovered over Schrimm's Jews. Were they not also tainted as "ostjüdisch" [Eastern Jewish]? But the term denoted greasy caftans, sing-song voices, speaking with one's hands, body odor, dishonest trading, meant being disdained by the Goyem, the Aryans, as they would soon be called. (Heym 1988: 7)

This explanation is written only one paragraph after he provides a list of his aunts, the five aforementioned sisters, three of whom were gassed by the Aryans, whose cultural level was supposedly superior to that found in lazy business and sing-song voices (Heym 1988: 6).

As we will see, Heym's sympathies always lay with those whose cultural norms lay out of the mainstream. This sympathy, coupled with a sense of responsibility, a characteristic feature of Scholem Aleichem's work, marks Stefan Heym's as well. It is to Heym's work to which I now turn.

Hostages

In 1942, when he was a 29-year-old German-Jewish refugee in the United States, Stefan Heym published *Hostages*, his first novel (Heym 1988: 206–209). *Hostages* explores Nazi moral and spiritual depravity, brutality, dishonesty, the psychological pressure of impending death, and the makeup of the emerging Communist personality. Written in the form of a detective novel, the book concerns the intertwining stories of a group of men taken hostage in a cafe by the occupation authorities "investigating" the supposed assassination of a German army officer, which was actually a suicide. The hostages were to be shot in several days as retribution. The hostages included a bourgeois intellectual (a psychiatrist), a writer, an actor, a capitalist, and Janoshik, a resistance fighter. Janoshik links this plot line with the novel's other central theme, Czech resistance to Nazi *Herrschaft*, appearing in the form of a sabotage operation against German supplies. In the end, the hostages are shot, the Nazis are exposed as stupid, rather perverse, greedy brutes, and the act of resistance succeeds.

Several characters of great interest emerge from this novel. The first of these is SS Colonel Reinhardt. Reinhardt embodies illegitimate power. He enjoys overly refined food, paints his fingernails, has no qualms about ordering the deaths of innocent bystanders, and enjoys rape as a sport. As we will see, refinement and perversion, coupled with unmediated brutality and enjoyment of violence, will emerge as a red thread in Heym's oeuvre. For Reinhardt, Germany's domination is rooted in its "economic, political and spiritual unity . . . administered by a generation of physically and psychically superb German warriors . . . led by the super-mind of the Führer" (Heym 1942: 326). Speaking in a voice that Sheyne-Sheyndl would recognize as her own, Milada, a woman loosely affiliated with the Czech resistance, responds that, "(w)e are people, humans! Certainly we're weak, and it's easy for you to get the jump on us because we prefer the tranquility of home and love, of working and singing and fishing, to years of planning and scheming war. But just this tranquility, this minding of our own business—this it is which people will rise to defend" (Heym 1942: 327). Probably speaking with Heym's voice, Milada recognizes the loneliness and spiritual emptiness of dictatorship. Nazism's success will ultimately destroy it (Heym 1942: 327).

Pitted against Reinhardt is the already mentioned Janoshik. A worker, emerging from the Czech people, Janoshik embodies physical, spiritual, and moral courage, wisdom and craftiness, and the vision of a better world to come. Caught in the hostage roundup which gives the novel its name, Janoshik concerns himself less with escape—which he realizes is impossible—than with trying to continue his work for the Resistance and with the morale of his fellow hostages. His success in these tasks is perhaps the book's greatest weakness. Janoshik never flags. Even torture to the point of near death barely slows him down. Although his party affiliation is never made explicit, Janoshik is undoubtedly a Communist. Janoshik is, in many ways, Tevye the Milkman transformed into a Czech Communist. Tevye understood that escape was not a possibility in his world. Like Janoshik, he was a devoted storyteller. His stories, indeed his entire life, were propelled by a sense of justice and belief in the possibility of a better world. Running through both Janoshik's and Tevye's stories is a love for humanity. On the other hand, Janoshik's understanding of politics is not unlike that of Menachem Mendl's, while his practical-mindedness reminds one of Sheyne-Sheyndl. His folksiness, wellsprings of courage, and ability to defeat Nazis with ease make this conclusion inescapable. As Heym matured as an artist and political thinker, his portraits of heroes would become more textured. He would never, however, lose his disgust of abusers of power, regardless of their political affiliation.

The Crusaders

The Crusaders is also a story of the fight against fascism, although here the victory is both more and less secure. The novel follows the American army's march across France from D-Day through the early occupation of Germany. The basic elements of the plot may be quickly recounted. Both during and after a hard-fought war to defeat Nazism militarily, a fight that encompassed the novel's first half, progressive elements within the United States military find themselves in a struggle against fascist attitudes in their own ranks. In their search for power, money, and prestige, a number of officers and enlisted men conduct themselves in ways morally indistinguishable from those of the Nazis. Others realize that the necessary struggle must continue for a very long time.

The Crusaders presents an interesting range of characters, reflecting Heym's views of moral and political possibilities. Among the first to be introduced is Lieutenant David Yates. Yates' moral and political development will characterize the novel as a whole. Indeed, it is a kind of *Bildungsroman*. Beginning as an "Assistant Professor of Germanic Languages at Coulter College, [he] was being changed into a soldier, for reasons and purposes which he could clearly perceive, but which did not blot out his belief that war was vicious, a throwback, a degrading attempt at solutions for problems that never should have been allowed to arise" (Heym 1948: 6). At the novel's end, he understood that fascism had to be combated at home as well as abroad.

Several characters exemplify the American brand of fascism. Sergeant Pete Dondolo, always on the lookout for advancement and profit, is utterly uninterested in any of the moral ramifications of the war. For him, rights mean nothing, favors—everything (Heym 1948: 35). The war is anything but a moral crusade:

> "Shut up!" he said. "Sure I'm fighting for my kids. I'm going to get back to 'em, too! It's because of people like you I had to leave 'em. If anything happens to them, I'll kill you. Bunch of Jews get themselves into trouble, and the whole American Army swims across the ocean. This fellow Hitler, he knew what he was doing, and Mussolini, he, too. Everything is wrong. We should be fighting with them, against the Communists. They're against the family, against everything . . ." (Heym 1948: 37)

In response to this, Heym puts the following story into the mouth of Sarkis Tolachian, a minor character: "When men with guns beat up men without guns, and women and children, that is not right. But me, I know this: When a thing like that happens somewhere, it will happen all over . . . When you see a bad weed, you tear it out, roots and all. Otherwise, it will swallow the whole field" (Heym 1948: 41).

David Yates' moral guides in the novel—guides who will lead him to Tolachian's conclusion—are two Jewish enlisted soldiers. The first of these is Sergeant Bing, a German-Jewish refugee. The second is Corporal Abramovici, a Rumanian Jew. At the novel's outset, Bing backs Yates into a series of political actions that gradually open his eyes to the real meaning of democracy. For example, the novel's first section, "Forty-Eight Rounds From Forty-Eight Guns," discusses the political machinations behind the July Fourth firing of a political pamphlet at German lines. Bing composes the pamphlet, which expresses his (and Heym's) sense of the best that America has to offer (Heym 1948: 63). The pamphlet is written in the language of the Enlightenment, encompassing rights, liberties, and "the dignity of man." The full horror of what Germany has become leads Bing, who as a German Jew was not able to deal with the revelation, first to lose his will to live and later his life. His role as moral center is taken on by Corporal Abramovici. Symbolically, this transference takes place when Abramovici finds himself

> standing, facing the wrecked hull of the tank, bending, straightening himself, and bending again. From his lips came words that rose and fell with his swaying.
> "Yiskadal veyiskadash shema rahboh. . . ."
> The sing-song increased in volume. It seemed to rise from the bottom of the ravine, from the tank with the nothing inside—to swing in the air, to die away only to be taken up once more by the odd little man. It was lulling and sad and comforting.

Abramovici stopped.

He turned to Yates and smiled, a wise, gentle smile.

"For the dead" he said, "a prayer." (Heym 1948: 503)

Certainly the use of the term sing-song, ironically denigrated in the opening pages of his memoirs, cannot be accidental. Rather, it shows the value of *Yiddishkeit*. Although fully versed in the tradition, Abramovici seeks to act in this world. Indeed, only three pages after saying Kaddish, Abramovici relates a saying of his father to Yates, "a war is absolutely no good unless you get through alive" (Heym 1948: 506). Here Heym seems to offer a cautionary note. Abramovici—small, squat, unsoldierly—combines the search for justice with a jaundiced realism that escapes Bing. The corporal is a Rumanian Jew who has experienced pogroms, has a quiet dignity and a sense of justice that is not to be denied. His personality, his slow storytelling ways—immediately recognizable to readers of Scholem Aleichem's Tevye stories—show how true victory is to be won. In short, Heym exposes the evils of fascism in its Nazi form, shows its underlying characteristics—characteristics that were present among the American "Crusaders," and offers a moral and political compass to achieve a lasting victory.

The King David Report and The Wandering Jew

In *The Wandering Jew* and *The King David Report*, the most directly Jewish of Heym's novels, readers confront an anti-Semitic Reformation-Era clergyman and a king who falsifies his father's personal history to ensure an unchallenged right to a throne. This pattern suggests Heym's acquaintance with the Jewish notion that evil degrades the evil doer as much as good deeds raise one's own moral worth. These two novels both explore Jewish identity and the questions of intellectual and spiritual freedom in an unfree world. Thus, even decades after his earlier works, Heym's earlier passions and interests continue to infuse his work.

The King David Report is the story of the commissioning of Ethan the Scribe to write the history of King David in such a way as to legitimize the rule of Solomon, David's youngest son. Ethan, unsurprisingly, immediately tries to assert his unworthiness for such an "honor." Being no fool, he understands that the preparation of such a work presents a series of choices, all problematic, some distasteful, others quite dangerous. This "King David Report," officially entitled "The One and Only True and Authoritative, Historically Correct and Officially Approved Report on the Amazing Rise, God-fearing Life, Heroic Deeds, and Wonderful Achievements of David the Son of Jesse, King of Judah for Seven Years and of Both Judah and Israel for Thirty-three, Chosen of God, and Father of King Solomon," would be the basis of Solomon's legitimate authority, yet the preparation of it would allow Ethan access to much knowledge that, if publicized, would threaten the dynasty's existence. Indeed, in the course of his research for the Report, Ethan uncovers so much that the state's security apparatus arrests and prepares to punish him. In the end, Ethan loses his concubine, his Jerusalem house, and his right to claim the report's authorship. Thus stripped, he rides to his home and eternal anonymity. Such a novel could lend itself to a strictly political interpretation. Indeed, Malcolm Pender sees it as offering "parallels between the totalitarian state of biblical times and that of the twentieth century" (1991: 67). For example, one could try to line up the biblical characters with Communist leaders from the past; David as—alternatively—Lenin, Stalin, or both. Solomon stands in for either Stalin or, perhaps, Walter Ulbricht. Joab, David's chief general, could be Trotsky, and so on. In such a reading, Davidic and Solomonic Israel are no more than stand-ins for the Communist world. Four issues loom large: the critical writer struggling for truth in a dictatorship; authority, oversight, and mediocrity in real existing socialism; life in a socialist society; and pervasive perversion. Ethan fully understands that too critical an engagement could lead to his having his "head cut off and [his] body nailed to the city wall" (Heym 1972: 11).

Nevertheless, Ethan's story is much more complicated than this. Ethan is interested in the nature of a Jewish God, his whims and actions. In his musings, he considers the nature of a God who "proclaimed laws but often was unjust; he was short-tempered at times and long-suffering at others; he played favorites, he contradicted himself: he resembled one of those tribal elders you can still meet in the back hills" (Heym 1972: 13). Such musings are not so far removed from Tevye's conversations with Scholem Aleichem. "Quickly put, what did I want to say? Yes, I was then, with God's help, a poor beggar. I died of hunger three times a day with my wife and children. I worked like a donkey . . ." (Aleichem 1921a: 7).

Ethan grasps the notion of two kinds of truth, historical and dogmatic—the latter more authoritative than the former (Heym 1972: 42). Indeed, legend, if useful to a regime, could also acquire the heft of documentary evidence (Heym 1972: 49–50). It goes without saying, however, that documentary evidence was not without its problems. Uncomfortable documents seemingly could not be destroyed, but could still be treated like horse manure, housed in a poorly preserved stable (Heym 1972: 100). Truth must be in the interest of the regime to be given official credence (Heym 1972: 82). Even in this though, Ethan—in some ways the stand-in for Heym—argues that wholesale disregard for truth would subject the regime to ridicule, weakening rather than strengthening it (Heym 1972: 84).

As the secondary literature reminds us, Tevye's grasp of scripture is imprecise. He frequently mangles biblical quotations, making them say what he thinks they should. Ethan finds himself inventing what will become biblical text. Like Tevye, Ethan believes in a God and finds himself both in and out of trouble because of his storytelling abilities. Unlike Tevye, Ethan is drafted into telling stories. Like him, he is on a quest for truth and justice. In his final confrontation with power and violence, Ethan hears that, as a historian, he is the equal of the Serpent in Gan Eden, providing mere poison to the masses. Serpents, he is reminded, are to be crushed under foot (Heym 1972: 251–52). Yet in the end, the truth that he is most interested in is the truth of the human condition. As Ethan observes,

> I am endowed with the gift of observing myself at times of inner stress, which helps in preserving one's sanity. And though I saw nothing pretty as I watched myself shuffle along beside that litter, I also recognized that I was caught up in my time and unable to go beyond its limitations. Man is but a stone in the middle of a sling, to be slung out at targets he knows not. The most he can do is to try making his thought last a little beyond him, a dim signal to generations to come. (Heym 1972: 238–39)

In 1981, Stefan Heym published *Ahasver* in West Germany. The following year, he published his own translation of it in English under the title *The Wandering Jew*. The novel, set in the heavens, biblical Israel, Reformation-Era Germany, and the GDR, presents the story of two angels, Ahasverus and Lucifer, whom God cast out of heaven. Both angels are troubled by the order to worship a being which was created later than they were. Lucifer's refusal turns to scorn and disgust. He is offended by God's creation of a creature who would "commit more sins than I could ever invent, and will be a mockery of [God's] image" (Heym 1981: 10). In both his angelic and human forms, Lucifer is a reactionary who understands that an ordered world is well suited to his purpose of human damnation (Temme 2000: 59). Ahasverus, on the other hand, would come to pity humans, indeed, to support them against God. Briefly told, the novel combines three intertwined tales.

One thread tells of (Prof. Dr. Dr.h.c.) Siegfried Beifuss, a second-rate GDR academic, director of the Institute for Scientific Atheism, and author of *The Best-known Judeo-Christian Myths as Seen in the Light of Science and History*, who begins a correspondence on the reality of the Wandering Jew with Jochanaan Leuchtentrager—the human incarnation of Lucifer—of the Hebrew University. Beifuss is the subject of pressure from his superiors to develop the correspondence in the direction of anti-Zionism. A letter from Würzner, of the Ministry of Higher Education, reminds him "to show the greatest firmness of principle, and our scientifically worked out and proven viewpoints are to be represented without deviation. Wherever feasible, the role of the State of Israel as an outpost of imperialism against our valiantly struggling Arab friends is to be stressed" (Heym 1981: 59). Beifuss, a careerist, is most concerned with advancement, and wishes to have others do his work for him. It is well worth noting that this episode is epistolary, reminiscent of the Menachem Mendel stories.

The second thread relates the story of Paulus von Eitzen, a Reformation-Era clergyman and understudy to Martin Luther who uses Luther's anti-Jewish attitude cynically for his career advancement. Eitzen, who seems never to have worked a day of his life, declaims, "how the Jews, full of false pride and heresy, were living in their midst not by the work of their hands but by usury and, to top this, were mocking and cursing those whom they exploited" (Heym 1981: 97). His actions are defined by lust and ambition.

Finally, it is the story of Lucifer and Ahasver—the Wandering Jew—and their duel with one another and with God to change the world. Lucifer consistently looks back at God's mistakes. In Ahasver's words, "Far be it from me to doubt your miracles, O Lord, or your little molecules; my doubts concern your divine justice and the claim that man, whom you made, was actually created in your image" (Heym 1981: 121). Ahasver looks forward, believing that if God will not act to improve the world, he himself must.

Critics often view this as a milestone in Heym's career, one that allowed him to explore German anti-Semitism since Martin Luther, GDR anti-Zionism, and the stultifying culture of the GDR bureaucracy. Pursuant to this, they emphasize the Christian origins of the myth of the Wandering Jew, a myth that is rooted in the presumption of Jewish guilt for the crucifixion of Jesus. In short, Heym is said to invert a Jewish stereotype to provide a structural critique of German society and culture. While the novel's sociological and political criticism is quite biting, its many Jewish perspectives have gone largely unseen.

For example, Heym does not forego the opportunity to criticize the stereotypes of Jews commonly found in anti-Semitic discourse, stereotypes which he refers to both in his memoirs and in *Hostages*. As he considers Jewish religious services, von Eitzen imagines that they:

> must be an annoyance to God . . . for the Jews arrive at their house of prayer whenever the mood strikes them, some sooner, some later, the one is putting on his *tallis* or prayer shawl while another is removing it from his shoulders and leaving the room, and at any rate most of the praying is done by a *chasen* or cantor who, unfortunately, hasn't the least talent for singing but stands there in front of the *aron hakkodesh*, the holy shrine inside which the parchment scrolls containing the Jewish laws are kept. With his head turned crazily and his thumbs stuck in his ears he shouts at the top of his voice a medley of Hebrew words, at times with such speed that no one can follow him, and then again straining and stretching each syllable and often laughing or weeping along with it; in short he acts as though he were beside himself until, finally, the other Jews are gripped by his mania and join their yowls to his bleating, or put up a low mutter and bow to the four corners of the world, or noisily clear their throats and spit, or start jumping up and own and twisting their bodies as though they were so many goats. (Heym 1981: 180–81)

From the opening scene, in which Lucifer and Ahasverus are expelled from God's presence, a Jewish tone is set. Lucifer's questioning of God's judgment in creating man introduces the possibility of God wrestling. In the tradition of the biblical Abraham, Isaac, Moses, and Tevye, Ahasverus challenges God's perspectives and decisions.

Lucifer, in his human guise, Leuchtentrager, influences Paulus v. Eitzen to state that Ahasverus, "wants to change the world as he believes it can be changed, and man along with it" (Heym 1981: 72). Certainly, this is a perspective alien to the Christian tradition. Indeed, when Ahasverus confronts God himself in heaven, God's wrath turned to a smile as Ahasverus "spread [his] arms to receive Him like a lover" (Heym 1981: 123). Leuchtentrager, in his twentieth-century incarnation as a professor at the Hebrew University, acknowledges Ahasverus's 'peculiar' relationship with God, but claims that God refused to answer him—a bald-faced lie (Heym 1981: 147).

Ahasverus's disdain for a religion of the next world manifests itself in his relationship to Jesus, referred to in the novel by his Hebrew name, Reb Joshua. Ahasverus, finding Reb Joshua in the wilderness, asks him "to take matters into his own hands, for the time had come to erect the true kingdom of God; but he replied to me: My kingdom is not of this world" (Heym 1981: 166). Upon hearing this, Lucifer argues that suffering alone is without merit, for "the lamb that lets itself be devoured strengthens the order of the wolves" (Heym 1981: 166). This sentiment is in keeping with a sympathy of Heym's that goes back to at least as early as *Hostages*.

Joshua finally understands this sentiment, confronting his father with the claim that creation is merely, 'a stinking morass in which everything alive is striving to devour one another, . . . a kingdom of horror in which all order and organization exist only for the purpose of destruction' (Heym 1981: 269). God is unwilling to act, leaving only one alternative: human action. With this we return to question the obituaries with which Stefan Heym's life was commemorated. Even a cursory study of his corpus reveals a writer deeply committed to humanity. Rather than being a hypocritical Marxist, Heym comes across as a Scholem Aleichem for the twentieth century.

Works Cited

Aleichem, Scholem. *The Further Adventures of Menachem Mendl*. Trans. Aliza Shevrin. Syracuse, NY: Syracuse University Press, 2001.

———. *Die Geschichten Tewjes des Milchhändlers*. Berlin and Vienna: Verlag Benjamin Harz, 1921a.

———. *Menachem Mendel*. Leipzig and Vienna: R. Löwit Verlag, 1921b.

Binder, David. "Stefan Heym, Marxist-Leninist Novelist, Dies at 88 on Lecture Tour." *The New York Times*. 18 December 2001.

Brenner, Michael. *The Renaissance of Jewish Culture in Weimar German*. New York: Columbia University Press, 1998.

Fox, Thomas C. "Stefan Heym and the Negotiation of Socialist-Jewish Identity." In *Stefan Heym: Socialist—Dissenter—Jew*. Ed. Peter Hutchinson and Reinhard K. Zachau. Oxford and Bern: Peter Lang. 2001.

Frei, Hannah Liron. *Das Selbstbild des Juden entwickelt am Beispiel von Stefan Heym und Jurek Becker.* Ph.D. diss., University of Zurich, 1992.

Gay, Ruth. *The Jews of Germany: A Historical Portrait.* New Haven and London: Yale University Press, 1992.

Gilman, Sander. "The Rediscovery of the Eastern Jews: German Jews in the East, 1890–1918." In *Jews and Germans from 1860–1933: The Problematic Symbiosis.* Ed. David Bronsen. Heidelberg: Carl Winter, 1979.

Gittleman, Sol. *Scholem Aleichem: a Non-Critical Introduction.* The Hague: Mouton, 1974.

Grossman, Jeffrey A. *The Discourse on Yiddish in Germany From the Enlightenment to the Second Empire.* Rochester: Camden House, 2000.

Heym, Stefan. *The Crusaders.* Boston: Little, Brown and Company, 1948.

———. *Hostages.* New York: Sun Dial Press. 1942.

———. *The King David Report.* Evanston, IL: Northwestern University Press, 1997. (Originally published 1972.)

———. *Nachruf.* Frankfurt am Main: Fischer Taschenbuch, 1990. (Originally published 1988.)

———. *The Wandering Jew.* Evanston, IL: Northwestern University Press, 1997. (Originally published 1981.)

Hutchinson, Peter and Reinhard K. Zachau, eds. *Stefan Heym: Socialist—Dissenter—Jew.* Oxford and Bern: Peter Lang, 2001.

Krutikov, Mikhail. *Yiddish Fiction and the Crisis of Modernity, 1905–1914.* Stanford: Stanford University Press, 2001.

Meyer, Michael, ed. *German-Jewish History in Modern Times: Renewal and Destruction: 1918–1945.* New York: Columbia University Press, 1998.

Pender, Malcolm. "Popularising Socialism: the Case of Stefan Heym." In *Socialism and the Literary Imagination: Essays on East German Writers.* Ed. Martin Kane. New York and Oxford: Berg, 1991.

Pinsker, Sanford. *The Schlemiel as Metaphor: Studies in Yiddish and American Jewish Fiction, Revised and Enlarged Edition.* Carbondale and Edwardsville: Southern Illinois University Press, 1991.

Tate, Dennis. "Stefan Heym, East German Dissident Author." *The Guardian.* 7 December 2001.

Tait, Meg. *Taking Sides: Stefan Heym's Historical Fiction.* Oxford and Bern: Peter Lang, 2001.

Temme, Marc. *Mythos als Gesellschaftskritik: Stefan Heyms "Ahasver."* Berlin: Karl Dietz, 2000.

Zachau, Reihnard. *Stefan Heym.* Munich: Beck, 1982.

4

ANTI-SEMITISM BECAUSE OF AUSCHWITZ

An Introduction to the Works of Henryk M. Broder

Roland Dollinger

I.

Few other writers and journalists in Germany elicit such strong reactions to their writing as Henryk Broder. Seen by many as a polemicist and provocateur with great skill for sarcasm and irony, Broder has attacked, criticized, and questioned the political and cultural opinions and actions of large segments of German society. He has not only incited and accompanied numerous debates about major events in recent German history, but also commented on less spectacular public utterances and actions by politicians, writers, intellectuals, and other journalists. Read together, Broder's books and collections of essays constitute an "archive" where important material about "things German" and "things Jewish" is stored. While Broder has established himself as a leading journalist, who since 1995 has been employed by the prestigious magazine *Der Spiegel*, he continues to write about German politics and culture from the position of an "outsider," a position that reflects his biographical story as a German of Polish-Jewish descent.

Broder was born in 1946 in Katowice. His parents, who survived the Holocaust in concentration camps, emigrated to West Germany in 1957 and settled in Cologne. In his essay *Heimat? Nein danke!* (Homeland? No, thanks!), Broder describes how this childhood experience as an outsider within a German-speaking environment brought forth his ambition to speak and write the German language better than the native Germans (Broder 1987: 187). Moreover, Broder sees in his desire for "belonging" the cause for his rebellious, anti-authoritarian behavior that created a lot of conflict with his teachers in school, and later, during his studies at the University of Cologne, with the police and judiciary system. While this provocative attitude toward figures of authority was typical for the generation of West Germans born after WWII because they rejected the cultural and political conservatism of the 1960s, Broder's defiant and insubordinate behavior was also an act of compensation that distinguished him from his German friends. Burdened with a feeling of guilt toward his parents who projected both their trauma and hopes for a better future onto their son, Broder compensated "the conflict with his parents that never took place" (Broder 1987: 192) with his antagonistic attitude toward the German state and its authorities.[1] While Broder found his political home for some time with the German New Left during the turbulent years of the Student Movement, his increasing alienation from the radical Left during the late 1970s led him to reevaluate his life in Germany in general. Broder's essay *Warum ich lieber kein Jude wäre; und wenn schon unbedingt—dann lieber nicht in Deutschland* (Why I would rather not be a Jew—and if I must, rather not in Germany)[2] in *Fremd im eigenen Land* (Stranger in your own country) (Broder 1979: 82–102), a collection of essays by Jews living in Germany that Broder co-edited with Michel R. Lang in 1980, describes his frustration about living in West Germany, whose authoritative structures and mentality he sharply attacked. From 1981 to 1990, Broder lived in Jerusalem, without ceasing to write about German "affairs." Working as an independent filmmaker, journalist, and author for the German media, Broder published several of his most famous books, such as *Der ewige Antisemit* (The eternal Antisemite, 1986) and *Ich liebe Karstadt und andere Lobreden* (I love Karstadt and other eulogies, 1987), during his stay in Israel. While Broder enjoyed his life in Israel because he was not constantly reminded of his Jewishness, his critical stance toward the religious Right in Israel and the inability of both Israelis and Palestinians to find a political solution to their conflict (before the beginning of the second *intifada*) became manifest with his publication of *Die Irren von Zion* (The Madmen from Zion, 1998). After moving back to a different Germany in 1991, Broder devoted many of his essays to the failure of the German public to deal critically with the history of the Stalinist dictatorship in the former East Germany. His numerous stories about informants for the East German Secret Police, published in *Erbarmen mit den Deutschen* (Have Mercy on the Germans, 1993) and *Schöne Bescherung! Unterwegs im Neuen Deutschland* (A nice mess! On the Road in the New Germany, 1994), not only demonstrate his desire to expose political perpetrators and side with the victims of totalitarian ideologies, but also reveal Broder's continued support for a consistent analysis of German history in the name of justice and democracy.

II.

In the summer of 1976, five Palestinian and two German terrorists, who belonged to a militant leftist group called Red Cells, hijacked an Air France plane on its way to Paris to obtain by force the release of some fifty "comrades" who were locked up in Israeli and German prisons. They redirected the plane first to Athens and then to Entebbe in Uganda. There were more than 250 passengers on board, among them about one hundred Israeli citizens and Jews from other countries. Within a few days, they released the non-Jewish passengers and extended the deadline of their ultimatum to further their negotiations with German and Israeli officials. This extension was used by the Israeli government to prepare a military solution. During the night of 4 July 1976, a special military unit attacked the airport in Entebbe, killed the hijackers, and freed the hostages. Thirty-one people died: three hostages, among them a concentration camp survivor, an Israeli major, the seven hijackers, and twenty soldiers from Uganda.

In his book *Der Ewige Antisemit*, Henryk Broder uses these events in Entebbe and the public response of the New Left in Germany as a case study for his exploration of leftist anti-Zionism since the late 1960s.[3] He writes about his horror and speechlessness at witnessing the public reaction of diverse leftist groups who were not enraged about the hijacking of the airplane and the "selection" of Jewish passengers by Palestinian and German terrorists, but by the liberation of the hostages through the Israeli military. *Unisono*, they condemned Israel as the aggressor and declared solidarity with Idi Amin's Uganda, whose national sovereignty the Israelis had supposedly violated. What united all the leftist groups in their protests against Israel, Broder concludes, was their shared anti-Zionism, which served as ideological and emotional glue for the heavily fragmented militant left in the Germany of the 1970s (Broder 1996: 64). This one-sided response to the violence in Entebbe also accelerated Broder's separation from his former leftist friends with whom he had demonstrated, for example, against the Emergency Powers Act in West Germany in 1968 as well as the war in Vietnam. At the same time, Broder's growing distance from the leftist ideologies in the wake of the Student Movement in West Germany seems to have awakened his interest in "things Jewish" and sharpened his perception of the militant left as deeply anti-Zionist.[4]

While Broder spent much time and ink to attack the hostile attitude of the radical Left against post–1967 Israel, it would be wrong to suggest that the radical Left has been his sole target during all of these years. With equally fervent zeal, Broder has also exposed anti-Semitic statements and opinions coming from all segments of German society. From his first publication in 1976 about leftist anti-Zionism (*Linke Tabus* (Leftist Taboos)) to his most recent book *Kein Krieg, nirgends: Die Deutschen und der Terror* (No War, Nowhere: Germans and Terror, 2002), which chronicles the public response of German intellectuals and celebrities to the events of September 11 in New York and Washington, Broder has led a public campaign against anti-Semitism that includes both the anti-Zionist bias against Israel within various leftist circles and the German Peace Movement of the 1980s and 1990s, and other expressions of a more "traditional" anti-Semitic rhetoric by German politicians, intellectuals, journalists, and representatives of various German institutions and groups. These anti-Zionist and anti-Semitic prejudices were expressed more strongly in the public sphere not only during military conflicts such as the Israeli invasion of Lebanon in 1982 or the Gulf War in 1991, but also at significant junctures of the relationship between Germans and Jews living in Germany, such as the controversies surrounding Fassbinder's play *Die Stadt, der Müll und der Tod* (City, Garbage and Death, 1985), the Bitburg affair, or more recently, the Walser-Bubis debate. Broder's books and essays are an archive of both anti-Zionist and anti-Semitic attitudes and manifestations in Germany since the 1970s, and thus call attention to the fact that anti-Semitic tendencies have not disappeared from German culture and politics after 1945. On the contrary, I will show how Broder interprets both anti-Zionism and anti-Semitism as German strategies to deal with a past that does not want to go away. According to Broder, anti-Semitism exists in Germany not *despite of* Auschwitz, but *because of* it (Broder 1986: 132). While the radical Left in Germany has consistently denied any links between anti-Zionism and anti-Semitism and ignored works by Améry, Sartre, and Poliakov dealing with this issue (Broder 1986: 66), and while unabashed anti-Semitism in postwar Germany has become a political and cultural taboo, Broder's writings reveal to what extent the tropes and stereotypes of the "traditional" anti-Semitic discourse continue to haunt the collective German psyche. In order to deal more systematically with these issues now, I will first explore Broder's analysis of leftist anti-Zionism and then discuss some of his more recent "public interventions" in the cultural arena of today's Germany where "things Jewish and German" are negotiated.

III.

Despite much textual and historical evidence of the existence of anti-Semitism of the political left since the ninteenth century, the myth that anti-Semitism belongs exclusively to the political right became one of the pillars of the self-perception of the New Left in Germany.[5] At the time of the Six Days War of 1967, a particularly vocal strand within the New Left, "the Third Worldists,"[6] began its about-face with regard to Israeli politics. Until the second half of the 1960s, the image of Israel within the leftist *milieu* in Germany was characterized by its appeals for reconciliation with Jews and the Israeli state, support for material reparations to Shoah survivors, efforts to establish diplomatic relations with Israel, and interest in the socialist efforts of the Kibbuzim, which served as practical confirmation for leftist criticism of West Germany's conservative politics. The following statement by Ulrike Meinhof, who was one of the intellectual leaders of the New Left in the 1960s before choosing the path of terrorism, is representative of this pre–1967 attitude toward Israel: "There is no reason for the European Left to cancel its solidarity with the persecuted; it includes the present and the State of Israel. . . . Whoever wants to question the existence of this state must know that it would hit once again the victims and not the perpetrators" (Meinhof 1980: 100).

Solidarity with the victims of National Socialism still included the state of Israel. The following resolution of a conference of the SDS (Socialist German Student Organization) in September 1967, however, already indicates the paradigmatic shift of the radical Left toward Israel, containing a plethora of anti-Zionist phrases that would dominate their "anti-imperialist" discourse on Israel for several decades:

> The war between Israel and its Arabic neighbors can only be analysed against the background of the anti-imperialist struggle of the Arabic peoples against the oppression by Anglo-american imperialism. . . . The SDS condemns Israeli aggression against the anti-imperialist forces in the Middle East. . . . The recognition of the right to exist of Jews living in Palestine must not be identical with the recognition of Israel as a bridgehead for imperialism and a zionist state. (Meinhof 1980: 100)

The reductive division of the world into imperialist powers and national liberation movements served the desire of the radical Left to identify with Palestinian liberation movements in their struggle against Israel, which was viewed as a "bridgehead" of Western, primarily American, imperialism. Moreover, their simplistic Marxist understanding of National Socialism along strictly economic lines (fascism as a necessary consequence of advanced twentieth-century capitalism) prevented the champions of a leftist politics from engaging in a serious analysis of the Nazis' racist anti-Semitism and made possible the charge that Israel's "imperialism" is but another manifestation of "fascism." The former victims of German National Socialism thus became "fascist" perpetrators and the Palestinian victims of Israel's policies were seen as the "new Jews." Slogans such as the "Final Solution of the Palestinian Question" and "Reversed Holocaust" from this point on characterized the radical Left's discourse on the Israeli-Palestinian conflict well into the 1980s and helped set off a wave of violence by various terrorist groups.[7] In addition, the positive identification of the conservative establishment and media (especially by the Springer publishing house) with the victorious Israeli army turned Israel into a suspicious country for the radical Left. The efforts of the Great Coalition in West Germany to establish "normal" political relations with Israel (ambassadors were exchanged for the first time in 1965) only confirmed the leftist opinion that Israel had become an ally of Western imperialism.

According to Broder, criticism of Zionism and the rejection of Israel's policies are as legitimate as that of any other government (Broder 1996: 69f.). However, Broder discovers in the one-sided support for the Palestinian liberation movements and the leftist negation of Israel's right of existence an emotional component that has more to do with Germany's past than with a rational critique of Israel's policies. He accuses the leftist critics of Israel of expressing, through their anti-zionist rhetoric, an unacknowledged anti-Semitism that continues to disseminate the "traditional" stereotype of "the Jews" as the origin of all "evil." While the anti-Fascism of the left *symbolically* identifies with the *victims* of the concentrations camps, leftist anti-Zionism finds no reason for solidarity with *living* Israelis. According to Broder, the routine expression of anti-fascist statements helps to produce a good conscience and the moral alibi for the use of anti-Semitic stereotypes, such as the tropes of "Jewish exploitation," "the Jewish lobby in New York," or "the power of the Jews" that constitute the vocabulary of anti-Zionism without creating a moral dilemma for the speaker. Broder uses an example from the so-called "Green Calendar" of 1983 to illustrate his point, and its hateful language is worth being quoted at full length:

> Although we had already asked people last year "Don't buy from Jews," because the Jewish, unjust state pursues an aggressive policy in the Middle East, bombards nuclear power plants, occupies land that is not its own, and harasses and kills the residents there, and has already been condemned several times by the UN, the "financial mafia of the world" struck again. Jewish mercenaries are preparing the "Final Solution of the Palestinian Question." . . . My ancestors killed six million Jews, and it is embarrassing for me to be German. But in comparison with Zionist crimes, Nazi-crimes and Neo-nazist scribblings pale, and not only I am asking the question when the Jews will be taught a lesson that makes them stop to murder other people. . . . (Broder 1986: 98)

The confession to be ashamed of being German because of Auschwitz serves as a moral high ground from which "Jews" are publicly threatened—this "instrumentalization" of Auschwitz by leftist and "alternative" groups in Germany never met any public resistance.[8] "Normal anti-Semitism" after 1945, writes Broder, does not consist in the fact that Jews are being persecuted and murdered. Its "normality:"

> is characterized by the fact that more is expected of Jews than of others and that they are allowed to take fewer liberties than others. This means that they must become more patient, defenseless, and more suffering as victims, and as perpetrators they will be judged more harshly. (Broder 1986: 148)

Israeli aggressiveness is measured differently and gets more strongly condemned by political groups and individuals on the left than military operations by other countries. The same people who took to the streets to protest the Israeli invasion of Lebanon and compared the massacres in the refugee camps of Sabra and Shatilla to *Auschwitz* were silent about the Soviet invasion of Afghanistan, the Chinese attack of Vietnam, or other invasions. Why is it that Israeli and Jewish crimes trigger an emotional reflex that other, comparable crimes are unable to excite?

To answer this question, Broder offers in *Der Ewige Antisemit* a political and psychological interpretation of leftist anti-Zionism that he also employs in his work on the Gulf War of 1991 and in his book about the public response in Germany to the terrorist attacks of September 11. Broder claims that the strong German condemnation of Israeli or Jewish aggression and German solidarity with the suffering of the Palestinians serve a national project that has united the New Left in Germany since the 1980s: the project of regaining a sense of "German normality," of overcoming the National Socialist legacy, of exculpating the generation of the parents and grandparents by putting the moral blame on Israelis and other Jews, thus relativizing the uniqueness of German guilt. Through the discursive association of Israeli crimes with German crimes during the Third Reich and by identifying exclusively with the Palestinian victims of Israeli aggression, the German left projected Germany's own criminal history onto the Jewish victims of German history (Broder 1986: 115). If the Israeli treatment of the Palestinians is but a "reversed Auschwitz" and the "Final Solution of the Palestinian Question," then the German collective psyche might conclude that German crimes from 1933 to 1945 were not so special.

Again, Broder does not question anyone's right to criticize Israel's policies. However, he takes issue with a certain German fascination for Israeli aggression in the Middle East conflict that all too often is clothed in a rhetoric of German *Betroffenheit* (moral concern) for the victims of Israeli violence while, conversely, Palestinian or Arab violence elicits no such reaction.

Almost ten years after the Israeli invasion of Lebanon that unleashed such an enormous indignation against Israel, the German Peace Movement celebrated its rise from the dead during the American-led war against Saddam Hussein. The end of the Cold War and the reunification of Germany seemed to have made the *raison d' être* of the Peace Movement—to fight for disarmament and against a nuclear war between the United States and the Soviet Union on German soil—obsolete. The Peace Movement's first commandment that "nothing justifies war" remained unheeded when Saddam Hussein attacked Kuwait, and the international community, led by American and British forces, responded militarily. Although Israel did not participate in the coalition against Iraq, it became a target of Saddam Hussein's aggression, who declared his desire to turn Israel into a crematorium and fired SCUD missiles at Tel Aviv. Although it had become public knowledge that German companies had delivered the military equipment to Iraq that allowed Saddam Hussein to threaten Israeli civilians with chemical weapons, the German Peace Movement demonstrated against the Gulf War, shifting the blame to the United States and making Israel responsible for Saddam Hussein's attacks on its citizens.

The historian Dan Diner has convincingly demonstrated that the history of German anti-Americanism has often been linked with anti-Semitism.[9] In his essay Unser Kampf (Our Struggle),[10] Broder, in a similar vein, characterizes the resistance of the German Peace Movement to the Gulf War with its anti-American and anti-Zionist attitudes as a projection of German resentment against the former enemy in World War II and the former victims of Germany's crimes against the Jews. Broder argues that this military conflict without direct German involvement (German soldiers were not fighting in Kuwait and Iraq) released memories of World War II that may explain the strong German identification with the Arab victims of an US-led air campaign against Iraq. Bagdad and Basra, it seems, became two German cities suffering from Allied air strikes.

> The friends of peace are not concerned about Iraq and the Gulf War, they are not concerned about the Iraqi people who perish in the air raids. They say Iraq and they mean Germany which, two generations after the last World War, must defend itself against the American aggressor. The more strongly they reject the comparison between "Hussein and Hitler," the more strongly they identify today's Iraq with the former Germany. (Broder 1994b: 30)

While the majority of German citizens supported the war against Iraq (according to a TV-poll, taken in February 1991), sixty-four percent agreed with the military action (Bitterman 1991: 105), public opinion makers, politicians from the opposition parties SPD and "the Greens," and many intellectuals supported the Peace Movement's conviction that there is no "just war." One of the leaders of the Green party, Hans-Christian Ströbele, gave Broder an interview on 15 February 1991, shortly before he and other members of his party traveled to Israel and Jordania with the intention to explain their radical pacifism. Ströbele told Broder that, "The attacks by Iraqi rockets are the logical, almost inevitable consequence of Israel's policies," thus blaming Israel for Hussein's desire to destroy the Israeli state (Broder 1994b: 21). Moreover, Ströbele voiced his opinion against the delivery of Patriot missiles to Israel (their purpose was to intercept Iraqi missile) by categorically declaring that there are no "pure defensive weapons" (Broder 1994b: 21) and that they could be used offensively in the next military operation. Israel, Ströbele believed, could achieve security only by a radical politics for peace (Broder 1994b: 22). Broder published this interview on 19 February 1991 in the Süddeutsche Zeitung and the Jerusalem Post. Obviously, Ströbele's remarks about Israel were not well received there. The Green party had to return from the Holy Land after two days because nobody wanted to talk to them, which led Ströbele to accuse Broder of having conducted the interview in a "perfidious" way and of being a "150 percent representative of the Israeli government's policies" (Broder 1994b: 28).

From his interview with Ströbele, who was just one of many people on the left opposing the war and weapons for Israel,[11] Broder draws a particularly provocative conclusion about a certain "segment of the Peace Movement":

> I do not believe that the majority of Germans wants the destruction of Israel. I only mean that within a relevant segment of the Peace Movement an unconscious but very strong desire determines its feeling, thinking, and actions, (hoping) that Saddam Hussein will use the historical opportunity and finish the job that the Nazis could not carry out to its end. . . . In other words: by dint of the second final solution of the Jewish question, the first one would finally disappear in the archives of history. (Broder 1994b: 35)

Do certain factions within the Peace Movement unconsciously wish for the annihilation of Israel in order to wipe off the bloodstain of German history on their otherwise morally pure conscience? Of course, Broder's thesis cannot be proven wrong or right. How is one to analyze the "unconscious desire" of the Peace Movement? When radical Leftists from other European countries expressed similar anti-zionist opinions, for example during the Israeli invasion of Lebanon, does that mean that they also wish for the destruction of Israel? And if yes, how does Broder explain the difference between German leftist anti-Zionism and, for example, Italian leftist anti-Zionism? While the Italians may have their own reasons to relativize certain chapters of their history, one certainly cannot argue that feelings of guilt for Auschwitz motivates their leftist anti-Zionism.

Broder's thesis that the lack of support for the US-led coalition against Saddam Hussein and the empathy for the situation of Israeli citizens within certain circles of the Peace Movement should be viewed as the psychologically motivated national project of an *Entsorgung* of German history (the phrase was originally coined by Habermas and means the storage of nuclear waste, but also implies that German history is "taken care of"), reappears in his most recent book. In *Kein Krieg nirgends: Die Deutschen und der Terror*, Broder accuses many German individuals (most of them are politicians, opinion makers, academics, or simply the "rich and famous") of experiencing the war in Afghanistan "retroactively":

> The peaceful Germans acted as if they talked about Afghanistan; in reality, they spoke about their own country and history. They condemned the bombardment of Afghan cities in order to protest retroactively against the air raids on Dresden and Hamburg; they delare their solidarity with today's victims in order to allude to the fact that yesterday they became the victims of the same powers. (Broder 2002: 12)

One of the many statements that Broder uses to unmask the manifestation of "total peace" as dangerous madness—the motto of his book is a threat by Karl

Kraus: "Dear Sir, if you are not silent, I will quote you"—is by Theodor Ebert, Professor of Political Science in Berlin and one of the intellectual leaders of the Peace Movement. According to Ebert, any person, who during the Third Reich sat in the bomb shelters, knows that even the opponents of Hitler could not declare their solidarity with those who bombed their houses (Broder 2002: 62). While Chancellor Gerhard Schröder declared his "unconditional solidarity" with the United States and the majority of German citizens supported the war in Afghanistan, the "peace-loving" Germans, according to Broder, linked their condemnation of terrorism and sympathy for the victims with a rhetorical "however," emphasizing American guilt or co-responsibility for what had happened (Broder 2002: 12). Time and again, Germans were inclined to ask: What have the Americans, the West, or sometimes the inclusive "we" done wrong that the Arabs hate us so much?

Broder's book makes clear that the public reaction of some prominent Germans to September 11 was still greatly influenced by a leftist anti-Americanism that sought the reasons for the terrorist acts in the economic, social, political, and cultural hegemony of the United States, and the Israeli-Palestinian conflict. Michael Lüders, for example, the Middle-East expert for the weekly *Die Zeit*, commented on the symbolism in one of Osama bin Laden's videos as such: "From his point of view he is making a peace offer in quotation marks to the West. He is saying, here is the Kalashnikov, I can use it, but I am offering you peace. I am telling you, solve the problems in Palestine, and then the Americans can live in peace and safety" (Broder 2002: 56).

Broder asks whether Lüders believes that Osama bin Laden is really interested in a peaceful Middle East, or perhaps in a Middle East *without* Israel. Is perhaps Israel the sacrifice that people like Lüders are willing to offer for bin Laden's "peace offer?" (Broder 2002: 56). While we will probably never know the answer because nobody in Germany today will ever admit to "sacrificing" Israel, Broder's question raises a broader issue: that the absolute rejection of war by the Peace Movement always comes at the cost of a third party's victimization. Was the war against Hitler not a "just war?" Did not the American and English air raids on Germany bring down the National Socialist regime and thus stop the deadly machinery in the camps? One can argue that either the German Peace Movement has not yet learned this important historical lesson or that it has drawn the wrong conclusions from the lessons of National Socialism, which are invoked so often to prove that Germans today are "different" from the generations of their parents and grandparents. Even if one does not agree with Broder's interpretation of leftist anti-Zionism as a form of "noble anti-Semitism"[12] harboring a death wish toward Israel in order to free Germans from their guilt complex, these anti-Zionist sentiments by Germans born after 1945 certainly manifest their desire to blur the moral differences between the perpetrators and victims of the NS regime or to blame the victims as being responsible for the crimes that were committed against them. This is, of course, one of the oldest anti-Semitic strategies and by no means used exclusively by the political left.

IV.

As mentioned earlier, Broder also explores numerous incidents in recent German history that testify to the desire to blame "the Jews" for the anti-Semitism that is directed at them. The public taboo of anti-Semitism after 1945 often becomes the reason for an anti-Semitic "backlash," allowing the potential perpetrator to view himself as being persecuted. This reversal of roles took place twice during significant historical moments in the 1980s: first, when Jews in Germany blocked the premiere of Fassbinder's play *Die Stadt, der Müll und der Tod* because they were offended by Fassbinder's protagonist, who is simply called "the rich Jew"; and for the second time during the Bitburg affair in 1985, when Germans read the Jewish protests against Reagan's and Kohls's visit of a Bitburg cemetery, where former members of the SS are also buried, as an obstacle to the German-American friendship. While in the first case, Jews in Germany were accused of silencing a necessary public discussion about such issues as "the taboo of anti-Semitism" or the power of "Jewish money," during the Bitburg controversy, they were criticized for manipulating the American people against Germany (Broder 1986: 8, 111).

Broder uses these two famous events from the 1980s to address the longevity of the traditional anti-Semitic charge that Jews themselves are to be blamed for anti-Semitism. In his essays, Broder repeatedly criticizes Germans as well as Jews in Germany for missing an important point: that anti-Semitism in Germany is not a Jewish, but a German, problem. Instead of asking what the performance of a play such as Fassbinder's, if it is indeed anti-Semitic, might mean for themselves, Germans asked instead what it signifies for the Jews in Germany. And the Jews in Germany, according to Broder, argued as if *they* had murdered the Jews, begging the Germans not to make it impossible for the Jews to continue the work of reconciliation (Broder 1986: 9). A more recent example for what could be called the "instrumentalization of Jews" for symbolic politics will illustrate this point.[13]

On 9 November 2000, the anniversary of *Kristallnacht*, 200,000 people followed the call by the German government and all major parties to demonstrate against "hatred of foreigners" and "right wing extremism." Paul Spiegel, President of the Central Council of Jews in Germany, was invited to deliver the keynote speech. Broder had written a letter to Spiegel on 10 October 2000, asking him to reconsider his participation, because he would send the wrong message to the German public. The point that Broder makes in this letter to Spiegel is that the German government, the major political parties, and institutions should act against the violence of neo-Nazis against foreigners. If Spiegel became the keynote speaker, the whole problem would be seen as a Jewish problem and not a German one. The German public, according to Broder, expects the Jews to be afraid of this violence and thus become politically engaged as proxy of all decent Germans (Broder 2001: 48). Spiegel ignored Broder's reservations and gave his speech, but to Broder's delight he refused to meet the expectations by asking the following question: "Is it German *Leitkultur* [the phrase refers to a guiding principle in German culture] to chase foreigners, burn synagogues, and kill homeless people?" (Broder 1986: 25). With his question, Spiegel particularly offended the CDU, whose minority whip in the Bundestag had previously initiated a public debate about the concept of a German *Leitkultur*, by implying that immigrants and foreigners in an increasingly multicultural society should follow German cultural values. By asking whether xenophobia and anti-Semitism are also part of this nebulous German *Leitkultur*, Spiegel attracted much criticism, some of which clearly contained anti-Semitic rhetoric. A member of the Bundestag, Martin Hohmann from Fulda, for example, wrote in a public statement that Spiegel's insinuation against the CDU is as wrong as making Spiegel co-responsible for the death of two innocent women and a twelve-year-old boy during the last Israeli retaliatory strike (Broder 2001: 26). Broder himself exchanged some letters with Günter Nooke, also a member of the German parliament, who called Spiegel's behavior "simply indecent" and wrote that his statements "had done no favor for democracy" (Broder 1986: 30). In his last letter to Nooke, dated 20 November 2000, Broder summarizes what he believes to be the main purpose of such public demonstrations of symbolic politics that seem to become more effective through the presence of a "token Jew":

> . . . and when they have to organize a big political rally for "humaneness and tolerance," which includes all parties, the participating parties can only agree on a Jewish speaker, because he is a quasi exterritorial figure. The Germans cannot do without the Jews. Sometimes they are the enemy of the *Volk* that binds the Germans together, sometimes they make possible the co-operation between the CDU and PDS. In any case, they contribute to the formation of a *völkisch* community. Unfortunately, Paul Spiegel has not understood the rules of this game; however, one day he will undertand them and then leave the struggle against Anti-semitism in the hands of the decent Arians. (Broder 1986: 39)

Broder refuses to become the modern day "Court Jew" (see his reference to Süß Oppenheimer in Broder 2001: 25) and support cultural or political events whose primary goal is to atone symbolically for German crimes in the past and satisfy the moral conscience of people whom Broder calls "the good Germans." This celebration of "symbolic anti-fascism" (Broder 1999: 8) all too often is nothing but a public display of empathy for the (dead) victims of the past, while at the same time important political issues in the present such as xenophobia and anti-Semitism are treated dilatorily. Like other critics of German *Betroffenheit* (moral concern), such as Cora Stephan,[14] Broder chastises German politicians for engaging in an emotionally driven politics; they like to show their concern in public, but do very little to produce significant changes in reality. What is the political purpose, Broder asks, when, for example, the Parliament of Rheinland-Palatinate holds a session in the former concentration camp of Osthofen on the anniversary of the liberation of Auschwitz, asking the participants to bring warm winter clothes "although the memorial site is heated?" (Broder 1986: 122). Sarcastically, Broder draws attention to the discrepancy between this public show of concern for former NS victims and the politicians' indifference to the problems of asylum seekers in Germany today:

> It is just a pity that during this meeting there is no discussion about a relevant issue, for example the deportation of asylum seekers to their home countries. For the representatives of parliament it will be sufficient to have acted against the "danger of repetition" symbolically. (Broder 1999: 122)

Broder clearly does not see his public role as journalist and critic to keep the memory of Auschwitz alive. In his essay *Auschwitz für alle* (Auschwitz for everyone) (Broder 1986: 87–91), he opposes the 51 million dollar project of the Ronald Lauder Foundation to preserve Auschwitz. He fears that Auschwitz will be turned into a *Freizeitpark* (Broder 1986: 88) and believes that the money could be spent more usefully, i.e., for the last survivors of the Final Solution in Eastern Europe. Similarly, Broder writes that the decision to build Peter Eisenman's Holocaust memorial in Berlin has very little to do with remembering the Jewish victims of National Socialism. Instead, he views the whole project as a synthesis of German *Sündenstolz* (pride in being a sinner) and Jewish *Opferstolz* (pride in being a victim) (Broder 1986: 168): Germans, he claims, merely pretend to be mourning Jewish victims while defending the singularity of their crimes, and Jews readily accept their singularity as victims at the expense of other groups that were persecuted by the Nazis. The new Holocaust memorial primarily serves to improve Germany's reputation abroad (Broder 1986: 173).

When Broder writes that his responsibilities do not lie in "keeping alive the memory and resistance against forgetting" (Broder 1986: 130), he does not, of course, make an argument against preserving the memories of the victims of the Shoah. Instead, he rejects all forms of sentimental expressions of German "mourning," in which false tears are shed for Jewish victims at no cost. With his great skill for satire and irony, Broder unmasks the official politics of remembrance by individuals and organizations as self-serving strategies. By positioning himself as a cultural outsider, who keeps his distance to both the German and Jewish establishment, he is able to point out some of the absurdities of the reification and commercialization of the memory of the Shoah. Hence, Broder's critique of the cultural politics of memory in Germany is a critique of the symbolic resistance to German crimes of the past that has great political value for the present.

There is an inherent correlation between Broder's work on the anti-Semitic anti-Zionism of some groups and individuals of the New Left and the Peace Movement and his criticism of this symbolic resistance to National Socialism by Germans of all political convictions: paying lip service to the memory of dead Jews can easily be instrumentalized for the justification of anti-Zionist attacks on Israel, as well as for the "normalization" of German-Jewish relationships during the reconstruction of a German national identity. Symbolic atonement for the crimes of the past does not guarantee the disappearance of anti-Semitism in the present. As Martin Walser's new novel *Tod eines Kritikers* (Death of a Critic) and the late Jürgen Möllemann's (a former leader of the Free Democrats) statements about the former Israeli Prime Minister Scharon and the German-Jewish talk show host Marcel Friedmann show, Broder's work about anti-Semitism in Germany has not lost its importance. While Walser's death fantasy about the Jewish critic Marcel Reich-Ranicki is replete with anti-Semitic stereotypes, Möllemann's attack on Israeli politics and Friedmann's character repeats an old discursive pattern: that Jews are to be blamed for anti-Semitism in Germany. Broder's "archive" of anti-Semitic occurrences in Germany since the 1970s is a useful tool to contextualize these recent anti-Semitic manifestations of the cultural and political center historically.

Notes

1. The Austrian writer Doron Rabinovici discusses the theme of guilt in the second generation of Jews after the Shoah in his novel *Suche nach M.* (1997).
2. An English translation appeared in Broder 2004: 1–20.
3. The concept of the "New Left" is refering here to those political forces of the Student Movement of the 1960s and their successors, who represented radical variations of a Marxist theory that was opposed to the "reformist" politics of Social democracy. Andrei Markovits has recently identified several strands within the New Left in his "The Minister and the Terrorist," an essay on the political development of Foreign Minister Joschka Fischer. The "Westerners" who endorsed liberalism, humanism, and democracy were opposed by the anti-Westerners, who according to Markovits, can be subdivided into the "Third Worldists, the orthodox Marxists, and the neonationalists" (Markovits 2001: 139). Chapters 4 and 5 of *Der Ewige Antisemit* had appeared in slightly different form two years earlier as "Linker Antisemitismus?", Broder's contribution to a seminar on leftist anti-Semitism held at the Evangelische Akademie Arnoldshain in 1984. The proceedings of this conference were published as *Solidarität und Deutsche Geschichte* (1984).
4. The simultaneity of a growing distance from the political left and the (re-)discovery of a more pronounced Jewish identity seems to be symptomatic for the second generation of Jews living in Germany or Austria. In her collection of essays *Unzugehoerig* (1989), the Austrian writer and filmmaker Ruth Beckermann comes to a similar conclusion. "The blacks in South Africa, trees, and women became *Jews*, but especially the Palestinians. Anti-semitism appeared in the garb of anti-Zionism" (Beckermann 1989: 125). And Esther Dischereit, born in West Germany in 1952, writes in *Mit Eichmann an der Börse* (With Eichmann at the Stock Market, 2001) that the beginning of her career as a writer followed her disillusionment with leftist politics (Dischereit 2001: 150).

5. For the relationship between the German Left and Israel, see Diner, "Täuschungen: Israel, die Linke und das Dilemma der Kritik"; Fischer, "Das dünne Eis der Geschichte. Israel und die deutsche Neue Linke"; and Heenen, "Deutsche Linke, linke Juden und der Zionismus."

6. According to Markovits, the "Third Worldists" were "vehemently anti-Zionist (although not necessarily antisemitic) and found in the Palestinians an emblem of noble suffering and anti-colonial resistance" (Markovits 2001: 140).

7. In 1969, a militant group calling itself "Schwarze Ratten/ Tupamaros Westberlin" wrote "Sha-lom und Napalm" and "El Fatah" on several Jewish memorials on the anniversary of the No-vember pogrom in 1938, implying that the pogrom during *Kristallnacht* was repeated by Zionists in the occupied areas; the RAF praised the attack of Israeli athletes at the Summer Olympics at Munich in 1972 by Palestinian terrorists who demanded the release of Palestinian prisoners in Israel and RAF members in Germany; in 1975, a group of terrorists, including the Germans Hans Joachim Klein and Gabriele Kröcher-Tiedemann stormed the OPEC-headquarters in Vi-enna, killing three people, and forced the Austrian government to broadcast an anti-Israeli declaration; in January 1982, an explosion in the Israeli restaurant "Mifgasch Israel" in Berlin-Wilmersdorf killed a 14-month old girl and wounded 24 people.

8. The term "instrumentalization" of the memory of Auschwitz has gained notoriety during the Walser-Bubis debate. In a different context, it was used by Y. Michal Bodemann, who writes in "Staat und Ethnizität": "It is my thesis that . . . the Jewish minority . . . must carry out intel-lectual work, and in various ways is being instrumentalized by this state for foreign and interior politics" (Bodemann 1986: 52).

9. See his *Verkehrte Welten* (1993), where he describes this nexus (Diner 1993: 29).

10. *Liebesgrüße aus Bagdad* (Loveletters from Baghdad), 7–36. This volume also contains essays by Enzensberger, Stephan, Oz, Giordano, Geisel, Friedrich, Bruhn, Siegler, Bittermann, and Wolf-gang Schneider. All authors in this volume are highly critical of the Peace Movement's goal to stop the war against Iraq.

11. Broder also mentions the singer and composer Franz Josef Degenhardt, Erich Modrow, Bishop Forck, the sociologist Ekkehardt Krippendorff, Walter Jens, and another member of Bündnis 90/Grüne, Vera Wollenberger.

12. See Jean Améry, "Der ehrbare Antisemitismus" where he states: "Anti-Semitism became hon-orable in the garb of anti-Zionism" (Améry 1982: 163). Améry's essay contains many ideas that are important for Broder: for example, that the "noble anti-Semite" enjoys his pure conscience because he is not aware of his anti-Semitism (Améry 1982: 164); and that the New Left uses different political standards for condemning Israel as reactionary and praising other dictatorial regimes in the Middle East and elsewhere in the name of a dubious Third World nationalism (Améry 1982:167).

13. The example is taken from Broder's essay "Nach dem Gang-Bang der Guten—über einen CDU-Abgeordneten aus Fulda, alias Schweinchen Oberschlau," in: Broder 2001: 24–26.

14. See Cora Stephan, *Der Betroffenheitskult.* In her analysis of the political culture of Germany in the 1980s, this moral concern for every crisis in the world has become an integral part of Ger-many's national identity (Stephan 1993: 17). At the same time, it produced very few concrete results: "Generally speaking, the 80s were dominated by 'symbolic politics' and 'soft issues': politics that did not creat or change anything in a substantial way" (Stephan 1993: 29).

Works Cited

Améry, Jean. "Der ehrbare Antisemitismus. Rede zur Woche der Brüderlichkeit." *Weiterleben—aber wie? Essays 1968–1978. Herausgegeben und mit einem Nachwort versehen von Gisela Lindemann.* Stuttgart: Klett-Cotta, 1982. 151–75.

Beckermann, Ruth. *Unzugehoerig. Österreicher und Juden nach 1945*. Wien: Löcker Verlag, 1989.

Bittermann, Klaus, ed. *Liebesgrüße aus Bagdad. Die "edlen" Seelen der Friedensbewegung und der Krieg am Golf*. Berlin: Edition TIAMAT, 1991.

Bodemann, Y. Michal. "Staat und Ethnizität." *Jüdisches Leben in Deutschland seit 1945*. Ed. Brumlik, Micha, Doron Kiesel, and Cilly Kugelmann. Frankfurt am Main: Athenäum, 1986. 49–69.

Broder, Henryk M. *Erbarmen mit den Deutschen*. Hamburg: Hoffmann & Campe, 1993.

———. *Der Ewige Antisemit. Über Sinn und Funktion eines beständigen Gefühls*. Frankfurt am Main: Fischer, 1986.

———. *Die Irren von Zion*. Hamburg: Hoffmann & Campe, 1998.

———. *Jedem das Seine*. Augsburg: Ölbaum Verlag, 1999.

———. *A Jew in the New Germany*. Ed. Gilman, Sander and Lilian M. Friedberg. Urbana and Chicago: University of Illinois Press, 2004.

———. *Kein Krieg, nirgends: Die Deutschen und der Terror*. Berlin: Berlin Verlag, 2002.

———. *Ich liebe Karstadt und andere Lobreden*. Augsburg: Ölbaum Verlag, 1987.

———. *Linke Tabus*. Berlin: Bär, 1976.

———. *Schöne Bescherung! Unterwegs im Neuen Deutschland*. Augsburg: Ölbaum Verlag, 1994.

———. "Unser Kampf—Die Deutschen und der Golfkrieg." In *Die Deutsche "Linke" und der Staat Israel*. Ed. Reinhard Renger. Merching: Forum-Verlag, 1994b. 145–58.

———. *www. Deutsche-Leidkultur.de*. Augsburg: Ölbaum Verlag, 2001.

Broder, Henryk M. and Michel R. Lang. *Fremd im eigenen Land. Juden in der Bundesrepublik*. Frankfurt am Main: Fischer, 1979.

Diner, Dan. "Täuschungen: Israel, die Linke und das Dilemma der Kritik." *Der Antisemitismus und die Linke*. Ed. Micha Brumlik, Doron Kiesel, and Linda Reisch. Frankfurt am Main: Haag und Herchen, 1991. 73–81.

———. *Verkehrte Welten. Antiamerikanismus in Deutschland: ein historischer Essay*. Frankfurt am Main: Eichborn: 1993.

Dischereit, Esther. *Joëmis Tisch. Eine jüdische Geschichte*. Frankfurt am Main: Suhrkamp, 1988.

———. *Mit Eichmann an der Börse. In jüdischen und anderen Angelegenheiten*. Berlin: Ullstein Berlin Verlag, 2001.

Fischer, Joschka. "Das dünne Eis der Geschichte. Israel und die deutsche Neue Linke." *Die deutsche "Linke" und der Staat Israel*. Ed. Reinhard Renger. Leipzig: Forum Verlag, 1994. 159–65.

Heenen, Susann: "Deutsche Linke, linke Juden und der Zionismus." *Die Verlängerung der Geschichte. Deutsche, Juden und der Palästinakonflikt*. Ed. Micha Brumlik. Frankfurt am Main: Verlag Neue Kritik: 1983. 103–12.

Markovits, Andrei S. "The Minister and the Terrorist." *Foreign Affairs* 80.6 (2001): 132–146.

Meinhof, Ulrike. "Drei Freunde Israels." *Die Würde des Menschen ist antastbar. Aufsätze und Polemiken*. Berlin: Wagenbach, 1980. 100–102.

Poliakov, Léon. *The history of anti-Semitism*. Tr. from the French by Richard Howard. New York: Vanguard Press, 1965.

Schneider, Karlheinz and Nikolaus Simon, ed. *Solidarität und Deutsche Geschichte. Die Linke zwischen Antisemitismus und Israelkritik. Dokumentation einer Arbeitstagung in der Evangelischen Akademie Arnoldshain, August 1984*. Berlin: Deutsch-Israelischer Arbeitskreis für Frieden im Nahen Osten e.V., 1987.

Stephan, Cora. *Der Betroffenheitskult. Eine politische Sittengeschichte*. Berlin: Rowohlt, 1993.

Part II

THE CASE OF AUSTRIA

5

"What once was, will always be possible"

The Echoes of History in Robert Menasse's Die Vertreibung aus der Hölle

Margy Gerber

"There is an echo, an eternal echo, and whoever doesn't hear this echo today simply isn't listening."

—Robert Menasse[1]

History, or more precisely, man's perception of history, is a red thread running through the four novels Austrian writer Robert Menasse (born 1954) has produced thus far. "History and, above all, our way of dealing with it"[2] is also a central theme of addresses, essays, and interviews. Menasse's philosophical and sociopolitically oriented interest in history began before the collapse of the Cold War order; it was heightened, however, by the political sea change of 1989/90, which, as Menasse has said, made the querying of history more urgent: "I think, if literature considers itself contemporary, and wants to reflect this, then it will simply have to concern itself more with the concept of history. What IS history?"[3]

Given the centricity of the notion of history in Menasse's writing, it is useful to place his new novel, *Die Vertreibung aus der Hölle* (Expulsion from Hell, 2001), within the context of his first three novels, his "trilogy of despiritualization (*Entgeisterung*)," and shorter texts in which he treats man's dealings with history. I will also attempt to situate Menasse's views within the contemporary discourse on history.

In the first two novels of Menasse's trilogy, *Sinnliche Gewißheit* (Meaningful Certainty, 1988) and *Selige Zeiten, brüchige Welt* (Wings of Stone, 1991), Hegel's *Weltgeist*—figuratively speaking—is one of the regulars in the Esperanza Bar in São Paulo, which its Austrian *Stammgäste* have dubbed *Bar jeder Hoffnung* (Bar without hope). Far removed from its full state of consciousness, the *Weltgeist* seems just as hopelessly stranded as the Austrian émigrés themselves, who spend long nights in the smoke-filled bar, imbibing innumerable caipirinhas and debating about Hegel's *Phänomenologie des Geistes* (Phenomenology of Spirit): Leo Singer, the "professor," a self-fashioned inverse Hegelian; Judith Katz, his sounding board and alter ego; and the young Viennese newcomer Roman Gilanian, in whom Singer finds a willing pupil. Leo Singer is convinced that the development of the human spirit is regressive, that consciousness has relapsed to the most basic level of development posited by Hegel: "*sinnliche Gewißheit*" (sensual perception), disconnected, unreflected consciousness. Historical "progress" is the process of ever increasing despiritualization.

Judith Katz illustrates Singer's theory of *Entgeisterung* by turning Walter Benjamin's angel of history around 180 degrees: while Benjamin in his well-known interpretation of Paul Klee's picture "Angelus Novus" perceives the angel as looking back toward the past, while the strong wind of progress unrelentingly propels him into the future, Judith Katz's angel of history is faced toward the future, and is being blown back into the past.[4] Her angel sees the goal of history, but cannot reach it. Assuming Benjamin's interpretive role, Roman Gilanian explains, with formulations paralleling those of Benjamin, an artist's rendering of Judith's angel:

> ... there he [the angel] sees the ideal, which, since it was never reached, disintegrates into rubble before him. He would like to stay on, awaken the dead and try once more to approach the ideal. But a strong storm is blowing from the paradise that was never reached. . . . This storm drives him relentlessly into the past, to which he has turned his back, while his goal disintegrates into ever more bizarre, incomprehensible rubble in front of him. This storm is what we call movement or history. (Menasse 1996a: 209)

The wind which thrust Benjamin's angel forward has changed its direction; the course of history has been reversed.[5] The goal of history is not only unreachable; it is disintegrating into ever less comprehensible rubble.[6] While in Benjamin's model it is the force of progress that prevents the angel from remaining in the past, here history itself pushes the angel ever further away from the ideal.

In 1991, the year in which the second part of the trilogy, *Selige Zeiten*, appeared—the work, which deals most extensively with Leo Singer's efforts to set his thesis down on paper, and which culminates in its (less than successful) publication—Menasse published a separate philosophical treatise, *Phänomenologie der*

Entgeisterung, under the name of his tragicomic fictional hero.[7] A sort of fourth part of the trilogy, it pretends to be the work which Leo struggled so long and so (self-)destructively to write—his continuation and inversion of Hegel's *Phänomenologie des Geistes*. Given the bungling, self-engrossed, and even murderous Leo, one may question the seriousness of Menasse's intentions with the treatise; it can be read simply as a clever Hegel parody, as a "serious carneval gag,"[9] especially since Menasse imitates the language and structure of Hegel's work. However Menasse later published the text under his own name, independent of the novel, as a philosophical essay.[9] Postulating that the peak of absolute knowledge, of consciousness, was reached in Hegel's time, the essay traces the historical and sociocultural steps of the ever-increasing *Entgeisterung* characterizing modern times.

Menasse's negative view of the progress of history refutes both the idealistic *Geschichtsphilosophie* of Hegel and the dialectical materialism of Marx, both of which posit a goal of history. And it stands in contrast to Fukuyama's more recently postulated "end of history," i.e., his claim that with the prevailing of Western democracy over Soviet-style state communism, the telos of history has in principle been achieved.[10] Menasse's notion of the regressiveness of history and the progressive *Entgeisterung* of the human spirit corresponds, on the other hand, to the pessimistic view of the progress of history, the critical revision of the dialectic model advanced by Horkheimer and Adorno as a reaction to fascism, to their theory that rational thought is in a self-destructive state of decline.[11] It is also in keeping with the application of the thermodynamic law of energy loss, measured as entropy, to human systems: the hypothesis of the inevitable and steady deterioration of society found in poststructuralist and postmodern theory. And it is akin to the cultural pessimism of Gehlen's post-histoire (see Gehlen 1956, 1957) and to Lyotard's postmodernist proclamation of the "end of the great narratives," i.e., the end of the philosophic constructs of historical progress based on rationalism (see Lyotard 1984). These congruencies would seem to put Menasse in the postmodern camp.

In the third novel of Menasse's trilogy, *Schubumkehr* (Reverse Thrust, 1995), the metaphorical angel of history meets a violent end. Cemetery angels, a leitmotif in both *Selige Zeiten* and *Schubemkehr*,[12] are unceremoniously dumped into an abandoned stone quarry, where they shatter at the bottom: history as bits and pieces, which—like Humpty Dumpty—cannot be put back together again.[13] This fragmentation of history is manmade; it is man who junks history, who rejects it as a system, whether teleological or entropic. The mayor of the economically depressed quarry town on the Austrian-Czech border, who orders the disposal of the angels, has a plan to revitalize the community by means of tourism. Historic Komprechts is to be turned into a grand open-air museum featuring certain fragments of its past, while ignoring others, thus presenting a complimentary "virtual" picture of itself. History becomes a postmodern construct. Against which, however, the archaic natural forces rebel! The town's lake once again fulfils its legend of claiming a life every eight years; and the massive boulder Teufelstein exhibits its age-old destructive powers. The shattered cemetery angels—the Angel of Death and the Angel of the Last Judgment—have the final word: tradition and myth counteract and avenge this falsification of history, destroying the mayor and his son, and jeopardizing the Disneyland plans for the town.

Menasse has often criticized the eclectic quoting and paraphrasing of history satirized in *Schubumkehr*, and which he and we associate with postmodernism.[14] He sees in it the *Entgeisterung* of contemporary culture: "postmodernism [quotes] from history, without being interested in the *Geist* of the quotations . . ."[15] "[They are] copies, without consciousness of the original . . . farces that have forgotten the tragedy."[16] In this aspect of *Schubumkehr*, at least, the *Geist* of history, the original, and tragedy prevail.

History was also the subject of Menasse's opening address at the Frankfurt Book Fair in 1995. In his speech, Menasse focuses again on the human dimension of history (and its philosophy). History, he states, is a response to the human need to make sense out of the world, to find order in the chaos of events ("to make sense of the senseless").[17] The teleological view of history reflects man's desire to believe in progress toward the good, in the happy ending; history as a fairy tale for adults—and with just as little grounding in reality. Man's assumption that history has "immanent meaning and a goal" (Menasse 1996b: 29) is only possible if we forget or suppress what has gone before. If there is progress, then only in the degree of technical sophistication with which the events of history reoccur.[18] Going one step further, Menasse blames man's fixation on the future and the historization of thought in general for the sequence of every increasing horror that we call history:

> It was the belief that history is a meaningful process with a goal which one can recognize and consciously work toward that turned the cycle of simple biological and social life of mankind on this planet into that sequence of atrocities of ever increasing quality which we study as history and simultaneously suppress. (Menasse 1996b: 28)

This leads Menasse to the conclusion already formulated in the title of his speech: "'History' was the greatest historical error."[19] He urges us to forsake our (Hegelian) concept of history and theorizes what the world would be like without its constraints.

History and historicism in disgrace? The abolition of history, "*Enthistorisierung*" (Menasse 2002: 57) as the key to a better world? Then how does one explain that Menasse's novel *Vertreibung aus der Hölle*, on which he was already working at the time of his Frankfurt speech,[20] deals with historical figures—the rabbi Manasseh ben Israel and other notable seventeenth-century Jewish and Christian intellectuals—and historical events—the Spanish Inquisition, the flight of

Portuguese and Spanish Jews from the Iberian peninsula to Amsterdam, which, freed from Spanish rule, became a haven for religious refugees, and the new blossoming of Sephardic Jewish culture in Protestant Holland? Menasse spent a year and a half studying the Inquisition and the life and writings of the rabbi and others of his time.[21] Moreover, the main character on the contemporary time level of the novel, the Viennese half-Jew Viktor Abravanel, is an *historian*. A university teacher (Dr. phil. habil.) specializing in early modern history, Viktor has done research on Rabbi Manasseh, and it is he, we must assume, who narrates the rabbi's biography. As Mario Scalla remarked in his review, the novel creates the impression that Menasse bade farewell to the philosophy of history only to turn to what was lying in the rubble of the theories of history, namely history itself.[22]

Menasse himself is quick to refute claims that he has written an historical novel.[23] And certainly not of the postmodern kind à la Umberto Eco.[24] If not an historical novel—a broad portrayal of past times—then what *has* he written? And how does it fit into his views on history?

Vertreibung aus der Hölle is two stories in one, two parallel biographies: the life story of Rabbi Samuel Manasseh ben Israel, the child of Portuguese Marranos, i.e., cryptic Jews, who, in spite of the forced conversion of Portuguese Jews to Catholicism, secretly practice their Jewish faith. We follow the rabbi's life from his birth during the historic auto-de-fé of cryptic Jews in Lisbon in 1604, the arrest and torturing of his father by the Inquisition, his forced Christian schooling in a Jesuit *Konfikt*, the flight of the family to Amsterdam, young Manasseh's Judaization and Talmud study in the new Jewish community there, his adult life as scholar and teacher—he was the first teacher of Spinoza—his diplomatic mission to Cromwell's England in the attempt to reverse the centuries-old banning of Jews there, and finally his death in 1657.

The other life story is that of Viktor Abravanel, born in Vienna in 1955 during the celebration following the proclamation of the Austrian State Treaty—the child of a Christian mother and a Jewish father, who, put on a *Kindertransport* by his parents, survived fascism in England in foster care. Viktor's own childhood is greatly marred as a result of his divorced parents' putting him in boarding school, where he lives from age eight to eighteen; "liberated" at last, the socially inadept Viktor joins the post–1968 student scene in Vienna, living in a commune, reading Marx and Wilhelm Reich, and becoming a zealous Trotskyite. We learn little about his life after he leaves the university, only that the now fortyish historian is divorced and has no children.

The stories of the rabbi and Viktor merge on the third time level of the novel—the end of the 1990s—the narrative plane, which is occasioned by a reunion of Viktor's school class, celebrating the twenty-fifth anniversary of their *Matura*. The celebration comes to a sudden and early end when Viktor announces the purported NSDAP membership numbers of his old teachers. The indignant teachers and former classmates storm out of the restaurant, leaving

Viktor and his old flame, Hildegund, alone in the banquet room: the scene is set for a long night of talking about the past. Their exchange of varying perceptions of common experiences in school and as student activists in Vienna in the 1970s is interspersed with narratives in the third person about Viktor's childhood, family, school and university life, *and* about the life of Rabbi Manasseh.[25]

It soon becomes clear that the lives, and even the personalities, of the rabbi and Viktor, despite the 350 years that separate them, are very similar; and it is equally obvious that the author Menasse is intent on our picking this up.[26] Both the rabbi and Viktor are the children of survivors, with attendant emotional scars; both were born under dramatic conditions, at a turning point in their respective country's history; both learn only later of their Jewish origins—both families conceal their Jewish heritage from the children; before learning that they themselves are Jewish, both "follow the pack," bullying Jewish children; both suffer physically as well as emotionally in the Catholic boarding schools they are forced to attend; both are humiliated by having to play the part of Mary in their school's Christmas play; as children and young men, both are naive, rather helpless and passive; they want very much to be accepted and come easily under the sway of others; both are overachievers; and both later experience the re-dogmatization of the liberal views they initially enjoy and support in seventeenth century Amsterdam and in Vienna in the 1970s. As a young rabbi, Manasseh angers his superiors by reconciling, in the spirit of tolerance, theological differences between Christianity and Judaism, but later he does not intervene to stop the censure and extreme humiliation of the liberal Jew Uriel da Costa, who dared to refute the authority of the dogmatic Amsterdam rabbis. Viktor undergoes a disillusioning Stalin-like show trial at the hands of his fellow Trotskyites, with no one inquiring about his possible innocence; yet Viktor himself, twenty years later, carries out a similar act of lynch justice when he reads out the NSDAP membership numbers he has made up for his former teachers, thus knowingly assigning guilt without proof. As Viktor tells Hildegund, his motivation for doing this was not a belated attempt at "*Vergangenheitsbewältigung*"; he simply wanted revenge for the affronts he suffered in school (Menasse 2001: 32).

Menasse even creates family ties between his two protagonists: Viktor's family name, Abravanel, links him to an illustrious Spanish Marrano family dating back to Ferdinand and Isabella; Rabbi Manasseh married into this same Abravanel family. The rabbi's son Joseph is buried in England, in Hampstead,[27] the town in which Viktor's father spent his childhood; and the very fact that England accepted Jews fleeing from fascism can be traced back to Rabbi Manasseh's efforts to end England's ancient ban on Jews. The story comes around full turn when at the end of the novel we learn that Viktor is to fly to Amsterdam the next morning to give a conference paper—on Rabbi Manasseh.

Why this obvious construct? We are left on our own to figure this out: there is no voice, no alter ego, of the author in the novel to tell us what to think.[28] But clearly, we are supposed to draw comparisons between the two life stories, and the two eras: the Spanish Inquisition and the carnage of Sephardic Jews, on the one hand; National Socialism and the Shoah, on the other; religious fanaticism, on the one hand, racial fanaticism, on the other; the lasting psychological effects not only on the survivors, but also on their children; the easy return to dogmatism in so-called free societies.

In the writings of the rabbi, as he has said, Robert Menasse came across the statement: "What once was, will always be possible" ("*Was einmal wirklich war, bleibt ewig möglich*") (Menasse 1996b: 26, 32). The rabbi had written this with reference to the Spanish Inquisition. Three hundred years later, Adorno used the same formulation with regard to Auschwitz. Menasse speaks of an echo, an eternal echo,[29] that is, the repetition of history that defies man's hope for historical progress. In a poignant scene in the novel, the boy Mané—Mané is one of the rabbi's childhood names—thinks he hears an echo when his father is saying evening prayers at a campsite on their flight from Portugal. He shouts, hoping to hear the echo again, which he does. He shouts again and again, louder and louder, more and more hysterically—until his father seizes him. The boy himself was producing the echo (Menasse 2001: 270f.). As Menasse wrote in an early sketch of his novel, this memory was recorded by the rabbi himself in an autobiographical text (Menasse 1997b: 334).

Elaborating on the rabbi's memory, Menasse comments: "Today every contemporary can hear the cry he [the rabbi] wrote about" (Menasse 1997b: 337). The events of history which man must suppress in order to believe in the progress of history continue to exist even if they have disappeared from man's consciousness. They return as echoes, uniting the past, present, and future. In the same sketch, Menasse quotes a second passage from the writings of the rabbi, in which the rabbi postulates the circular movement of history:

> "History is short," the rabbi wrote: "We believe that we have received a relay baton and are able to carry it to the finish line. In reality we run in circles, and often even back to pick up the baton which was lost. We want to think that what was, what appears to be over and past, has no meaning, and take the resounding noise for fading echoes. In reality we run shouting to the place where others shouted before us." (Menasse 1997b: 334)

One of Menasse's aims in writing this novel, as he has often stated, was to treat the beginning and the end of an historic era: the age of rationalism, the European Enlightenment.[30] He sees the Spanish Inquisition as a catalyst of the Enlightenment.[31] The Jews who survived its horrors yearned for a societal system based on reason and rationality, and produced thinkers such as Manasseh and, more importantly, Spinoza. In Menasse's novel Spinoza appears only as a boy, the Talmud pupil of Manasseh. The child of Portuguese Marranos, who, like the rabbi's family, had fled to Amsterdam to escape the Inquisition, young Spinoza questions rabbinical authority and rejects the dogmatism which has established itself in the rabbinical community in Amsterdam,[32] insisting instead on the freedom of rational inquiry, a position which leads to his break with Judaism and foreshadows his later critique of revealed religion that made him a pariah in both Jewish and Christian traditions.

The Enlightenment ended with the bankruptcy of rationality in National Socialism, when reason reverted to irrationality and fanaticism, a repeat of the Spanish Inquisition with greater technical sophistication. The horrors of the Third Reich, however, have not led to a new "Enlightenment," but instead to the discrediting of reason and rationality. As Menasse has written, the postfascist consciousness is postmodern: "Postmodern thought is . . . essentially postfascist thought, a consciousness that is the logical consequence of the caesura in the development of the superstructure caused by the fascist era" (Menasse 1990: 174). Quotations, paraphrases, excerpts devoid of spirit and of history, and copies without reference to the original.

The *Entgeisterung* of the human spirit that was the subject of Menasse's trilogy, his "*Verkümmerungsromane*" (Neuber 1997: 297), is thus also a theme in *Vertreibung aus der Hölle*. The regression is evident both in the individual life development of the two protagonists, i.e., from liberal and tolerant young men to dogmatic, resentful established scholars, and in the diminished qualities of Viktor vis-á-vis the rabbi. Victor is in many respects a pale, banal copy of Rabbi Manasseh, as is Viktor's world in comparison with seventeenth century Amsterdam.[33] As Menasse maintains: "Modern societies on the whole are becoming ever more infantile, ever more regressive."[34] The historic strand of the novel, the Spanish Inquisition, the horrors of its anti-Judaism, the rebirth of Jewish life in Amsterdam, serves as a foil for the contemporary plane in the second half of the twentieth century; it is "the gauge of the significance of our dramas and tragedies" (Thuswaldner 2002).

Menasse has frequently commented on the banality of his own life and of contemporary society in general in comparison with earlier times:

> I have the feeling that I, judged by my wishes, had to suffer great tragedy in my lifetime, but that I, judged by the tragedies of my ancestors, have been able to lead a pleasantly banal, almost comical life, so that the tragedy that I feel and which has sufficiently depressed me during my modest life span . . . is tragicomic. . . . My generation wanted to leave its childhood behind. . . . But we can't grow up. My generation has never learned to grow up. When you get down to it, we are zombies.[35]

In order to portray his generation, as he writes, he needs the "depth of focus (*Tiefenschärfe*) of history."[36] "On the one hand, it really bothered me, on the other hand, it was fascinating to familiarize myself with an historical biography that—only in its 'structure,' of course, not in the details—could have been my own" (Stolz 1997: 329).

On the seventeenth-century level of the novel, the rabbi's pupil Spinoza is the harbinger of a better future, the light which the rabbi himself constantly pursues, but never reaches.[37] Given the novel's parallel structure, one asks: is there no such sign on today's horizon? For whom is Spinoza the code word on the contemporary plane?[38]

In his Frankfurt address, Menasse read an excerpt from his then work-in-progress on Rabbi Manasseh, a text dealing with the petrified embryo found in the body of the rabbi's mother when it was autopsied—the long since calcified fetus of an abdominal pregnancy. The rabbi preserves the embryo in a glass jar in his study. At one point, Rabbi Manasseh plans to leave Amsterdam for the New World, where he hopes to better his financial situation. The trunks are packed, the furniture covered, and the Rabbi walks back and forth in his study trying to think of a way to safely transport the glass-enclosed embryo. In the end, he stays in Amsterdam. "It is . . . not possible to undertake a journey to a new life without damaging the glass [with its petrified contents]" (Menasse 1996b: 35). Menasse goes on to explain the metaphorical meaning he attaches to this scene: "In this image I see contained all of our misery . . . in the indecisiveness to separate one's own life from a virtual history, to accept (*in Kauf nehmen*) the latter's destruction" (Menasse 1996b: 36).

"[T]o separate one's own life from a virtual history, to accept the latter's destruction." This is, I believe, Menasse's hope for the future: the equivalent of the promise of Spinoza. Menasse's novel, although it deals with the past, is very much a novel about the present—and hence not an historical novel, in Menasse's definition.[39] Consider for a moment Menasse's title *Vertreibung aus der Hölle*:[40] there are certainly any number of greater and lesser hells in the novel. But "*Vertreibung*," expulsion, implies "against one's will," a seemingly illogical combination with hell. Our association with "Vertreibung" is of course not "Hölle," but "Paradies." The apparent paradox can be explained by substituting "history" for "hell," and expulsion from the optimistic view of history, the adult fairy tale. It is from this "hell"—which only reproduces other hells—that man must be expelled, against his will. Once "hell" has been left behind, one will recognize "*Heimat*" (home) for what it was: "We always recognize hell only in retrospect. After having been expelled. As long as we stew in it, we call it home."[41] Menasse's mission is to drive us out of the hell of history that we call home—to risk breaking the jar with the petrified embryo.

"What once was, will always be possible"—the emphasis is on "possible" (see Menasse 1996b: 86). The repetition of history is possible, but not inevitable. This is, of course, not only a philosophical or a historiographical position. It is an eminently political stand, one that encourages activism and individualism. History is the product of free human agency. The only way to counter the repetition of history—the echoes and the copies—is man's realization of his role in it and his knowledge of the original.

The answer to history is political activity, a challenge that Menasse readily assumes. In essays,[42] and in the print and electronic media, Menasse frequently speaks out on Austrian politics and history, criticizing Austria's encrusted policy of national reconciliation ("*die versteinerten Verhältnisse*"[43]), the unparliamentary and therefore undemocratic system of *Sozialpartnerschaft*, which crippled the growth of a political culture, its clinging to the national myth of having been a victim of German National Socialism, and, in general, its hypocrisy.

In his Frankfurt address and more recently in his speech accepting the Hölderlin prize, Menasse imagines what we would be like without history. His answer: contemporaries (see Menasse 1996b: 29 and Menasse 2002). Without the burden of the past and without the focus on the end of the rainbow, we would live in the present:

> The recognition of the irretrievability of every single life would be the only legitimation for all of our actions; the happiness that can be realized within our lifetime would be our goal, and our limits would be not to produce a reality which threatens future generations. . . . We would not be without a past, but it would not be an eternally contentious legacy, and we would not be without a future either, but it would not be an eternally threatening bequest. (Menasse 1996b: 29–30, Menasse 2002)

Where does all this place Menasse in the historical discourse? Is he a postmodernist? A modernist? Something else? Menasse shares the postmodern rejection of telos, he too deplores the entropic societal process, but he refutes postmodern arbitrariness and the utter relativization of history and being. Still, by juxtaposing the two life stories in *Vertreibung aus der Hölle*, he demonstrates multiple possibilities for interpreting, or constructing, the past, an idea reinforced by the lack of an authorial voice in the novel. Menasse's emphasis on individualism and activism is a modernist position, as is his hope of learning from the past; his cleaving to the original. Although acutely aware of the dangers of history, Menasse nevertheless wants to recognize meaning and patterns in it. He ultimately places his faith in man's reason. In the final analysis, he is espousing a new emergence from man's self-imposed tutelage, a renewed self-responsibility in our postmodern age.

Notes

1. Stolz 1997: 338. The text was originally published in *Sprache im technischen Zeitalter*, no. 140 (1996), 377–81. All English translations are my own. The English titles of Menasse's first three novels listed in parentheses after the German titles represent the titles of published English translations of these works: *Meaningful Certainty*, *Wings of Stone*, and *Reverse Thrust*, which, all

translated by David Bryer, appeared in Calder Publications, London, in 2000. *Die Vertreibung aus der Hölle* has not yet been translated into English.

2. Quoted from Menasse's speech in acceptance of the Hölderlin prize in June 2002 (Menasse 2002: 57).

3. Interview with Ernst Grohotolsky, "'Mit avanciertem Kunstanspruch erzählen,'" in Stolz 1997: 315. First appeared in *Provinz, sozusagen. Österreichische Literaturgeschichten*, ed. Ernst Grohotolsky (Graz/Wien, 1995). In the same interview, Menasse predicts that authors will now deal with larger historic time frames (as he was about to do).

4. Benjamin 1977: 255. For more in-depth analyses of Menasse's adaptation of Benjamin's angel of history, see Meyer 1996, Müller-Tamm 1997 and Feijóo 2001.

5. Menasse commented on his reversing of Benjamin's angel in a 1988 interview:

> The angel of history has turned around; previously he was driven into an unknown future while looking into the past; at the moment when he sees his face in the mirror, when he turns around, he is driven back into the past with every beat of his wings; now he can no longer arrive—knowing where; and he returns—having forgotten, to where. That is so to speak the theme of the novel [Sinnliche Gewißheit]. (Stolz 1997: 290)

First appeared under the title "*Engel der Geschichte*. Robert Menasse über sein Romandebüt," in *Die Presse*, 30/31 July 1988.

6. Jutta Müller-Tamm calls Judith's angel not the angel of history, but rather the "Engel der Posthistoire" (Müller-Tamm 1997: 53).

7. Leopold Joachim Singer, "Phänomenologie der Entgeisterung. Geschichte des verschwindenden Wissens," *manuskripte* 111 (1991), 91–110. See Konrad Paul Liessmann's comments on the speculations the text evoked in intellectual circles: "Das absolute Wissen. Die Roman Gilanian-Trilogie," in Stolz 1997: 277; first published in *manuskripte* 117 (1992).

8. As Konrad Paul Liessmann writes: "the *Phänomenologie der Entgeisterung* is . . . both a lucid Hegel reflection and an aesthetic ironization of Hegel; it can be read as a serious discursive text, but also as a serious carnival gag. . . ." (Liessmann 1995: 279).

9. Menasse 1995b. See Konrad Paul Liessmann's review of the book publication: "Am Anfang war die Kopie. Über Robert Menasses Hegel-Parodie 'Phänomenologie der Entgeisterung,'" *profil*, 20 February 1995, and Peter Bürger's reprinted *Zeit* review in Stolz 1997: 214–19.

10. Fukuyama 1992. Although he doesn't name him specifically, Menasse criticized and rejected Fukuyama's theory of the end of history in his address at the Frankfurt Buchmesse in 1995: "It is not the insight that history was the attempt to make sense of the senseless that shapes the present discourse on 'the end of history,' but rather once again the belief that it is now finally being realized . . ." (Menasse 1996b: 31). The speech was first published in *Die Zeit* (12 October 1995). It is also included in Stolz 1997: 27–34.

11. Max Horkheimer/Theodor Adorno, *Dialektik der Aufklärung* (Frankfurt: S. Fischer, 1986); first edition 1944/47; Theodor Adorno, *Negative Dialektik*, in *Gesammelte Schriften*, ed. Rolf Tiedemann (Frankfurt/Main: Suhrkamp, 1973), vol. 6; first published in 1965.

12. In *Selige Zeiten*, the cemetery stonecutter Zahradnik has his shop in the courtyard of Leo Singer's apartment house in Vienna. The cemetery angels are frequent objects of reflection. In *Schubumkehr*, Zahradnik's sister, the widow of a quarry worker in Komprechts, receives two large stone angels bequeathed to her by her brother.

13. Jutta Müller-Tamm equates the stone quarry with the "rubble heap of the future" which Judith Katz's angel sees before it (Müller-Tamm 1997: 60–61); Jaime Feijóo, on the other hand, views it as a synonym for the "rubble of history" which Benjamin's angel would like to mend (Feijóo 2001: 75).

14. Especially in his essay "Der Name der Rose ist Dr. Kurt Waldheim. Der erste postmoderne Bundespräsident," in Menasse 1990: 166–74. Essay originally published in *Falter*, 1987. In the preface of *Phänomenologie der Entgeisterung*, Menasse speaks of the "path from *absolute knowledge* to modern disparate 'anything goes' (a form-democratic euphemism for what is really means (*"dessen Wahrheit"*): 'nothing comes')" (Suhrkamp edition, 8).

15. Interview with Wolfgang Neuber, "Die seltsame Lust an falschen Zusammenhängen," in Stolz 1997: 298. First appeared in *Neue Zürcher Zeitung*, 7/8 October 1995.

16. Menasse, "Der Name der Rose ist Dr. Kurt Waldheim," 173. In his use of "original" and "copy," Menasse is indebted to Walter Benjamin (*Das Kunstwerk im Zeitalter seiner technischen Reproduzierbarkeit*). Cf. allusion to Karl Marx, "Der achtzehnte Brumaire des Louis Bonaparte": "Hegel remarks somewhere that all great historical facts and persons happen twice so to speak. He forgot to add: the first time as tragedy, the second time as farce."

17. Menasse, "'Geschichte' war der größte historische Irrtum," in Menasse 1996b: 31. Cf. the title of the Jewish philosopher Theodor Lessing's text *Geschichte als Sinngebung des Sinnlosen* (1919), which he wrote in response to WWI. Lessing calls the supposed rational progress of history a construction; man ascribes meaning to historical events.

18. Cf. Horkheimer and Adorno, *Dialektik der Aufklärung*. Adorno: "No universal history leads from the primitive to the humane, but one *does* lead from the slingshot to the megabomb," *Negative Dialektik* in his *Gesammelte Schriften*, vol. 6, 314.

19. The statement is repeated in the body of the speech (Menasse 1996b: 27). A more drastic phrasing follows: "If there is 'a manure pile of history' then the most urgent thing to throw on this manure pile is our concept of history itself" (Menasse 1996b: 29). In his 1995 interview with Wolfgang Neuber, Menasse repeats the statement, changing "our concept of history" to simply "history" (Neuber 1997: 300).

20. Menasse's idea for the novel dates from 1992, when, viewing the exhibit "Jüdische Lebenswelten" in the Gropius-Bau in Berlin, he came across Rembrandt's painting of Rabbi Manasseh and became curious about this figure, whose name was so similar to his own (Kaindlstorfer 2001: 25). See also Menasse's interview with Anton Thuswaldner in Thuswalder 2002.

21. Interview with Dieter Stolz, "Es passiert alles mögliche," in Stolz 1997: 329. Menasse will have had access to archival material on Rabbi Manasseh in Amsterdam and also to the archives of the Spanish Inquisition. In Menasse 2002 he discusses two works he studied on the Spanish Inquisition, both entitled *Geschichte der Inquisition*, one published in 1932, the other in 1952.

22. Scalla 2001. Menasse himself uses a similar image in regard to history and rubble in his 1995 interview with Ernst Grohotolsky: "The second half of the century will probably be shaped by the mood ("Stimmung") evoked by the clearing of the debris that flies around when history simply occurs. . . ." (Grohotolsky 1997: 315).

23. For example, in his 1997 interview with Dieter Stolz, "Es passiert alles mögliche," Stolz 1997: 329. In a ZDF Nachtstudio discussion (10 October 2001) with Harry Mulisch and F.C. Delius about the historical novel, Menasse again refuted having written an historical novel: "There are two things in life that have especially not interested me: I never wanted to write an historical novel and I never wanted to read an historical novel." In his interview with Anton Thuswaldner in the *Salzburger Nachrichten* ("Verlust der Utopien"), Menasse maintained: "When I read in a review that it's an historical novel, I stop reading. The critic hasn't understood anything."

24. ZDF Nachtstudio, 10 October 2001.

25. Viktor's life is told in conversation with Hildegund and by a third-person omniscient narrator. The rabbi's biography is narrated by a third-person omniscient voice. At times, identification numbers of (apparently) historic documents from archives are cited in connection with narrated events on the seventeenth-century time level.

26. The parallel episodes are often (especially in the beginning of the novel) immediately juxtaposed; frequently the "he" of one episode flows without interruption into the "he" of the other

character, so that the reader is not immediately aware that the protagonist and the time frame have changed.

27. Although Menasse has often repeated (most recently in his *Salzburger Nachrichten* interview with Anton Thuswaldner) that the rabbi's son Joseph is buried in Hampstead, where Menasse's own father lived as a child, this may well be one of the several deviations from history in the novel. A standard biography of Manasseh (Cecil Roth, *A Life of Menasseh ben Israel. Rabbi, Printer, and Diplomat*, 1934) does not corroborate this information. According to Roth, Joseph died while on a trip to Poland in the 1640s. Manasseh's second son Samuel (in the novel, this child dies as a baby) accompanied the rabbi to England and died there, but at the son's request—he did not want to be buried in England—Manasseh brought the coffin back to Holland and buried Samuel in Middleburg. Other discrepancies between the novel and Roth's biography: in Menasse's story, the rabbi has only a sister (Esther); according to the historical account, there was a second son (Ephraim), who lived through adulthood and carried out various business activities for Manasseh. In the novel, this child was conceived but never born, as will be explained below. The rabbi Aboab, Manasseh's successful arch rival, did not return immediately from the New World (Recife), snatching the chief rabbi position back just as Manasseh was about to assume it; instead, Aboab remained in Recife for thirteen years (1641–754) returning only when Portugal regained control of the Dutch holding. In the novel, it is claimed that Shabbetai Zevi, the messianic East European Jew, was never supported in Amsterdam; according to Roth, Aboab and most of the Amsterdam Jewish community supported Shabbetai Zevi; also, Menasse sets Zevi's messianic movement earlier than it actually took place: it began in 1665 (Aboab was one of the signatories of a letter of allegiance to Zevi in 1666); the historical Rabbi Manasseh died in 1657. Nor is there in Roth's biography any suggestion that Rabbi Manasseh was poverty-stricken; in the novel, the rabbi's publishing house soon goes under—another financial failure, whereas, according to Roth, Manasseh continued publishing at his Hebrew press until his death. Nor are there indications in the Roth biography that Manasseh became so dissipated in his failure, drinking, taking drugs, vegetating, a spineless opportunist, as Menasse portrays the rabbi in his last years.

28. Pointed out by Menasse himself in the ZDF Nachtstudio discussion, 10 October 2001.

29. "What is a sentence that is not a quotation but which has the exact same wording as an earlier one? It is an echo, an eternal echo . . ." (Robert Menasse, "Die Geschichte ist kurz und ewig. Romanprojekt," in Stolz 1997: 338). Both the statement of the rabbi and that of Adorno may well be fictional. Extensive searching failed to locate the quotation in Adorno's writings.

30. See Menasse 1996: 26–27; Menasse's 1997 interview with Stolz, "Es passiert alles mögliche," Stolz 1997: 328; his interview with Thuswaldner in the *Salzburger Nachrichten*; and the ZDF Nachtstudio discussion.

31. ZDF Nachtstudio.

32. Here, young Spinoza stands in contrast to the now opportunistic/indifferent Manasseh, who does not intervene in the punishment of Uriel da Costa. Spinoza loses all respect for Manasseh as a result.

33. One indication of the intended banality is Menasse's choice of the name Viktor for his protagonist—Viktor, as Menasse has said, is a "trend name" (*Modename*) of his generation (ZDF Nachtstudio). "Viktor" stands in contrast to the three names the rabbi has during his lifetime: Manoel (the name of the Portuguese king who ordered the conversion of all Jews—conformity, disguise), Mané (naive), Samuel (the seer).

34. Interview with Neuber, 1997: 297. Menasse goes on to remark: "In the beginning was the spirit (*Geist*), at the end is the despiritualization (*Entgeisterung*)" (Neuber 1997: 297).

35. ZDF Nachtstudio. See also Menasse's interviews with Neuber (1997) and Thuswaldner (2002).

36. ZDF Nachtstudio.

37. Menasse's narrator describes the sensations of the dying rabbi:

    > It was the beginning, the start, but he manifested this sense of finality, this restlessness and despair that one has when there is only a little time left. Soon this chubby child would have to run home, as fast as he could. He ran, and got bigger and bigger, and fatter and fatter, and blacker and blacker. He ran and didn't arrive. Someplace up ahead there was light. (Menasse 2001: 492)

38. Mario Scalla asks this question at the end of his review ("Klassentreffen mit Spinoza"), without attempting to give an answer.

39. In his 1997 interview with Stolz, Menasse speaks of the novel's ". . . many contemporary implications" (Stolz 1997: 328). The novel is "not an historical novel" but rather "a radically contemporary one" (Stolz 1997: 329). "It shows the present in its vulnerable spot: its relationship to its past (Gewordenheit)" (Stolz 1997: 329). As he said in the ZDF Nachtstudio discussion in October 2001: "the novel treats today's dealing (Umgang) with history." In his review of Vertreibung aus der Hölle, Klaus Nüchtern speaks of "memories of the present"—"Erinnerungen an die Gegenwart" ("Signatur des Wahnsinns. 'Die Vertreibung aus der Hölle': Erinnerungen an die Gegenwart," Falter, 25 July 2001, 54).

40. The title occurs in the novel in connection with Viktor's surreptitious entry into the secret archives of the Vatican, where he is able to look at documents regarding the Abravanel family, his supposed Marrano forefathers: "The history was hell. I saw informers' reports and torture protocols. People were broken there and souls put together again new. . . . Hell—and die expulsion from Hell!" (Menasse 2001: 144). The working title of the novel was "Seelenfabrik" (Soul Factory) (Stolz 1997: 328).

41. Quoted from the book jacket of the novel.

42. Three volumes of essays should be mentioned here: Die sozialpartnerschaftliche Ästhetik. Essays zum österreichischen Geist (Sonderzahl: Vienna, 1990; 2nd ed.: Überbau und Untergrund, Frankfurt/Main: Suhrkamp, 1997); Das Land ohne Eigenschaften. Essay zur österreichischen Identität (Vienna: Sonderzahl, 1992; 2nd rev. ed.: Frankfurt/Main: Suhrkamp, 1995); Erklär mir Österreich. Essays zur österreichischen Geschichte (Frankfurt/Main: Suhrkamp, 2000). Menasse speaks of Austria as the "country of the either and or" ("Land des Entweder-und-Oder") (Menasse 1995a: 14ff.). He uses the metaphor of the Punschkrapfen (an Austrian pastry) to describe the Second Republic ("pink outside, brown inside") (Menasse 1995a: 31).

43. Menasse 1995a: 13. Jaime Feijóo makes the connection between the regressive historical development, which Menasse theorizes and illustrates in his first three novels and the situation in Austria since 1945 which he explicitly criticizes in his essays (Feijóo 2001: 71).

Works Cited

Adorno, Theodor. Negative Dialektik. In Gesammelte Schriften, ed. Rolf Tiedemann. Frankfurt/Main: Suhrkamp, 1973, VI.

Benjamin, Walter. "Über den Begriff Geschichte." In Benjamin. Illuminationen. Ausgewählte Schriften I. Frankfurt/Main: Suhrkamp, 1977.

Bürger, Peter. "Gesellschaftskritik heute." In Die Welt scheint unverbesserlich. Zu Robert Menasses "Trilogie der Entgeisterung." Ed. Dieter Stolz. Frankfurt/Main: Suhrkamp, 1997.

Feijóo, Jaime. "Verkehrte Geschichte(n): Erkundung eines österreichischen Grundmotivs in Robert Menasses 'Trilogie der Entgeisterung.'" Modern Austrian Literatur, nos. 3/4 (2001): 64–78.

Fukuyama, Francis. The End of History and the Last Man. New York: Macmillan, 1992.

Gehlen, Arnold. Urmensch und Spätkultur. Bonn: Athenäum, 1956.

———. Die Seele im technischen Zeitalter. Reinbek: Rowohlt, 1957.

Grohotolsky, Ernst. "'Mit avanciertem Kunstanspruch erzählen.'" In *Die Welt scheint unverbesserlich*. Ed. Dieter Stolz. Frankfurt/Main: Suhrkamp 1997.

Haider, Hans. "'Engel der Geschichte.'" In *Die Welt scheint unverbesserlich*. Ed. Dieter Stolz. Frankfurt/Main: Suhrkamp, 1997.

Horkheimer, Max, and Theodor Adorno. *Dialektik der Aufklärung*. New ed. Frankfurt/Main: S. Fischer, 1986.

Kaindlstorfer, Günter. "Robbis Irrtum. Robert Menasse über seinen Roman 'Vertreibung aus der Hölle.'" *Stuttgarter Zeitung*, 28 August 2001: 25.

Lessing, Theodor. *Geschichte als Sinngebung des Sinnlosen*. Munich: Matthes & Seitz, 1983.

Liessmann, Konrad Paul. "Am Anfang war die Kopie. Über Robert Menasses Hegel-Parodie 'Phänomenologie der Entgeisterung.'" *profil*, 20 Feb. 1995.

———. "Das absolute Wissen. Die Roman Gilanian-Trilogie." In *Die Welt scheint unverbesserlich*. Ed. Dieter Stolz. Frankfurt/Main: Suhrkamp, 1997.

Lyotard, Jean-François. *The Postmodern Condition*. Minneapolis: University of Minnesota Press, 1984.

Menasse, Robert. *Die sozialpartnerschaftliche Ästhetik. Essays zum österreichischen Geist*. Sonderzahl: Vienna, 1990. 2nd edition: *Überbau und Untergrund*. Frankfurt/Main: Suhrkamp, 1997.

———. *Selige Zeiten, brüchige Welt*. 2nd ed. Frankfurt/Main: Suhrkamp, 1994.

———. *Das Land ohne Eigenschaften. Essay zur österreichischen Identität*. 2nd rev ed. Frankfurt/Main: Suhrkamp, 1995a.

———. "Der Name der Rose ist Dr. Kurt Waldheim. Der erste postmoderne Bundespräsident." In *Die sozialpartnerschaftliche Ästhetik. Essays zum österreichischen Geist*. Sonderzahl: Vienna, 1990, 166–74.

———. *Phänomenologie der Entgeisterung. Geschichte des verschwindenden Wissens*. Frankfurt/Main: Suhrkamp, 1995b.

———. "'Geschichte' war der größte historische Irrtum. Rede zur Eröffnung der 47. Frankfurter Buchmesse 1995." In Robert Menasse. *Hysterien und andere historische Irrtümer*. Wien: Sonderzahl, 1996b.

———. *Sinnliche Gewißheit*. 2nd rev. ed. Frankfurt/Main: Suhrkamp, 1996a.

———. "Die Geschichte ist kurz und ewig. Ein Romanprojekt." In *Die Welt scheint unverbesserlich*. Ed. Dieter Stolz. Frankfurt/Main: Suhrkamp, 1997b.

———. *Schubumkehr*. 2nd ed. Frankfurt/Main: Suhrkamp, 1997a.

———. *Die Vertreibung aus der Hölle*. Frankfurt/Main: Suhrkamp, 2001.

———. "Igel, Hase und die Lehre des Rabbi." *Frankfurter Allgemeine Zeitung*, 15 June 2002: 57.

Meyer, Jürgen, "Von Engeln und Puppen. Walter Benjamins Geschichtphilosophie in der Philosophie Geschichten Robert Menasses." In *Freiburger Universitätsblätter*, No. 31 (March 1996), 135–49.

Müller-Tamm, Jutta. "Die Engel der Geschichten. Zu einem Motiv in Robert Menasses Romantrilogie." In *Die Welt scheint unverbesserlich*. Ed. Dieter Stolz. Frankfurt/Main: Suhrkamp, 1997.

Neuber, Wolfgang. "Die seltsame Lust an falschen Zusammenhängen." In *Die Welt scheint unverbesserlich*. Ed. Dieter Stolz. Frankfurt/Main: Suhrkamp, 1997.

Nüchtern, Klaus. "Signatur des Wahnsinns. 'Die Vertreibung aus der Hölle': Erinnerungen an die Gegenwart." *Falter*, 25 July 2001: 54.

Roth, Cecil. *A Life of Menasseh ben Israel. Rabbi, Printer, and Diplomat*. Philadelphia: The Jewish Publication Society of America, 1934.

Scalla, Mario. "Klassentreffen mit Spinoza. Intellektuellenmärchen. Robert Menasses neuer Roman 'Die Vertreibung aus der Hölle,'" *Freitag*, Literaturextra, 12 October 2001.

Stolz, Dieter. "Es passiert alles mögliche." In *Die Welt scheint unverbesserlich*. Ed. Dieter Stolz. Frankfurt/Main: Suhrkamp, 1997.

Thuswaldner, Anton. "Verlust der Utopien." *Salzburger Nachrichten*, 3 August 2002.

Wischenbart, Rüdiger. "Was sonst noch geschieht. Nachwort." In Robert Menasse, *Hysterien und andere historische Irrtümer*. Wien: Sonderzahl, 1996.

6

THE GLOBAL AND THE LOCAL IN RUTH BECKERMANN'S FILMS AND WRITINGS

Hillary Hope Herzog

Contemporary Austrian-Jewish writing, to a far greater extent than its German-Jewish counterpart, adheres closely to the tradition of city writing. The city of Vienna plays a crucial role in the themes explored by a number of significant Jewish writers of the post-Shoah generation. For these writers, Vienna serves as a more powerful referent than Austria. Indeed, their approaches to the difficult task of negotiating an identity as an Austrian Jew are crucially bound up with a primary identification with Vienna. However important, it is, nonetheless, a highly complex relationship between Jewish writers and the city in which they live, work, and which they recreate in their literature. As they seek to create new narratives of the Jewish experience of the past and present, they are continually confronted with a city that exists at once as a lived experience in the present and is at the same time located in the past—as a space of both personal and collective Jewish history.

The writer and filmmaker Ruth Beckermann lives much of the time outside of Austria, yet Vienna is central to her explorations of Jewish history. In an interview with Andrea Reiter, she commented on her relationship to Vienna: "The most pleasant thing about living here is that one can partake of whatever one pleases of its literature, its music. . . . I love Vienna, and I will never have as much understanding for another literature as I have for that of Schnitzler. That is quite clear" (Reiter 1998: 162). It is striking that when commenting on her current living situation and work in Vienna in the 1990s, Beckermann should evoke an image of the city as a cultural space located in the past. The comment reveals a deep attachment to Vienna, but it is a relationship that is culturally rather than geographically defined. Maintaining some distance to the city enables her to be selective in embracing only certain aspects of Viennese life in a relationship marked equally by attachment and distance.

As Beckermann seeks to explore the experience of European Jews since the Holocaust in her films and writings, she departs from the very personal question of why her parents and others of their generation chose to return to Vienna after the war, a city that was hardly welcoming of Jewish returnees. Her reflections on the Jewish Diaspora begin in the streets of Vienna. An important early publication is *Die Mazzesinsel* (The Mazza Island, 1984), a historical essay on the Jews of Vienna's second district. Her more recent film, *homemad(e)* (2000), presents a slice of the lives of Jews who settled in the street in which Beckermann lives. Throughout Beckermann's work, Vienna is at the center of a process of exploration marked by a dynamic of departure and return, distance and proximity, and the fluid movement between the past and present. This essay considers Beckermann's relationship to Vienna in the context of her examinations of Jewish history and memory. What kind of climate does the city offer an artist who wishes to examine topics previously taboo or underexamined? What sorts of stories can be told in this city? How does Beckermann see the link between Jewish experience in the present and the legacy of Jewish Vienna? As I hope to show, the city is a constant and significant presence in Beckermann's work, and she requires both access to and distance from Vienna in creating her narratives of Jewish history and memory.

In the essay *Unzugehörig* (Non-Belonging, 1989), Beckermann reflects on the complexity of the generational conflicts between survivors of the Holocaust and their children, describing her generation's struggle to come to terms with their parents' decision to return to Vienna, a city that clearly did not welcome their return, but seemed merely to tolerate it. Beckermann writes, "In order to remain in Vienna, Jews have to follow certain conditions, which state: repress your own history; consider the case closed; Begin at ground zero; act as if all that were possible" (Beckermann 1989: 111). Beckermann characterizes the postwar atmosphere as one in which the presence of Jews was an unwelcome reminder of a past that the dominant culture was eager to forget, and which therefore required that this presence remain undetectable. Those who wished to return were to do so as Austrians, and not as Jews.

Beckermann's critique is directed not only against the culture that established this strict set of conditions and constraints upon Jewish life in postwar Austria; she also discusses the negative effects of Jewish compliance with these imposed conditions. She characterizes the silence of her parents' generation on the Nazi era as contributing to the erasure of Jewish history, and further suggests that living in Vienna under such conditions has produced a selective relationship to the past, corresponding to the official version of Austrian history of the Second Republic:

> Viennese Jews made every possible effort to preserve the peace by remaining silent about sensitive issues—and every issue that has to do with Jews can become sensitive. They mythologize their own history, clinging to the great musicians and poets that Jewish Vienna produced, while forgetting the dark side of emancipation and assimilation. They fantasize that they are back in the sanitized past, without being clear with themselves that this era gave rise to the era of National Socialist persecution. (Beckermann 1989: 109)

This mythologization of history depends on the elision of the First Republic, the *Anschluss*, and the Second World War in order to reconnect to a nostalgic and sanitized image of Vienna: "It also appears to be no coincidence that the Jews who remained in Vienna after their liberation continued to frequent precisely those spaces that corresponded to their image of the former monarchy, such as the Meierei in the Stadtpark, Cobenzl, and Semmering" (Beckermann 1989: 102). When Beckermann suggests that her parents' generation has clung to the great Jewish musicians and poets of a hundred years ago and developed a deep attachment to the architecture of Habsburg Vienna, she sees them as projecting a harmonious and productive Austrian-Jewish symbiosis onto the *fin de siècle*. The creation of an idealized image of Vienna in 1900 offers them the psychological means for coping with Vienna in the present. Turning to the Vienna of Freud and Schnitzler, Mahler and Schönberg, they effectively create bridges to the past, establishing connections between nostalgic memories and present reality that obscure the experience of the war and the Holocaust.

The essay *Unzugehörig* is characteristic of Beckermann's work in its placement of this discussion of the experiences of the postwar generation within the broader framework of Central European Jewish history. Historiographical concerns— both personal and collective—are central to Beckermann's critique of both Jewish and non-Jewish society in Austria, playing a prominent role in her work in film, as well as in her writing.

Ruth Beckermann's 1987 film *Die papierene Brücke* (The Paper Bridge) exemplifies her very personal approach to documentary filmmaking. The boundaries between history and memory, between the personal and the collective, are fluid in this film, as they are in a number of her other works. In a voiceover at the beginning of the film, Beckermann explains her motivations for making the film. Having spent the summer reflecting on her family history, looking at old photographs, and asking questions of her living relatives, Beckermann then left Vienna in the early winter, heading East to trace in reverse the path that brought her family to Austria. It is evident that she approaches this personal history in the context of a broader concern with central European Jewish history, as she notes that she was perplexed to read recently that the fate of the Jews would only become the focus of study for scholars once there are no longer any living survivors. Beckermann comments later in the film that her own fear of forgetting this story needing to be further explored is bound up with a fear of her parents' death. She seems compelled to document a history that is at once personal and collective. Beckermann states, "It is a strange feeling when the experiences that determined the course of your life become history—when you become an object of scholarly investigation" (Beckermann 1987).

But just what does Beckermann seek as she leaves Vienna, traveling to first Romania and then into Yugoslavia, before ultimately pushing on to the Russian border? As she describes her reasons for undertaking this film project and the journey the film records, both the spoken and visual narratives of the film underscore the impossibility of telling the story she wishes to tell from within the city of Vienna. Dismissing months of intensive study and reflection on her family history, Beckermann concludes, "I gained no further understanding during this summer" (Beckermann 1987). As we hear these words, the camera captures an unfolding street scene, filmed from inside a tram traveling along the Ringstrasse of Vienna's central first district. The street is immediately recognizable, and even before Beckermann states that her intellectual engagement with the Central European Jewish experience often makes her head spin, we can clearly see that she is, quite literally, going in circles.

Ceasing this circular motion and breaking out of the bounded space of Vienna, Beckermann travels east in pursuit of the stories her relatives told her during her childhood. Her film suggests that the telling of and listening to the stories in Vienna is somehow inadequate to her relatives' experiences. Her attempts to remember, record, and understand are insufficient, requiring a different approach—Vienna is not a space in which these stories can be fully explored. As the tram moves around the Ring, Beckermann tells the story of her Grandmother Rosa, who survived the war in Vienna in hiding. Oma Rosa was able to escape detection not by disappearing, but by remaining in full view, erasing only her voice. Pretending to be dumb, she was not recognized as a Jew. In a sense, Beckermann's film seeks to fill the void created by her grandmother's silence, searching out the stories her grandmother did not tell her.

Beckermann addresses the spectator directly in this voiceover early in the film, asking "The story of Hagazussa—do you know it?" (Beckermann 1987). She then relates the story of an outsider who has little contact with the villagers among whom she lived. Gradually, Hagazussa became nearly invisible and was able to move unseen through the attics and cellars of the homes in the village. Thus moving freely, Hagazussa learned many stories, such as the tale of the paper bridge that gives the film its title. In many of her films, Beckermann makes use of this freedom of movement to trace the narratives she wishes to depict, moving among various sites of memory to produce a coherent narrative.

The film has two parts, the travel narrative of the trip to Romania and, upon Beckermann's return, an exploration of Jewish life in Vienna. The first part is a documentary of the Jewish communities encountered in the East. The Viennese portion of the film includes her parents' accounts of their experiences of the war and postwar return to Vienna, as well as a fascinating record of an American production of a Holocaust film being shot in Vienna.

Underlying the trip to the East is the notion that those Jewish stories that remain unfinished or unsatisfying in Vienna will be completed. More specifically, Beckermann seeks out Eastern Jews whose recent history is not marked by assimilation, accommodation, and silence, pockets of surviving Jews whose identity as Jews appears to be self-evident. In Radautz, Romania, she visits a community composed of ten Jewish men, all advanced in years, who meet daily in a small temple. Beckermann is candid in describing her impressions. She notes, "Just like pictures—that's how they appeared before me" (Beckermann 1987). The film-maker's desire to integrate the scenes and images she encounters into a stream of memory and fantasy are foregrounded in the film, playing as important a role as the scenes and images themselves. In another village, she attends the synagogue at Hanukkah, finding the community very welcoming, happy to include "the visitors from abroad, who just want to take a quick look at where they come from, where their parents and grandparents and all of their stories came from" (Beckermann: 1987).

Yet Beckermann is also aware that this apparent simplicity and clarity is largely the projection of her own desires. In this last village, where the synagogue is full and lively and young people study Hebrew, all is not as it first appears. The community is challenged in its attempts to preserve itself and its traditions by the continual drain of emigration. There are only two young students in the Hebrew class. Adults both young and old are all asking themselves whether they should make a new start in Israel. As she travels further, Beckermann reflects, "the land-scape drew me in. I traveled right up to the Russian border. Still, the closer I got to my goal the less attainable it became" (Beckermann 1987). While the film's interviews and scenes like the one in the temple suggest the continued presence of small Jewish communities in the East, these are gradually overshadowed by a focus on empty spaces that visually depict the loss of community.

The pursuit of history and memory becomes more personal as Beckermann returns to Vienna to film interviews with her parents recounting what brought them to Vienna. Her father came to Vienna after the war from Czernowitz, eventually opening a clothing store and becoming a successful and respected businessman. Beckermann films her father in his clothing shop, neatly refolding his merchandise as he describes his experiences. The interview contains a number of comments on his relationship to his chosen city and to Austria. He tells her that there is a picture of the Emperor Franz Josef hanging in his office, a linger-ing symbol of a once enthusiastic and unreserved identification by Jews with the

Habsburg monarchy. His relationship to Vienna and the nation in the present is less clear; a sentence in which he begins to describe his relationship to Vienna after living there for so many years breaks off without conclusion. When asked how he dealt with anti-Semitism after the war, Beckermann's father shrugs and states that he has always known how to defend himself, with words and when necessary, with force.

Although the father downplays these experiences, the film seems to appraise them differently. The interview with Beckermann's father is intercut with contemporary footage of an anti-Waldheim demonstration on Vienna's central St. Stephen's Square. Beckermann films the arrest of one anti-Waldheim protestor, while the protestor shouts to the police officers, the crowd, and the camera, proclaiming his right to a peaceful demonstration. Beckermann's father appears, arguing with Waldheim supporters who unleash a stream of anti-Semitic comments, each one more brazen than the last. In a voiceover, Beckermann asks ironically, "Who says that the Viennese don't recognize Jews anymore? They unmasked my father as a Jew instantly" (Beckermann 1987).

Beckermann's mother's story is not explored as extensively in the film as that of her father. The film does contain an interview, however, in which she tells of her own return to Vienna after the war. She sees her own fate as having been determined by meeting and falling in love with Beckermann's father. She settled in Vienna with him because he was determined to make a new life there. Although born in Vienna, she did not feel at home upon her return and would gladly have left. Yet she never felt she had the right to force her husband to leave. She reflects that because she had children, she was never able to justify to herself living among the perpetrators. Even after so many years, she feels at home in Israel, and not in Austria.

In Vienna, as in Romania, the film takes up the experiences of other Jews outside of Beckermann's family. While she films her parents at home, at work, and in the street, Beckermann captures other Jews in a most unusual situation far removed from everyday life in Vienna. Forty Viennese Jews assemble on the set of an American movie production (the filming of Herman Wouk's *War and Remembrance*) to serve as extras inhabiting a fictional Theresienstadt ghetto created at the outskirts of the city. As they shuffle past a sign announcing the ghetto marked with the proclamation "No Loitering," the film visually establishes a contrast between the impossibility of remaining still and the surreal quality of their movements—a visual commentary on the Diaspora experience. In spite of the blunt prohibition, these Jews are rooted in Vienna, while at the same time their experience is one of movement.

Warming themselves in a tent on the set, some are reluctant to speak to Beckermann of their experiences, objecting to talking about it in that space, while others feel compelled to speak about the difficult memories evoked by the set. Beckermann notes that she finds herself thinking nostalgically of Romania, "where everything seems so simple" (Beckermann 1987). For these Jews, things are clearly not at all simple. Unable to tell their own stories in a city that long made these stories taboo, they end up as extras in an American version of their story—a narrative only possible because of the spatial and temporal distance that Americans have to the Holocaust, a distance that is impossible for Austrian Jews. The unreal space of the film set, bringing the past eerily into the present, becomes a site of memory, a site at which for some, new narratives are possible. Beckermann films for a long time, commenting that she cannot get enough of their stories of survival.

Beckermann's pursuit of stories of both loss and survival continually draws her in and out of Vienna. The movement of *Die paperiene Brücke* is paralleled in other films. In fact, the film may be seen as part of a trilogy, each segment of which is in effect a travel narrative. In *Die papierene Brücke*, Beckermann travels from Vienna to the shtetl, tracing in reverse the migration of her relatives. *Wien Retour* (Return to Vienna, 1983) details the reverse, telling the story of Franz Weintraub-West, a Jewish communist who settled in the second district, as he moves from the shtetl to the city. This earlier film, shot in Vienna before the Waldheim scandal unfolded in Austria, is not marked by the isolation and vulnerability of *Die papierene Brücke*. Dagmar Lorenz has stressed the interiority and intimacy of this film, with its exclusive focus on Weintraub-West (Lorenz 2003: 159). When the film moves out of the private space of Weintraub-West's apartment, it is also a movement into the past, as Weintraub-West's reminiscences on a walk through the Prater are intercut with historical photographs of Red Vienna. The third film, *Nach Jerusalem* (Toward Jerusalem, 1990), depicts a journey between Tel Aviv and Jerusalem with a panorama of Israeli life unfolding along a single street. The centrality of this travel motif has been noted by Lorenz, who sees the filmmaker as traveler occupying a position as a deterritorialized outsider, an appropriate vantage point from which to explore the central European Jewish experience (Lorenz 2003: 164).

While these earlier films continually shift between the past and present, Beckermann's more recent film *homemad(e)* (2000) is more firmly rooted in the present. The film captures a pivotal moment in contemporary Austrian life as the FPÖ coalition is assuming power. In this film, Beckermann moves not only into the present, but back to the street in which she grew up and still lives. A voiceover at the beginning of the film foregrounds the film's homemade quality reflected in its production and subject matter: "Just back from a big trip with a big camera, I am now going to take a small camera on a small trip, venturing no further than just outside my front door right in the middle of Vienna" (Beckermann 2000). The smaller camera limits the distancing effect between the photographer and subject. Similarly, a more limited use in this film of voiceover narrative distinct from the visual track keeps the viewer focused on the film's subject, the people who live and work in the Marc Aurel Strasse, while also shifting Beckermann's position from a detached perspective outside of the filmic images to sometimes being captured in or partly in the frame. Beckermann herself is thus nearly as much a visual as an aural presence in *homemad(e)*. This film shares with her other documentary work a highly personal quality, but here the filmmaker is a part of the film in a new way. Filming her neighbors and acquaintances, she engages in dialogues with the subjects of her interviews. They joke with her, ask her questions, draw her into a conversation. No longer the deterritorialized solo traveler, Beckermann is clearly a part of this community. But is she really at home? The "(e)" of the film's title, creating the unsteady adjective "home-mad," suggests that there is no simple answer to this question. For Lorenz, this film is a continuation of Beckermann's "search for the appropriate cultural and geographical space" (2003: 170).

On one level, the film does seem to be an affirmation of Jewish life in contemporary Vienna. The film depicts vital, interesting people who form a community anchored by the sidewalks of the Marc Aurel Strasse and the Café Salzgries. Beckermann's identification and personal engagement with this world is underscored by the intimacy of her portraits of the street's inhabitants. Her interviews are conversations on intimate matters. She asks the interviewees about how they live, where they see their friends, how they get ready to go out, why they visit the café and what it means to them.

While the familiarity between Beckermann and the people she films shows the filmmaker to be a part of the community she depicts in the film, when the discussion shifts from the intimate and personal to the public and political, it is no longer clear the extent to which Beckermann or her subjects feel at home. The sense of belonging and community revolves around the street. With Jörg Haider's rise to political prominence at the national level, this attachment is not integrated into a greater sense of municipal or national community. Is it possible to feel a part of this broader community when, as Beckermann's voiceover states, every third Austrian and every fourth Viennese voted for Haider?

As the regular customers at the Café Salzgries relate their opinions about the election results on film, one man laments the artificial simplicity and clarity that Haider's party projects, and wonders whether he can identify with this image of Austrian life. Another posits that the Café Salzgries will remain the same no matter who is in power, but concludes on a more pessimistic note, looking ahead to the new century with a sense of foreboding. An unchanging Café Salzgries may continue to provide a respite for the people of the Marc Aurel Strasse. One of the film's subjects describes the role of this street in the life of the city, likening it to a village created within the city in order to be able to bear the stresses of city life. Still, the Marc Aurel Strasse does not shield its inhabitants from a confrontation with the nation of which they are a part. A number of the interviewees are actively involved in political resistance against Haider and thus play an active, if oppositional, role in civic life beyond the street.

Ruth Beckermann's work is underscored by a perspective that is at the same time cosmopolitan and very much rooted in Vienna. The themes of her films and writing require this dynamic of exploration and return, and both elements seem to be equally important in her work. Like other Austrian-Jewish writers, such as Doron Rabinovici, Robert Schindel, and Robert Menasse, Beckermann makes Vienna her home and a focus of her work. Unlike German-Jewish writers of the same generation, the space of one particular city plays a crucial role in Austrian-Jewish literature, without rendering it provincial. These other writers share with Beckermann a heavy travel schedule. All have strong ties to another place—Menasse to Brazil, Rabinovici and Schindel to Israel. In order to continue to write and be productive, it seems these writers need to be in Vienna and, at times, *not* to be. Beckermann has used the term "uncannily at home" (*unheimlich heimisch*) to convey this sense of being simultaneously at home and unhomed in Vienna. This feeling is constitutive of these artists' experience of living in Vienna, and it provides them a unique point of access to the culture about which they write.

An image from the film *Die papierene Brücke* illustrates the uneasy yet familiar position these writers occupy. Near the end of the film, there is a scene shot in a Viennese café in which Beckermann and these other writers spend a great deal of time together. Of all of the cafés in the city, this group of Jewish writers, the children of survivors, chooses to be regular patrons of the Café Prückl, located on Karl Lueger Platz. The windows of the café look out at a statue of Lueger, the famous pragmatic politician who successfully campaigned for mayor of Vienna in 1895 on a platform of popular anti-Semitism and who is fondly remembered and memorialized in the present. Rather than avoid the square and its statue, these Austrian-Jewish writers have carved a place for themselves alongside it, where it stands as a reminder they seem to welcome, *unheimlich heimisch* in their Vienna.

Works Cited

Beckermann, Ruth. *Die Mazzesinsel. Juden in der Wiener Leopoldstadt 1918–38.* Wien: Löcker Verlag, 1984.

———. *Unzugehörig: Österreicher und Juden nach 1945.* Wien: Löcker Verlag, 1989.

———. *Wien Retour.* Documentary film. 1983.

———. *Die papierene Brücke.* Film essay. 1987.

———. *Nach Jerusalem.* Film essay. 1990.

———. "Auf der Brücke: Rede zur Verleihung des Manes Sperber-Preises, Wien, 16/10/2000." *The German Quarterly* 74.1 (Winter 2001).

———. *homemad(e).* Film essay. 2003.

Lorenz, Dagmar. "German and Austrian Jewish Women's Writing at the Milennium." In *Unlikely History: The Changing German-Jewish Sumbiosis, 1945–2000.* Ed. Leslie Morris and Jack Zipes. New York: Palgrave, 2002. 277–90.

———. "Post-Shoah Positions of Displacement in the Films of Ruth Beckermann." *Austrian Studies* 11, no. 1 (2003). XX.

Markovits, Andrei S. "Austrian Exceptionalism—Haider, the European Union, the Austrian Past and Present: An Inimical World for the Jews." In *Unlikely History: The Changing German-Jewish Symbiosis, 1945–2000*. Ed. Leslie Morris and Jack Zipes. New York: Palgrave, 2002. 119–40.

Posthofen, Renate. "Ruth Beckermann: Re-Activating Memory—In Search of Time Lost." In *Out from the Shadows: Essays on contemporary Austrian Women Writers and Filmmakers*. Ed. Margarete Lamb-Faffelberger. Riverside, CA: Ariadne Press, 1997. 264–76.

Reiter, Andrea. "Ruth Beckermann und die jüdische Nachkriegsgeneration in Österreich." In *'Other' Austrians: Post–1945 Austrian Women's Writing*. Ed. Allyson Fiddler. Berne: Lang, 1998. XX.

Part III

Transatlantic Relationships

7

THE HOLOCAUST SURVIVOR AS GERMANIST

Marcel Reich-Ranicki and Ruth Kluger

Benjamin Lapp

Ruth Kluger and Marcel Reich-Ranicki are members of the "second generation" of German-speaking Jews, writers and intellectuals who survived the Holocaust in their youth and began to give voice to their experiences in the post-Nazi period (Schlant 1999: 247). Both have written memoirs that, I will argue, reflect on the end of a tradition, the tradition of the German-Jewish *Bildungsbürgertum* and on the historical event—the Holocaust—which destroyed that tradition. Each of them is a significant voice in contemporary German culture. Reich-Ranicki plays a prominent role in German literary life as a leading newspaper and television critic. His autobiography *Mein Leben* (1999, translated into English as *The Author of Himself*, 2001) was a bestseller in Germany. Ruth Kluger lives in the United States, and is a Professor Emeritus of German literature at the University of California, Irvine. She does not live in Germany, but is nevertheless actively engaged in cultural and literary debates in that country. Her book, *Weiter Leben* (1992, translated as *Still Alive*, 2001), was originally published in German in 1992 and was also a major success. Reich-Ranicki and Kluger each seek in his and her own way to engage the Germans in a dialogue about the past.

The concept of *Bildung* has come to play a key role in our understanding of the specific characteristics of German-Jewish identity before the Holocaust. *Bildung*, George Mosse writes, signified the transition from superstition to enlightenment by means of the cultivation of the individual through reason. This was "an ideal readymade for Jewish assimilation, because it transcended all differences of nationality and religion through the unfolding of the individual personality" (Mosse 1985: 3). *Bildung* thus allowed German Jews "to accomplish in two or three decades a journey that their peers elsewhere, especially in Eastern Europe, would take much longer to complete: from a hermetically closed system centered on divine sacraments to an emancipated agnostic culture centered on man" (Elon 2002: 66). Indeed, for German Jews, *Bildung* became synonymous with their Jewishness. The "romance" with *Bildung* led to a German-Jewish love affair with German culture itself. "Quotations from Goethe were part of every meal," writes Marion Kaplan (Kaplan 1997: 126). German-Jews embraced the notion of the German-Jewish symbiosis. To be sure, the unproblematic identification with German culture could not withstand the shock of the Holocaust. Gershom Scholem proclaimed the "myth of the German-Jewish dialogue" (Scholem 1976: 61). And the survivor Jean Amery, formerly Hans Maier, stated that the link to Germany and the Germans was based on an "existential misunderstanding" (Amery 1990: 50).

This did and does not mean, however, that the relationship to Germany and to the issue of German-Jewish identity was in any sense resolved. In fact, in the case of Reich-Ranicki, it is precisely the ongoing love affair with German culture—before, during, and after the Holocaust—which distinguishes his memoir. Born in 1920 in Poland into a middle class Jewish family, Reich's upbringing was unabashedly pro-German. The Reich family subscribed to the *Berliner Tageblatt* and enrolled the children in German school. His mother had been raised in Germany and, unlike his father, could not speak Yiddish and only spoke elementary Polish, and "wanted me to be educated in the German language." Although she was descended from a long line of rabbis, she was disinterested in Jewish religion and culture and was totally enraptured with German culture. Even after the German invasion, she continued to believe, Ranicki writes, in "German order and German justice" (Reich-Ranicki 2001: 26).

In 1929, the nine-year-old Reich-Ranicki was sent to Berlin, and here he, as he puts it, "fell under the spell of German literature, of German music." "I was in love with German literature" (Reich-Ranicki 2001: 26). By contrast, the rituals of Judaism held no interest for Reich-Ranicki: he saw them as antiquated and superstitious, and writes only of his deep identification with the Jewish commitment to learning (Reich-Ranicki 2001: 37). Nor was his love of German culture diminished by his experience of the Nazi dictatorship. His memories of his youth in Nazi Germany were relatively benign; his teachers treated him fairly, and he was not subjected to anti-Semitic abuse from his classmates. "Surprising as this may sound today," he writes, "I never suffered any hostility in Berlin, and never witnessed any" (Reich-Ranicki 2001: 103).

In October 1938, his time in Berlin came to an abrupt halt. Like other Jews with Polish passports, he was arrested and deported to Poland. However, he

writes, ". . . from the country from which I had been expelled I had taken a language with me, the German language, and a literature, the German literature"
(Reich-Ranicki 2001: 109). Throughout his autobiography, he continually reaf-
firms that his *Heimat* (homeland) is culture, and, particularly, German culture.

Nevertheless, there is another Germany, and that is at the center of this
memoir. In the Warsaw ghetto, Reich-Ranicki encountered the ugliest face of
Nazism:

> Any German who wore a uniform and had a weapon could do whatever he wished
> with a Jew in Warsaw. There was no one to spoil the fun of those German troops,
> no one to stop them from maltreating the Jews, no one to make them answerable
> for what they did. It revealed what human beings are capable of when they are
> granted unlimited power over other human beings. (Reich-Ranicki 2001: 129)

Here, he witnessed the deportation of his parents and relatives to Treblinka.
Nevertheless, despite the suffering perpetrated upon him by the Germans,
throughout this period, his connection to and love for German literature and
culture remained strong. Reich-Ranicki and his wife Tosia read German poetry
to one another in the ghetto and he speaks eloquently of the powerful effect of
Beethoven's music on himself and others in the ghetto; the music brought him
a feeling of solace, a counter-world. Because of his fluency in German, he was
employed as a translator and interpreter for the Jewish Council and worked directly under the tragic chairman of the Jewish Council Adam Czerniakov, who
ultimately committed suicide rather than help organize the deportation of the
ghetto inhabitants to the extermination camps. What is Reich-Ranicki's reference point for Czeniakov's tragic end? Reich-Ranicki writes, "When shocked and
bewildered, I heard of Adam Czerniakow's lonely death I thought . . . of the great
Polish romantics and the great German classics" (Reich-Ranicki 2001: 175).

With the help of a Polish couple who gave him and his wife shelter outside
of the ghetto, Reich-Ranicki survived the war and, following the defeat of Nazi
Germany, enthusiastically joined the Polish Communist Party. The Stalinist policies of the late 1940s, however, led to his expulsion from the party and a brief
imprisonment. After his release, he began to work as a translator and reviewer of
German fiction and poetry, and, as such, developed relations with German writers such as Brecht, Seghers, Lenz, and Böll. In 1958, wary of rising Polish anti-
Semitism, no longer believing in Polish Communism, and feeling, in any case, an
ongoing deep affinity with German culture, he made the decision to emigrate to
the Federal Republic of Germany.

Upon his arrival, Reich-Ranicki was invited to participate in the meetings
of the celebrated literary circle "Group 47," and he quickly found himself at the
center of German cultural life. His extraordinarily successful career as a literary critic for the *Frankfurter Allgemeine Zeitung* and as an eloquent advocate and

popularizer of literature on German television is well known. Known as the "pontiff of German letters," Reich-Ranicki's judgments of contemporary German literature became extraordinarily influential. How does he view his own role in post-Holocaust Germany? "Was it my ambition" he writes, "to continue, perhaps in a very demonstrative manner, the tradition of Jews in the history of German literary criticism to which I had long since adhered in a leading position and in great public view? Certainly. Did my passion have anything to do with my yearning for a home country, that home which I was lacking and which I had believed to have found in the German literature? Yes, and possibly in a much greater degree than I was even aware" (Reich-Ranicki 2001: 349). At the same time, he is clear about his refusal to adopt a German national identity: despite a strong attachment to German culture, he says, "I am not a German and I shall never be one." "I have no country of my own, no homeland, no fatherland."[1]

Thus, despite his continuing love of German literature, his relationship to the political culture of postwar Germany is one of critical distance. He relates how the founder of Group 47, Hans-Werner Richter, studiously avoided any reference to Reich-Ranicki's Jewish background: "His attitude to Jews was inhibited and tense even forty years after the end of the Second World War. This, I believe makes him a typical figure of his time" (Reich-Ranicki 2001: 292). He mentions how in 1964, after his testimony in the criminal proceedings against SS-man Karl Wolff concerning the conditions in the Warsaw Ghetto, he was first asked about his own experiences in the Warsaw Ghetto; prior to that, no one had been interested (Reich-Ranicki 2001: 328). And he discusses his outrage and disappointment at the position that the publisher of the *Frankfurter Allgemeine Zeitung*, Joachim Fest, took in the famous historians' dispute of the 1980s. Fest defended those conservative historians who argued against the uniqueness and singularity of the Holocaust: "The political and moral consensus which had existed between us regarding the Third Reich and its consequences, the consensus that was fundamental to my work on *Frankfurter Allgemeine*, and indeed my whole existence in the Federal Republic—that consensus was needlessly . . . destroyed by Joachim Fest" (Reich-Ranicki 2001: 387). Reich-Ranicki was clearly deeply troubled by signs of historical revisionism and resurfacing anti-Semitic resentments in Germany. Nevertheless, Reich-Ranicki recalls how Chancellor Willy Brandt knelt before the Warsaw Ghetto Monument in 1970, and how moved he was by this highly charged symbolic act: "I thought to myself," he writes, "that my decision to return to Germany in 1958 and to settle in the Federal Republic of Germany was not false but correct. The historians debate . . . while an important symptom of the mood of the times, has not changed my mind . . ." (Reich-Ranicki 2001: 390). In other words, he seems to suggest that, despite everything, Germany has acknowledged its past in the public sphere in ways that enable him to stay and participate in German culture—not, however, as a German, but as an outsider. Still, he defines himself by his special affinity with German cultural traditions.

As Jack Zipes has pointed out, Reich-Ranicki's project is characterized by a central paradox: Reich-Ranicki has argued that the German-Jewish cultural symbiosis has long since ended. Yet, despite the end of that symbiosis, he sees himself as having a distinct mission in German society: to preserve the integrity of German literature, something the gentiles cannot be trusted to do. Reich-Ranicki is, Zipes concludes, "unwilling to surrender Germany to the Germans." Indeed, he "seeks to outdo or out-German Christian Germans and to become the major spokesman for German literature in the public domain" (Zipes 2002: 185).

Ruth Kluger's autobiography *Weiter Leben* is a more complex book than Reich-Ranicki's *Mein Leben*. The narrative is constructed on several levels; on the one hand, it is a deeply personal and brutally honest Holocaust testimony, which describes the author's life from her childhood in Vienna to her deportation to the camps, and finally to her life in Germany and in the United States after her liberation. While organized chronologically, the narrative is by no means straightforward; it goes back and forth from the present to the past and very self-consciously complicates the stereotypical views we have of survivor literature. In many ways, her book represents a dismayed response to the "Holocaust" discourse that has developed in both Germany and the United States since the 1980s. It offers a female and feminist perspective on the Holocaust in a field dominated by the narratives of male survivors. It deconstructs the sanctification of the survivor, and the author painfully confronts her own deeply ambivalent feelings toward her father, who died in the Holocaust, and especially toward her mother, who was with her in the camps and afterward. To quote Pascale Bos, the memoir "provides testimony while commenting on the impossibility of testimony, and it problematizes the recall of memory, the constructed nature of survivor narratives and the function of writing." (Bos 2002: 221). The German and original version of her book is also expressly directed to a German audience, but she is writing as a Jewish survivor who—while deeply connected to the language and culture of Germany—is also no longer part of that culture. Not unlike Reich-Ranicki, albeit from a different perspective, the book can be viewed as an attempt to open a difficult and painful dialogue with the Germans about the Holocaust.[2]

In contrast to Reich-Ranicki, who has fond memories of his childhood in Berlin, Kluger's memories of Vienna are deeply disturbing. Born in 1931 into a middle class family, she was seven years old during the *Anschluss* of Austria. The family was very Jewish, "emancipated but not assimilated," Kluger writes, and very much a part of the Austro-German-Jewish *Bildungsbürgertum* (Kluger 1992: 41). Kluger's early memories of Vienna are inextricably connected with images of popular anti-Semitism and Nazi policy. "Vienna," she writes, "was my first prison" (Kluger 2001: 26).

I have heard a Jewish woman who is about my age tell how she first experienced the Nazis in Vienna. It was the sandbox she says, She was playing in the sandbox and one of the Aryan mothers simply threw her out. She thought at first it was a new game and promptly piled back in. The "game" was repeated. After the third time she understood. Jewish children are notoriously good learners. . . . And yet being thrown out of our sandbox for no apparent reason by the parents of the other kids—that was the quintessential experience of my generation of preschoolers and first graders in Hitler's Vienna. (Kluger 2001: 41)

Her postwar visits to Vienna are rare and uncomfortable. "Everyone felt that they had been victims of the Nazis, whereas to me, they had been the arch-Nazis." It is noteworthy and striking that Ruth Kluger's relations to the German-speaking world are not in Austria or Vienna but in Germany, and she is quite open about her ongoing sense of acute discomfort on her occasional trips back to Vienna.

Responding defiantly to her anti-Semitic surroundings, Ruth Kluger took on her middle name Ruth, in place of her first name Susi. "Jewish self-contempt wasn't for me. I had discovered the opposite: Jewish pride" (Kluger 2001: 23). As a young girl, she responded angrily to Jewish teachers and relatives who warned that bad manners or unruly behavior causes *Rishes* (anti-Semitism): "I wanted to see myself as in opposition rather than simply as a victim" (Kluger 1992: 50). On the other hand, her relationship to Judaism itself is highly ambivalent. She regards herself as a "bad Jew" and the religion as patriarchal and oppressive (Kluger 1992: 42). Nor did religion help her deal with the Holocaust; in the face of mass extermination any belief in a Jewish God crumbled. "I would have become an agnostic anyway, but the Nazis added to my disappointment the feeling of having grasped a rotten plank during a shipwreck" (Kluger 2001: 45).

What, then, does her Jewishness consist of? She writes of Thereseienstadt that here, despite the horrors of the camp, "the only good was what the Jews managed to make of it, the way they flooded this square kilometer with their voices, their intellect, their wit, their playfulness, their joy in dialogue. The good emanated from our sense of self. And I learned for the first time who we (that is the Jews) were, what we could be, this people to whom I belonged" [Kluger 2001: 86–7]. In a poignant reference to the German-Jewish belief in culture, she recalls reciting Schiller to help her endure the roll call at Auschwitz. And in the English-language version, Kluger proclaims her pride in a particularly German-Jewish tradition of critical intellect and *Bildung*, attempting to problematize many of the anti-German stereotypes common among American Jews. "Consider that until the Holocaust, most of the worlds prominent secular Jews spoke and wrote German: Kafka, Freud, Einstein, Marx, Theodor Herzl, and Hannah Arendt, to name the first that come to mind" (Kluger 2001: 205). She does not, however, embrace what she, speaking of Rabbi Leo Baeck, calls the futile idealism of German Jews (Kluber 2001: 85). Kluger remembers as ridiculous a central European Jew in Birkenau who pronounced on the incompatibility of genocide and

European culture: "I, too, liked culture . . . but I didn't believe that it compellingly mandated a certain line of conduct . . . Poetry wasn't connected with the outside, the real world. Its value lay in the comfort it provided, in that profound consolation that could fill the mind when a malevolent environment tried to suck it dry" (Kluger 2001: 100–101). Culture remains central to Kluger, but it no longer holds any redemptive promise.

Much of the book, of course, is about the camps and about the specific realities that she confronted there. "People don't want to hear," she writes, "that for me life was better in Theresienstadt than it had been during the last months in Vienna, because to digest this bit of admittedly subjective information would mean that they'd have to rearrange a lot of furniture in their inner museum of the Holocaust" (Kluger 2001: 73). In fact, she seems to suggest, much of the discourse about the Holocaust is wrapped up in preconceived ideas, clichés, and simplistic slogans. "Nothing offended me more than the generalization that the camps turned us all into brutal egotists, and whoever survived them must be morally defective." To be sure, the clichés and slogans have changed—the survivor is now sanctified—but the difficulties in confronting the event itself remain. A goal of her book is to "break through the curtain of barbed wire with which postwar sensibility has surrounded the camps . . ." (Kluger 2001: 71).

Although there is now an English version of the book, *Weiter Leben* was originally written and published in Germany in 1992. The English-language edition (2001) was written for an American audience, and avoids many of the references to the German literary tradition as well as addressing specifics of the American relationship to Holocaust memory. The first edition, by contrast, is clearly intended to address a German audience, an audience with which she has a special relationship: "Memory connects us, memory separates us" (Kluger 1992: 218). Who am I writing this book for, she asks at one point? For those who can read German, namely the Germans. And yet the dialogue that Kluger starts is a complex and difficult one. A recurring character in *Weiter Leben* is Gisela, the German wife of a Princeton colleague. Gisela "felt smug about belonging to a younger generation of Germans who couldn't be blamed for anything." Gisela responds to Kluger with defensive and self-serving clichés; she is quick to draw attention to the sufferings of the Germans, going so far as to suggest that Ruth and her mother had it relatively easy. They were, after all, not that long in Auschwitz, and "they were able to leave Germany after the war and miss the hardship of post-war Germany" (Kluger 1992: 92). With Germans such as Gisela, Kluger makes clear, any sort of dialogue is impossible.

Kluger's ongoing conversation with her friend, the novelist Martin Walser (called Christoph in the German version), is in fact, a genuine dialogue; it too, however, is characterized by misunderstandings and conflicting memories, a conversation, she writes, than can never "have a satisfactory end" (Kluger 2001: 165). He acknowledges her Jewishness, which pleases her; at the same time, although he met her in 1946, he claims later not to have known that she had been in Auschwitz. He describes Nazi anti-Semitism as deriving from primeval thought patterns and as a variant of xenophobia that comes naturally to all men; she, by contrast, insists that Nazism was the product of a highly developed civilization and was freely chosen (Kluger 1992: 215–17). "He leaves out too much and defends the omissions. He doesn't whitewash the past, but he straddles a fence," she writes, "Not untypical of his countrymen" (Kluger 2001: 169). And yet she is clearly drawn to Walser, who somehow becomes representative of Germany, and she seeks to continue the dialogue, no matter how difficult it is for both.[3] Until an open conversation about the past has taken place, Kluger implies, Germans and Jews cannot find "sufficient common ground" to meet in the present. She writes at one point to her German readers that they should not "identify" with her, but neither should they avoid confrontation with her; rather they should embrace difference and disagreement and seek out dialogue (Kluger 1992: 141).

Both Reich-Ranicki and Kluger have attempted to reestablish a link to a German culture that had become impossibly tainted by Nazism. As Geoffrey Hartman has pointed out, the political liberation of Germany meant far more than simply restoring freedom of speech: "Not only the material and psychic powers of Germany were exhausted but also its cultural heritage—squandered by a shameless appropriation." "But," Hartmann goes on to say, "if we anticipate . . . the possibility of hope, it has to come from a renewed understanding of language or art, including Germany's contribution" (Hartmann 2003: 234, 243). The two memoirists discussed here are engaged in precisely this project. Through their interventions and participation in the cultural life of contemporary Germany, both Reich-Ranicki and Kluger actively seek to preserve and to redeem the humanistic elements of the German cultural tradition. In the case of Reich-Ranicki, this engagement with Germany follows from his love for German literature and his desire to play a role in contemporary German culture without, however, losing his outsider status. Ruth Kluger, by contrast, participates from a distance; despite lengthy stays in Göttingen, her home base is in California. Nevertheless, she too, is actively engaged in and continues to seek out German discussions about the past and the present. Both Kluger and Reich-Ranicki are calling for a discussion based not on denial or false affirmation, but rather on the knowledge of the enormity of the crime perpetrated on German and European Jewry in the Holocaust. Irrespective of where they live, these two survivors will never again call Germany/Austria their homeland, but they are willing to engage in a dialogue.

Notes

1. Quoted in Zipes, "The Critical Embracement of Germany," in Morris and Zipes, *Unlikely History: The Changing German-Jewish Symbiosis*, 196.

2. While I quote from both texts, there are in fact significant differences between the German and the English editions of the book; the latter is not simply a translation of the former. For a discussion of the difference between the two texts, see Caroline Schaumann, "From *weiter leben* (1992) to *Still Alive* (2001): Ruth Kluger's Cultural Translation of Her "German Book" for an American Audience," *The German Quarterly* 77.3 (Summer 2004): 324–339.

3. To be sure, this relationship to Walser has been called into question following the publication of his novel *Tod eines Kritikers* (2002). In this novel, Walser caricatured Marcel Reich-Ranicki in unmistakably anti-Semitic ways. In an open letter published in the *Frankfurter Rundschau* (June 27, 2002), Kluger repudiated the book and accused her friend of espousing anti-Semitism.

Works Cited

Amery, Jean. *At the Mind's Limit: Contemplations by a Survivor on Auschwitz and its Realities*. Bloomington: Indiana UP, 1998.

Bos, Pascal. "Return to Germany: German-Jewish Authors Seeking Address." In Morris and Zipes, *Unlikely History: The Changing German Jewish Symbiosis*. New York: Palgrave, 2002. 203–32.

Elon, Amos. *The Pity of it All: A History of Jews in Germany, 1743–1933*. New York: Metropolitan Books, 2002.

Hartmann, Geoffrey. "Holocaust and Hope." In Moishe Postone and Eric Santner, eds, *Catastrophe and Meaning: The Holocaust and the Twentieth Century*. Chicago: University of Chicago Press, 2003. 232–49.

Kaplan, Marion. "The German romance with *Bildung* begins, with the publication of Rahel Levin's correspondence about Goethe." In Sander L. Gilman and Jack Zipes, eds, *Yale Companion to Jewish Writing and Thought in German Culture, 1096–1996*. New Haven, CT: Yale UP, 1997. 124–28

Kluger, Ruth. *Weiter Leben. Eine Jugend*. Gottingen: Wallstein, 1992.

———. *Still Alive: A Holocaust Girlhood Remembered*. New York: Feminist Press at the City University of New York, 2001.

Mosse, George. *German Jews beyond Judaism*. Bloomington: Indiana UP, 1985.

Reich-Ranicki, Marcel. *Mein Leben*. Stuttgart: Deutsche Verlags-Anstalt, 1999.

———. *The Author of Himself: The Life of Marcel Reich-Ranicki*. Princeton: Princeton UP, 2001.

Schaumann, Caroline. "From *weiter leben* (1992) to *Still Alive* (2001): Ruth Kluger's Cutural Translation of Her "German Book" for an American Audience." *The German Quarterly* 77.3 (Summer 2004): 324–39.

Schlant, Ernestine. *The Language of Silence*. New York: Routledge, 1999.

Scholem, Gershom. "Against the Myth of the German-Jewish Dialogue." In *On Jews and Judaism in Crisis: Selected Essays*. New York: Schocken Books, 1976. 61–70.

Morris, Leslie and Jack Zipes. *Unlikely History: The Changing German-Jewish Symbiosis*. New York: Palgrave, 2002.

Jack Zipes. "The Critical Embracement of Germany." In Morris and Zipes, *Unlikely History: The Changing German-Jewish Symbiosis*. New York: Palgrave, 2002. 183–202.

8

TRANSATLANTIC SOLITUDES

Canadian-Jewish and German-Jewish Writers in Dialogue with Kafka

Iris Bruce

There have been numerous studies of artists all over the world who were in-spired by Franz Kafka's writings. However, apart from a few sporadic references, there has been no scholarship on the transatlantic dialogue between Kafka and Canadian Jewish writers. This in itself is a noteworthy absence in contempo-rary scholarship. More importantly, it is worth examining the Canadian Kafka reception in literary circles in relation to their German Jewish counterpart: the former soon found an original voice in Canada's increasingly multicultural liter-ary community, whereas German Jewish writing did not achieve this until the third generation.

Kafka's famous line about the predicament of German Jewish writers in his time ("their hind legs were bogged down in their father's Judaism and their front legs could find no new ground. The resulting despair was their inspiration") can be said to resonate through both Canadian and German Jewish fiction. In *Typ-ing: A life in 26 keys* (2000), Matt Cohen (1943–1999), for instance, remarks:

> How familiar such complaints sound to a Canadian writer whose origin or sensibil-ity lies outside the Canadian cultural mainstream. One of the strange things about being a writer in Canada–or at least, being this writer in Canada–is the gradual realization that if one is not writing books that represent the white, conservative, middle-class and Protestant values of the literary establishment, one is forever

destined to be seen by that establishment . . . as unimportant and marginal. . . . (Cohen 2000: 231)[1]

If Jewish writers felt marginalized in Canada—a country of immigrants that became even more diverse after WWII—how much more marginalized would German Jewish writers feel, whose world became more homogeneous after the war than it ever was before? German Jewish writers had virtually no voice. Only today (after the fall of the communist Eastern bloc and with a growing Jewish community in Germany's and Austria's increasingly multicultural world) has German Jewish writing found an equally original voice, depicting themes of marginalization, self-assertion, and the problem of (re-)constructing a Jewish identity— issues that Canadian Jewish writers addressed long before them. What is striking, though, is that the German Jewish writers drawn to Kafka seem to be mostly male.

My focus will be largely on Montréal, the birthplace of Canadian Jewish literature, because of its pronounced multiculturalism: French, Anglo, and Allophone. Beginning with A.M. Klein, the "father" of Canadian Jewish literature, I will also discuss writers of the second generation after the holocaust: Leonard Cohen, Régine Robin, Irena Eisler, and Gabrielle Goliger. As for the European counterpart, I will briefly examine the postwar impact of Kafka on German Jewish writers, discuss the second generation's politics of identity construction, and for the third generation, focus on the novel *The Search for M.* by Doron Rabinovici, set in contemporary multicultural Vienna.

For A.M. Klein (1909–1972), Kafka's *In the Penal Colony* exemplifies the experience of anti-semitism and the holocaust. In 1948, he remarks that it "may be a story of Devil's Island" (Klein 1987: 274), immediately linking it with European anti-semitism, i.e., the famous trial in France of Alfred Dreyfus (1859–1935), who was banished to Devil's Island off the coast of South America from 1895–1901. He then argues that Jews "without the benefit of formal school education have not escaped political instruction; *they*, like that wretched victim in Kafka's *Penal Colony*, learned it writ large, and annotated, upon their very own persons" (Klein 1982: 371). Moreover, Klein describes Gregor Samsa, the traveling salesman in Kafka's *The Metamorphosis*, as bringing home "the fact of insectitude to the reader"; Samsa is a "nobody," lacking an identity (Klein 1987: 277).

The quest for reestablishing Jewish identity after the holocaust is depicted in Klein's subsequent novel, *The Second Scroll* (1951): here an unnamed narrator, who has grown up in Canada, follows the trail of his uncle, Melech Davidson, whom he has never met. The nephew's messianic quest (in search of his uncle, his roots) takes him through Europe, North Africa, and eventually Israel. His quest is a "trial," for the uncle continually eludes him, and the nephew finds himself in many paradoxical *kafkaesque* situations. Each time he thinks he is close, it turns out he has just missed his uncle. These "almost meetings" (to borrow a phrase from another Canadian novelist, Henry Kreisel)[2] seem about to end when the two are finally in the same country, the newly established state of Israel. But Klein's protagonist is no more successful than Joseph K. in his search for the Law in *The Trial* or the land surveyor in his repeated attempts to enter the Castle. Ironically, the nephew's entrance into the Promised Land is accompanied by failure. Before the two can meet, the uncle undergoes a final metamorphosis: the victim of an Arab attack, he dies a martyr and leaves the nephew to attend his funeral.

As in Kafka, irony is pervasive in Klein. The quest for the uncle had grown out of the nephew's desire to find "instances" of "metamorphosis and rejuvenation" (Klein 1951: 84), especially in Israel. But the wished for apotheosis turns into a great disappointment when the Zionists whom the nephew meets are "objectionable in the patronizing airs they put on" (Klein 1951: 80). Uncle Melech represented a different kind of Truth because "He wanted to feel in his own person and upon his own neck the full weight of the yoke of exile" (Klein 1951: 55). Claiming the uncle as "kin" when he is saying the prayer at the funeral, the nameless nephew claims neither traditional religion, nor nationalism, but the yoke of exile as his heritage. Kafka, too, is 'kin' in this regard; by writing about "insectitude," he chose the yoke of exile as well. Klein's relation to Kafka, then, is one of affinity: what the two writers share is the theme of exile. There is no rejuvenation for the nephew in the new land of Israel, but unlike Kafka's protagonists, the nephew has an alternative by making Canada his home.

However, Klein goes farther than exploring Kafka's themes of exile and homelessness. Deeply rooted in Jewish tradition, he also attempts to give Kafka a Jewish identity. Significantly, he does not associate the adjective *kafkaesque* with the holocaust alone, but rather with the "labyrinth of [Kafka's] prose" in which he recognizes Kafka's search for Truth. Thus, Klein insists on a broader reading of Kafka, while at the same time anchoring his writing in Jewish tradition: ". . . its meaning encompasses the globe; it is, in truth, a nineteenth-century *Maggid-of-Dubnow* who speaks, with a sophistication unknown to the Preacher, and of the Preacher's faith utterly bereft, through these essentially simple anecdotes of insights and realizations touching nothing less than the human situation" (Klein 1987: 275). Though Kafka, to Klein, is clearly not a religious writer, he believes Kafka shares with the famous eighteenth century Jewish preacher the quest for Truth in a paradoxical world. This idea is so central for Klein's reading of Kafka that he turns him into a modern Maimonides: "It is in this sense that Kafka is a sort of latter-day Maimonides, but it is no *Guide* to the Perplexed that he writes. His entire opus is the *Song of Perplexity* itself" (Klein 1987: 276). Klein's attempt after the holocaust to anchor Kafka in Jewish tradition is something Kafka would have never done himself. Kafka's *Song of Perplexity* may represent a Jewish existential commentary for Klein, but other Canadian Jewish writers will interpret his song differently—they will leave the voice of Tradition behind and construct modern identities across cultural boundaries.

Kafka is an important and obvious intertext in the work of Leonard Cohen (1934–). Making Kafka his spiritual muse in "Last Dance at the Four Penny," Cohen links Kafka's Prague to Québec when he revives the rabbis of Prague and Vilna to dance a "freilach" "in this French province,/ cold and oceans west of the temple" (Cohen 1964: 69). Similarly, in the collection of poetry, *Let Us Compare Mythologies*, the poem "Jingle" associates the experience of love and death with Kafka's writing/torture machine in the *Penal Colony*: ". . . torn and stretched for the sun,/to be used for a drum or tambourine,/to be scratched with poetry/by Kafka's machine" (Cohen 1956: 59). Moreover, the novel, *Beautiful Losers* (1966), which is especially rich in allusions to Kafka, places him within a cross-cultural framework, as Cohen mixes narratives from seventeenth century Native/Christian history with twentieth century Jewish/Christian history. Michael Greenstein remarks: the narrator's "fascination with the tribe of 'A–s' and his best friend F, bring to mind Kafka's initialed anti-heroes. Similarly, Cohen's System Theatre and Telephone Dance metamorphose from Kafka's Penal Colony; and just as 'The Hunter Gracchus' and 'Josephine the Singer, or the Mouse folk' are, and are not, about the Jews, so *Beautiful Losers* is about a lost Jewish folk" (Greenstein 1989: 136). Greenstein's argument is well taken; the echoes here are also to the Theatre of Oklahoma in Kafka's *America* novel and to the telephone 'dance' in *The Castle*. The *Penal Colony* is indeed a central intertext for *Beautiful Losers*. The narrator's quest is for a tormented young Native girl, Catherine Tekakwitha (1656–1680), who experiences the pain of exclusion after her conversion to Christianity and becomes a martyr for her faith. Catherine Tekakwitha has consciously constructed a new identity for herself. What this saint shares with Kafka is the purist aestheticism with which she pursues her goal, crossing cultural and religious boundaries and breaking taboos in the name of Truth. Her voluntary submission to martyrdom is reminiscent of *The Penal Colony*. When Catherine is dying, she is asked: "What do we sound like?" She replies, "You sound like machinery," which, she admits, "is beautiful." When asked again, "What kind of machinery?" she answers "Ordinary eternal machinery" (Cohen 1966: 204). Like the helpers who assist the old Commandant in the *Penal Colony*, or the butchers in *A Hunger Artist*, her religious superiors will stand there "for a long time" (they admit it themselves), "watching" (Cohen 1966: 204), as she well knows, i.e., not understanding her. Her dying words reveal how far she has always been removed from most people, who have never understood and never will understand her sacrifice.

However, for Catherine Tekakwitha, there is beauty in the fact that the sound of those around her represents "ordinary eternal machinery." Cohen's machinery does not fall apart like the machine in the *Penal Colony*, but is relentlessly rotating and inscribing her, allowing her to decipher her punishment. Thus, the machinery has a function and meaning. We can see this when Catherine's death is described as an apotheosis: "At that precise moment the girl entered the eternal machinery of the sky. Looking back over her atomic shoulder, she played a beam of alabaster over her old face as she streamed forward on the insane grateful laughter of her girl friend" (Cohen 1966: 211). Here we might well have Kafka's machine in its days of glory, if it were not for the insane laughter. Yet, as with Kafka, the machine has ironic overtones. Like Klein, Cohen links the *Penal Colony* with the holocaust through his many references in the novel to human soap, newsreel Belsen (Cohen 1966: 194), the birch trees (Buchenwald concentration camp), etc. Since Cohen's machinery keeps moving, we now have, side-by-side, Catherine's Native/Christian sacrifice and the slaughter of millions of Jews during the holocaust. Finally, Cohen foregrounds the sexual attributes in his depiction of the 'machinery.' Likewise, the humming telephones in Kafka's *The Castle* have an erotic dimension: we hear that there is "uninterrupted telephoning" in the Castle and that the humming sound "drummed against one's ears as if demanding to penetrate more deeply into something other than one's wretched hearing" (Kafka 1998: 20). From this Cohen coins the sexual metaphor of the 'telephone dance,' another 'machinery' that never breaks down in either text.

Following Catherine's path, the narrator and his wife Edith experience the various "machineries" which bring pleasure and pain (or rather pleasure through pain), and which range from ordinary thorns to telephones to high tech Danish Vibrators that move the protagonists beyond the limits and thresholds of civilization (Cohen 1966: 230). F., the supposed friend and healer of the husband and wife, wants them to feel and understand their eroticized bodies. He describes himself as Oscotarach, a metaphorical "Head Piercer" (Cohen 1966: 184)—an allusion to the Mohawk myth of Oscotarach, whose function it was "to remove the brains from the skulls of all who went by, 'as a necessary preparation for immortality'" (Cohen 1966: 183), as well as to the *Penal Colony*. Since Oscotarach's hut represents the "legendary crossing place" to the hereafter,[3] Cohen intimates that the protagonists are on the threshold of a new world with their initiation into sado-masochistic pleasures through machinery such as the Danish Vibrator (1996: 178). In another sexual adventure, they unite with Hitler himself in an orgy, who makes them kiss the whip and baptizes F. and Edith with a bar of soap, "derived from melted human flesh" (Cohen 1996: 182). Edith ends up killing herself later, but the cycle of "rejuvenation" continues for her husband when F. takes him under his wing after Edith's death, until F. himself disappears.

The ultimate goal in this novel seems to be rejuvenation through pain and destruction. At the very end, the old narrator enters the system theater, like the Commandant in Kafka's *Penal Colony* who places himself under his own machine. Cohen's narrator finds himself in a postmodern Theatre of Cruelty, with its "apathetic anarchy," "Out of Order signs," and "jammed electric shooting galleries." Though it looks as if the machinery is finally breaking down, the old man is actually going through a climactic metamorphosis: "He disintegrated slowly . . . [but] his presence had not completely disappeared when he began to reassemble himself" (Cohen 1966: 241). In fact, his presence is likened to an hourglass, "strongest where it was smallest," and where he was most absent, "that's when the gaps started, because the future streams through that point, going both ways" (Cohen 1966: 241). However, his apotheosis is depicted like Tekakwitha's ultimate sacrifice and is as ambiguous and transfused with irony as Kafka's ending of *Amerika* (The Man Who Disappeared). Since the meaning of Tekakwitha's sacrifice and of his final metamorphosis is lost and both of them disappear, the scene becomes theatrical: "Just sit back and enjoy it, I guess.—Thank God it's only a movie," are the comments from the audience.

Though Kafka is an important intertext, Cohen's postmodern novel places religions, mythologies, cultural histories, and literatures side-by-side, crossing cultural borders (American/Canadian/European /Native /Christian/Jewish) and transgressing traditional moral boundaries (religious, moral, historical) in a Canadian setting. It is important to note that Cohen does not attempt to connect them: "Connect Nothing: F. shouted. Place things side by side on your arborite table, if you must, but connect nothing!" (Cohen 1966: 17). Connecting these cultures and histories would amount to appropriating or imprisoning the narrative from a certain point of view. This is exactly what happened to Catherine's history, when it was written by the Church, a narrative from which the narrator tried to liberate her all along ("I have come to rescue you from the Jesuits" [Cohen 1966: 5]).

Régine Robin (1939–) places Kafka within contemporary Québec society in her novel *The Wanderer* (1983). Kafka's well-known definition of the "four impossibilities" serves as an epigraph to the novel: "The impossibility of not writing, the impossibility of writing German, the impossibility of writing differently . . . the impossibility of writing." In *The Wanderer*, writing and identity are connected with recording the experience of immigration and marginality, specifically within the context of Québec nationalism, which marginalized even French native speakers if they were not Québécois. For a French writer from France, therefore, writing in French in Québec might well suggest "the impossibility of writing French" as well as all of Kafka's other "impossibilities." Robin uses Kafka as an authority to legitimize and support her theme of transatlantic solitude: the discrimination experienced by Jews and allophones in Québec society from which the French Jewish protagonist increasingly retreats as she comes to identify with immigrant allophones. For instance, her imaginary father-in-law is "going to enroll his son in school, where he would have seen nothing but nuns and crucifixes everywhere" (Robin 1983: 21). Her imagined response is rebellion: "He would have seen red and stormed out—and discovered a little later that the English were willing to accept the child without imposing any Protestant religiosity" (Robin 1983: 22). Thinking of the Montréal landscape, especially with a cross on top of Mount Royal representing a symbol of cultural dominance, one might expect—if we follow Matt Cohen's argument—that Canadian Jewish writers would engage in a *kafkaesque* search to gain admittance to their castle on the hill: the Anglo or Québécois cultural mainstream. However, by contrast, neither Klein's nor Cohen's protagonists are interested in storming the castle on the mountain in order to gain admittance to the Anglo or Québécois cultural mainstream. Klein, who struggled most with recognition and fell silent many years before his death, represents Canada as a place of refuge. The narrator mentions his father's "gratitude to the place of his adoption. This land hadn't given him much, mainly because he hadn't been a taker, but it had given him—this was no cliché to my father—freedom" (Robin 1983: 24). And the father defends the country "whenever one of his . . . compatriots took it in his mind to run down Canada" (Robin 1983: 24). Similarly, Leonard Cohen has not had much recognition in his own country, but is widely admired elsewhere, especially in Europe. His sensibility seems to indeed lie, "outside the Canadian mainstream," as Matt Cohen put it. But for Leonard Cohen, as for Klein, this has meant an enrichment of his art, which shows itself in the original mix of mythologies and intertexts from many cultures.

Ironically, despite her immigrant status, the "academic" Régine Robin (a professor at the Université du Québec, Montréal) is more integrated into the intellectual Canadian mainstream than Klein or Cohen; but it is for her narrator that the metaphor of storming the Catholic French Castle is most appropriate. Her weapons are Kafka and the contemporary rhetoric of otherness and alienation, all of which thrive in our contemporary environment. For Robin, Kafka's name is like a signpost. Her narrative of marginalization may use Kafka as a muse, but she is less subtle than Cohen or Klein. Her narrator puts a great deal of emphasis on finding an "anchor" for her words, which echoes Kafka's statement about "hanging on to his diary": "Would it be possible to find a position in language, . . . a fixed point of reference, a stable point, something that would anchor the words when there was only a tremulous trace of text, a mute voice, twisted words?" (Robin 1983: 8). But rather than an "anchor" for this text, Kafka is merely a hook on which to hang the novel.

To be sure, Robin's critique of Québec society represents a picture of a beleaguered Québec in the nineteen-eighties when the dogmatism of French nationalism polarized Québec society. There are indeed historical similarities to Kafka's Prague, which was as multicultural as Robin's Montréal, though his experience with different kinds of nationalisms (German/Czech/ Jewish) was more complex. The Czech nationalism, which he knew, was often violent; it also had its language police (even before the end of WWI, and certainly after 1918), which insisted that street names and family names be changed to Czech. However, just as Klein and Cohen sympathized with the situation of the Natives and the French in Canada, Kafka too sympathized with Czech and Jewish nationalism. Cohen's rejection of the Governor General's award for poetry in 1968, for instance, coincides with his identification with the rise of Québec's nationalism.

And granted, there are obvious links between various forms of nationalism and totalitarianism exposed in *The Wanderer*. Québec has had a long history of Anglo and Franco discrimination, one which Klein and Cohen were also certainly familiar with; but they never "compare" the suffering of the Natives or the experiences of a holocaust survivor with the forms of discrimination in Montréal. Similarly, they (like Kafka) did not fall prey to contemporary rhetoric, and rather employ ironic distancing devices in their representation of martyrs, be they Uncle Melech or Catherine Tekakwitha. Klein especially respected Kafka for avoiding melodrama. The Hunger Artist's final words, "I always wanted you to admire my fasting" (Kafka 1971: 277) may serve as an example here, when Kafka makes him realize at the end of his life that this wish was presumptuous and a mistake. Catherine Tekakwitha was never deluded like the Hunger Artist, who in his pride sought recognition. Similarly, when Klein turns Uncle Melech into a martyr, there is no melodrama. Melech ("king" in Hebrew) is meant to represent a deposed King of a Castle who is true to himself and his ideals, devoting his whole life to a quest for justice, wandering from country to country in his search. In true *kafkaesque* fashion, he is depicted with distanced irony. Most importantly, there is no rebirth for him: ironically, after he has survived the holocaust and more, he is brutally murdered in Israel, a place politically (and thus artificially) created for a cultural rebirth of the Jewish people. In contrast, one cannot say of Robin that she avoids melodrama when she claims and celebrates a kinship with Kafka in order to elevate the modern victimized self.

A less combative female voice emerges in Irena Eisler's story, "Chestnuts for Kafka," where the two transatlantic solitudes—the second-generation children of mixed Jewish and non-Jewish parentage—meet in Prague and together honor the dead in their family. Here, a firm but quiet European Jewish identity is juxtaposed with its more vocal North American counterpart. Emma, on a visit from San Diego, returns to her old home, Prague, where she attends a conference on Exile. She meets her older sister Eva, who remained in Prague after WWII and is a novelist and "translator" of Kafka's letters (Eisler 2001: 208). They have come to visit their families' graves on All Souls' Day. The Christian and the Jewish cemeteries are situated across from each other: "The black shiny street was lined with cemeteries on both sides—Christians to the right, Jews to the left" (Eisler 2001: 202). The father's side of the family is on the Christian side and the mother's is on the Jewish side.

The North American Emma resists when Eva also wants to go over to the Jewish cemetery, because, after all, All Souls' Day is a Christian holiday. Once there, Emma insists on placing pebbles on the Jewish graves, while Eva has no problem with the flowers she brought for the Jewish relatives: "So what, we are Mischlings . . . we don't have to do it by the book," she says. For Emma, both gestures—pebbles or flowers—are equally meaningful, especially when one considers that this is not a real grave. Though there is a family tomb, in front of it is a "large stone arch" and all the names on it have "the same terse postscript—'perished in exile, Lodz, 1943'" (Eisler 2001: 209). "Their grave was no grave, it was a cenotaph, a place with no bodies in it, with nothing to conjure, but the last trains full of shadows going out into the void" (Eisler 2001: 210). On their way out of the cemetery, Eva makes one last stop to visit Kafka's grave. This time especially Emma feels "a great urge to put a pebble on his grave . . . After all, *he really was* buried there" (Eisler 2001: 211). However, when she cannot find any pebbles, she realizes the futility of her search and proves that she too is capable of moving beyond institutionalized "Jewish" or "Christian" gestures of mourning. Instead of the traditional cold stones, she buys some roasted chestnuts and places them on his grave. "So what, we are Mischlings . . . we don't have to do it by the book" (Eisler 2001: 211) are her final words, echoing her sister.

Kafka's grave here becomes a symbol of reconciliation. For Kafka in his time, a *Mischlings identity*—in his fantasy of the Devil at the Hearth from 1923—was confused and traumatic:

> And now the child of this marriage is standing here looking all around and the first thing he sees is the devil at the hearth, a terrible apparition which didn't even exist before the child was born. At any rate it was unknown to the child's parents. In general, the Jews who had reached their—I almost wrote: happy—end did not know this particular devil; they could no longer differentiate among various infernal things, they considered the whole world a devil and the devil's work . . . But on the other hand, the child sees the devil standing over his hearth very exactly. And now the struggle of the parents begins in the child, the struggle of their convictions trying to escape the devil. Again and again the angel hauls the Jews on high, to where they should defend themselves, and again and again they fall back down and the angel has to return with them if he doesn't want them to be swallowed up completely. (Kafka 1990: 229)

The Devil, who is torturing the offspring of a Jewish-gentile couple, is an extraordinary personification of anti-semitic discourses about the *Mischling*, who, "in German racial science [is] alternately a psychologically unbalanced hysteric lacking a stable identity and a dangerous monster whose 'repressed' identity returns in an even more concentrated form" (Herzog 1997: 2–3). Therefore, it is all the more relevant that Eisler's post-holocaust story constructs the *Mischlings* identity as a positive model, one which can cross boundaries and overcome racial distinctions. The more "Jewish" North American Emma in the end learns from her older European sister Eva to gently and firmly accept both cultures.

In Gabriella Goliger's (1949–) story, "A Morning in Prague," we visit Kafka's cemetery again. This is the last story in her first book, *Song of Ascent* (2000)—a collection of short stories that is more adequately described as a novel. Goliger recounts the lives of the Birnbaum family, German-speaking holocaust survivors who first settle in Israel and then in Montréal. The father, Ernst Birnbaum, is originally from Marienbad, the resort town outside of Prague, where Kafka himself went many times. Two of his brothers, Thomas and Martin, their wives and one young daughter perished in the holocaust. The book deals with the first generation's inability to discuss the holocaust and the second generation's attempt to construct an identity for themselves which includes their parents' past history. Ernst was always unable to talk about his relatives, nor could he visit Auschwitz, where his family perished. As he tells his daughter Rachel of his failed attempt to go there, they rest by a lake, Lac St. Louis, and she just happens to observe— the symbolism is rather obvious—that, "The factory smokestacks across the lake barely smudged the air" (Goliger 2000: 142). In multicultural Québec, Rachel has not experienced any discrimination as a Jewish woman (nor is discrimination an issue for her 'allophone' parents), but with her father's impending death, Rachel's view of her family's past history—and of her own part in it—is rapidly changing: "The point of the story of Thomas and Martin, she used to think, was her father's survival, not their demise. He got out because he was the youngest, the luckiest, the dreamiest. . . . His escape from danger gave her wings, made her own life inevitable" (Goliger 2000: 148). The daughter's dismal final insight occurs when she crosses the Atlantic and is recounted in the surreal narrative of "A Morning in Prague," which concludes the volume.

The time is after the communist rule, when we see "signs of restless industry, a hunger to erase years of communist neglect, a frenzy of restoration" (Goliger 2000: 170). The holocaust is long forgotten, and everyone is busy erasing the most recent, Communist, history. At this point in time, the ghost of Kafka rises from his grave in the New Jewish cemetery because of "a vast formless shadow pressing on the mind" (Goliger 2000: 169). In contrast to Eisler's conciliatory Kafka, Goliger's Kafka finds facing the Christian burial ground on the other side unsettling: he "decides to take a break from the acres of burial grounds that stretch before him. They unsettle the spirit, all these stately groves, rows of crosses, cultivated lawns, and plaques dedicated to revolutionary heroes. The medieval centre of town is what he wants" (Goliger 2000: 169). He boards a tram and heads for the picturesque Old Jewish Cemetery, which dates back to the fifteenth century and was in use for 300 years until its closure at the end of the eighteenth century. Kafka's cemetery was the second Jewish cemetery, founded in 1890, after the old one was no longer used. In the post-communist era, the Old Jewish cemetery is now a big tourist attraction. As the story recounts, two hundred thousand people are buried here and the tombs are situated at twelve different layers. Goliger plays with Kafka's gatekeeper theme, when "a muttering old woman" (Goliger 2000: 170) cannot open the gate without Kafka's help. Then we meet the ghosts from the past, "Thomas and Gretl Birnbaum and their daughter Louisa" (Goliger 2000: 175), Rachel's relatives who perished and never had a grave. No one understands them any longer, because they speak only German. Kafka becomes their advocate and pleads with the gatekeeper to give them temporary refuge in one of the big tombs. But she wants to keep them out and asks, why these three and not any of the others?

> Armies of them pressed up against the walls, mouths gaping in every crack. Long lineups in ditches and gutters across the country and every one of them has a story, why he or she or their child should be allowed in. And they've been told ages ago it's useless, there's no room, they'd overrun this place in a flash and spoil it for the visitors. And don't they all say what your friends here say? . . . That they just want a temporary refuge when you know full well that if you let them, they'll dig in as deep as they can and it would be hell to root them out again. (Goliger 2000: 177)

One of the reasons, in these difficult economic times after the fall of the communist system, is that the gatekeeper does not want to lose her job and spoil the place as a tourist attraction. In addition, the continuing anti-semitism is obvious; and also, the fact that nothing has changed, while one history after another is being erased. Dead Jews are good for business and the place for Judaism is in the museum: "All is in State Museum with interesting explanations and displays" (Goliger 2000: 177). By this time, an ashamed Kafka is already on his way back to his own "comfortable resting place . . . not as picturesque as this one, perhaps, but perfectly adequate, and a place he can return to whenever he wishes. What petulant, childish dissatisfaction drove him to wander?" (Goliger 2000: 177). He is lucky to have a plot. Out of Kafka's gatekeeper theme, Goliger creates a narrative of exclusion that serves to confront the daughter's innocent Canadian identity with the legacy of the past.

On the other side of the Atlantic, in the German-speaking world, Jews during and after WWII frequently associated Kafka with the holocaust. The administration in concentration camps was likened to Kafka's bureaucracies (Neff 1979: 883), and for first generation Jewish writers in general, Kafka was an obvious intertext. The existential Kafka in Paul Celan (1920–70) comes to mind, as does the political Kafka in the work of Peter Weiss (1916–82), especially in his novella *Abschied von den Eltern* (1961), the novel *Fluchtpunkt* (1962), his major work *Die Ästhetik des Widerstands* (1975),[4] as well as the play *Der neue Prozeß* (1982). Like Weiss, the Nobel Prize winner (1981) Elias Canetti (1905–94), author of *Masse und Macht* (1960), explores Kafka in terms of power and class constellations in *Der andere Prozess* (1969). Moreover, Wolfgang Hildesheimer (1916–91), who worked as a translator for the Nürnberg trials, integrates Kafka and the holocaust into his novel, *Masante* (1973). None of these writers chose to live in Germany or Austria: Celan wrote from Paris, Weiss from Sweden, Canetti from England, and Hildesheimer returned to Europe from Israel and lived in Switzerland from 1957 until his death.

The situation is rather different for the next generations of Jewish writers who grew up in Austria or Germany, such as Rafael Seligmann (1947–), Esther Dischereit (1952–), Barbara Honigmann (1949–), Lothar Schöne (1949–), Maxim Biller (1960–), and Doron Rabinovici (1961–). Critics have found it surprising that they do not seem to draw on the tradition of German Jewish literature before WWII (see Herzog 2002: 208–9). Jack Zipes uses an analogy with Franz Kafka to describe their position in German society today: "Certainly, not all Jews in Germany today are Kafkas, or like Kafka. But Germany for Jews is like Kafka's trial or castle, and in their search for justice and God they have certainly left traces of what can be considered a Jewish minor culture marked by and marking the indomitable force of German culture" (Zipes 1994: 41). But they do not seem to feel a connection with Kafka the way their Canadian counterparts do. Sander Gilman, too, has argued that "the visible invisibility of Jews in contemporary German society replicates in many ways the situation of the Jewish, tubercular, male, German language writer, Franz Kafka, in the Prague of his time" (Gilman 1995: 46–47). We just saw several (male and female) Canadian writers who used Kafka effectively and creatively for their own narratives of exclusion and identity in various inter and transcultural contexts. But many of the German writers spend much time and energy protesting against their "visible invisibility" and their main theme is very limited and always the same: the (re)construction of a Jewish identity in the German-speaking world. To be sure, Kafka was sympathetic to "minor literatures" struggling against the mainstream and saw the "Literatur der kleinen Nationen" (Literature of Small Nations) as a necessary form of self-assertion (whether this was Czech or Yiddish literature). Yet Kafka discussed his own identity problems in his personal writings and did not make them the explicit subject of his literary texts. Perhaps Kafka cannot be an inspiration to some contemporary German Jewish writers, because he did not see his literature as Jewish self-exploration, but aimed instead for the highest literary quality.

Helene Schruff points out that Kafka's significance for the young writers is remarkable, but the only texts she cites are Rafael Seligmann's *Rubinstein's Versteigerung* (Rubinstein's Auction) (1989), where the father-son conflict reminds us of Kafka's *Letter to His Father* (1919) and Schruff also points out *kafkaesque* situations that occur in Lothar Schöne's *Das jüdische Begräbnis* (The Jewish Funeral) in relation to the protagonist's search for his identity. She especially highlights a scene which recalls Kafka's parable *Before the Law*, but remarks on a significant change: "In contrast to Kafka's Man from the Country, the first person narrator overpowers the doorkeeper in this imagined situation and makes sure that the entrance, the gate which provides THE answer to his identity, remains open forever" (Schruff 2000: 234). Here again we are back to identity construction—all of these writings, in one text or another, "revolve around a character's detective work in searching for clues to his/her identity" (Herzog 1997: 13).

As a matter of fact, the model for the outspoken male Jewish writers in asserting their visibility in German culture—especially Seligmann and Biller—was the American novelist Philip Roth, for whom Kafka is indeed of central importance.[5] Schruff therefore rightly argues, "Kafka could be seen as a link to another influencing factor, namely American-Jewish literature" (Schruff 2000: 27). She is correct: if there is a Kafka influence on these writers, it is mediated largely through an American vision of Kafka, or to be more precise, through Roth's "male fantasies" about the tubercular, visionary, lonely Kafka who encourages the self-pity of Portnoy in *Portnoy's Complaint*. Among the Canadian writers, we saw a "woman's complaint" in Régine Robin's *The Wanderer*, who used Kafka in her battle against the mainstream, dominant, culture. But Robin felt a connection with Kafka, whereas Seligmann and Biller identified with Philip Roth, and it is only through Roth that Kafka became paradigmatic for them. It seems that German Jewish writers felt they had no right to the Jewish tradition because "authentic" Jews were perceived to exist only outside of Germany, especially so in the United States (see Herzog 2002: 208–9). Thus, initially these male authors imitated Roth to legitimize their own Jewishness, which paved the way for the next generation of writers to explore their identity. But a polarization still exists: "The self-consciously Jewish characters in texts by Rafael Seligmann and Doron Rabinovici stand in contrast to the first person narrators in the works of Esther Dischereit and Lothar Schöne, who either define themselves as Jewish only after going through long identity crises or decide they do not wish to define themselves as Jewish after a long deliberation of what, if any, meaningful solution this might offer them . . ." (Schruff 2000: 232). German Jewish women writers especially do not have a base in mainstream (male) European society to speak from, nor would they necessarily identify with Roth's male discourse or be interested in his appropriation of Kafka. Yet, in her latest collection of essays, *Mit Eichmann an der Börse* (With Eichmann at the Stock Market, 2001), Esther Dischereit is as confrontational and provocative as some of the German male writers without needing the mediation of a Philip Roth.[6] At the same time, one of the youngest male Austrian Jewish writers, Doron Rabinovici, seems to have reached a position in between the hesitant and the dominant, confrontational, "male" Jewish discourse, when he makes a subtle distinction for himself in a recent interview: "I am a Jew. And I am a writer in Vienna. I do not want to be a Jewish writer."[7] His novel, *Die Suche nach M.* (The Search for M., 1997),[8] indeed moves beyond Jewishness, but not beyond maleness.

In Rabinovici's *The Search for M.*, guilt and revenge fantasies abound as families of holocaust survivors living in Austria struggle with the legacy of the past. The children are torn between their parents' past suffering and the fact that they have to live in the country of their families' former murderers: "No one here had called back those who had been driven away" (Rabinovici 1997: 55). Though not born of mixed Jewish-gentile parentage, these children exhibit the signs of a

German/Austrian–Jewish hybrid, as discussed earlier, who "in German racial science [is] alternately a psychologically unbalanced hysteric lacking a stable identity and a dangerous monster whose 'repressed' identity returns in an even more concentrated form." The struggle of the parents manifests itself in opposite ways in two of the children, Arieh Arthur Fandler and Dani Morgenthau: Arieh Arthur leaves Austria and becomes a 'Lion' King Arthur on a quest, while Dani(el) remains in the Austrian lion's den. Without knowing it and without knowing of the other, the two represent "a murder conspiracy on tour" (Rabinovici 1997: 74) and complement each other. Arieh rebels and transforms himself into a psychopathic agent for the Israeli secret service, hunting down enemies of the Jewish people all over the world, and Dani soaks up his parents' survivor guilt (Rabinovici 1997: 54), first becoming a lawyer, and then metamorphosing into a benevolent (not dangerous!) golem-like Frankenstein monster, Mullemann, who has the astounding ability to enter the psyche of every guilty person who has not acknowledged his/her guilt.

Though it has been argued that the postwar Jewish writers display no direct "connection with the German-Jewish literature before 1933" (Schruff 2000: 27), in the case of this novel, a sophisticated intertext from German culture is suggested by the title. *The Search for M.* no doubt refers to the search for Mullemann, but the allusion is also quite obviously to Fritz Lang's and Thea von Harbou's first sound film M (1931). The film is about a famous child murderer in Berlin at the end of the nineteen-twenties, and there is a direct echo in the novel when Mullemann claims to be the murderer of a child in the nineteen-thirties in Berlin (Rabinovici 1997: 162). This is a very appropriate intertext, considering that the title of the original film script was "Mörder unter uns (Murderers are Amongst Us)," a title that applies well to postwar Germany and Austria. In the film, we repeatedly hear, "Any man in the street could be the murderer." A similar kind of paranoia exists in postwar Austria. Here, a whole country absolved itself from guilt by arguing that they were, after all, invaded by the Nazis and should therefore be seen as innocent bystanders: "Guilty parties were just not to be found in a country that claimed to be without blemish" (Rabinovici 1997: 29). In this kind of set up, where many murderers were allowed to remain at large, the victims, simply by existing, represent "guilt": they are walking reminders of the perpetrators' crimes. This claustrophobic feeling extends to the second generation. Dani knows that he "reflected the past simply by his mere presence" (Rabinovici 1997: 55). To help his son with his identity problems, Dani's father goes from one authority to another to obtain some proof that he is indeed a victim, but he is only put off (Rabinovici 1997: 169)—there is no compensation for survivors (Rabinovici 1997: 55) and no acknowledgment of guilt (Rabinovici 1997: 169). The narrator speculates that if Dani had lived in another country, he might not have developed these guilt problems and his obsession with tracking down the guilty and bringing them to justice (Rabinovici 1997: 55).

In regards to the film M, the life story of the main actor is also significant for the novel because the child murderer, Peter Lorre (pseudonym for Ladislav Löwenstein [1904–64]), was Jewish. When we begin to "see" him in the film as a human being, he is hunted and running from his persecutors. Someone uses chalk to paint the letter M on his coat so that he cannot escape. Though the film was made before the Nazis came to power, from a post-holocaust perspective, the analogy to Nazi Germany and the star of David as a marker of difference and the sign of persecution is obvious. Like Fritz Lang, Lorre emigrated when the Nazis came to power and eventually continued his career in Hollywood. Later, the Nazi propaganda film, *Der Ewige Jude* (The Wandering Jew, 1940), by Fritz Hippler, used "Lorre's final monologue from M . . . billed as an admission by the Jews that they were incapable of controlling their desires and were therefore unfit to live in a 'moral society.'"[9] Rabinovici exploits the fact that Lorre symbolizes the Jew as murderer and victim (of himself and society), by making his own Jewish protagonists oscillate between both identities.

Individuals who are innocent and guilty at the same time, caught in a machinery of power, rejection, condemnation, domination, and humiliation—all of this sounds very *kafkaesque*. While these are themes that Kafka shared with Fritz Lang and Expressionism, at the same time, Kafka is not absent from this novel. After all, there is a major "trial" and there are many "metamorphoses." In the trial, which Dani attends as a member of the jury, an innocent man, Yilmaz Akan, is accused of the murder of a Turkish man who sexually harassed his wife, and though there is no evidence, he is pronounced guilty. The murder is "a Turkish affair" (Rabinovici 1997: 57), where racial presuppositions and prejudice are responsible for the outcome of the guilty verdict. The judge makes it clear that he has nothing against Turks, "but the relationships and customs in Middle Eastern families—blood reprisals, feuds between clans, a husband's rights over his wife—these would remain a puzzle for a European" (Rabinovici 1997: 45). Before the verdict, the defense lawyer uses the same argument: "'You have to empathize with the customs of these people,'" he states. "The crime was manslaughter committed from cultural motivations . . ." (Rabinovici 1997: 57). The irony is that the accused's wife, Gülgün, is the murderer, but no one would suspect her because everyone believes that Turkish women are subordinate to their husbands. In addition, the accused Yilmaz does not share the masculine ideals of "blood reprisals" and "feuds between clans"; when previously asked about this, the accused used to say with a smile, "these practices were outdated" (Rabinovici 1997: 49). In fact, he and his wife knew very well what was expected from them by Tradition, but they chose not to antagonize the man who made the sexual advances (Rabinovici 1997: 52). At the same time, Gülgün also knew—from her experience of living in racist and sexist Austria—that she would likely get away with the murder. Indeed, she was immediately sent to Turkey with her child and does not even have to appear in court (Rabinovici 1997: 53).

As a point of comparison, in Kafka's story A *Fratricide* (1917), a ritualistic murder is committed and the ritual murderer apprehended by the justice system. Ritual murder belongs to the discourse of anti-semitism, originating in the medieval superstition that accused Jews of killing gentiles at Passover/Easter for ritual purposes. The myth reached well into Kafka's time, which saw many ritual murder trials. A *Fratricide* brings these anti-semitic fantasies to life, reenacting the murder for the passive voyeuristic neighbor, a witness to the crime. Kafka stresses the complexity of the question of guilt or innocence by highlighting the complicity of witness and murderer in the crime. The justice system fails to serve justice. In *The Search for M.*, there is a witness as well, afraid of getting involved, while the justice system is outsmarted and exposed as a farce. Yilmaz Akan's Turkish wife Gülgün can laugh at the German/Austrian justice system, which acts in a very predictable fashion—in accordance with racial prejudice and cultural presuppositions.

Moreover, the trial scene reveals a new kind of racism that is hidden in 'politically correct' phrases by philo-semitic and philo-Turkish Germans or Austrians. Because of the veneer of political correctness, individuals are rendered helpless: the racism is not visible and therefore cannot be proven. The jury, including Dani (who knows very well that Yilmaz is not guilty), unanimously judges the accused guilty. In Austria's multicultural environment, Jews are not the only ones who experience this new form of racism. Gilman has therefore criticized writers like Seligmann whose

> notion of 'Germany' is defined in terms of their self-identified Jewishness. . . . their Germany is peopled by 'Germans'—a rather risky generalization given the fact that there are over a million and a half people of Turkish descent in contemporary Germany who may or may not be included in any legal definition of the 'German' but who certainly complicate the simple dichotomy of 'German' and 'Jew.' (Gilman 1995: 19–20)

In Rabinovici's novel, anti-Jewish and anti-Turkish racism are juxtaposed, and in the trial scene, anti-semitism is mirrored and refracted by the racism which is displayed toward the Turkish accused. Significantly, as a member of a minority, Dani understands the language of the accused and the murderess' thinking. Both Jews and Turks live "in the dual tonality of various harmonies" or "in the reverberations of foreign melodies" (Rabinovici 1997: 49)—from the voice of Tradition to the voice of Modernity.

Torn between the voices of the past and present, the protagonists Arieh and Dani, like several of Kafka's protagonists, initially split into two. Arieh refers to his second identity as a "metamorphosis" (Rabinovici 1997: 32). Beginning with the murder of Wernherr, a neo-Nazi whom Arieh 'accidentally' kills in the early nineteen-eighties (Rabinovici 1997: 34, 38), Arieh discovers that a split personality is a necessity for him, "since Arieh *was* another person and would never find his true identity as long as Wernherr remained undefeated" (Rabinovici 1997: 37). In his work for the Israeli secret service, Arieh changes identities (by taking on new names) more frequently than his father did before him (Rabinovici 1997: 94). Dani, on the other hand, absorbs other people's identities when he senses their guilt. Both of them become sick.

Even as a small child, Dani was obsessed with taking responsibility for crimes and pronouncing himself guilty: "It was me. I did it. I'm the guilty one" is the *leitmotif* in the novel. As an adult, his body eventually succumbs to the mental stress: every time he hears a racist or philo-semitic remark, he starts itching, and he develops an itchy skin disease which finally covers his entire body. Gregor Samsa is never admitted to the hospital, but Mullemann is hospitalized, "lies motionless, fettered to his bed. Gauze bandages lashed up in several layers are wound around his body. He can move neither of his legs, none of his limbs nor any of his joints" (Rabinovici 1997: 69). The narrative perspective at this point keeps switching from omniscient to first person, underlining Dani's split character into Dani and Mullemann. It just so happens that Arieh, too, has been hospitalized in his hometown, because his body has broken down and he and Mullemann are in adjacent rooms. When Arieh hears Mullemann's Morse codes (Rabinovici 1997: 75) over the radiator—revealing all secrets, all crimes, including Arieh's own—he becomes paranoid, like the animal in Kafka's The Burrow: "Maybe it was an enemy who was trying to drive Arthur Bein crazy" (Rabinovici 1997: 76). Mullemann's unrelenting Morse code signals confront Arieh with the crimes he was directly responsible for through his work, and this becomes the beginning of his final transformation: a return to his own self. Arieh realizes that he was in danger of losing himself, and after his release from the hospital, he decides that he cannot live with himself if he continues to assume further identities and becomes responsible for even more murders. On his next assignment, when he discovers his Palestinian enemy's German wife and daughter, Arieh, as well as the Palestinian agent who was ordered to spy on him, decide not to carry out their duties and retreat with their families.

When Dani is released from the hospital, he emerges as Mullemann, who from now on haunts the streets of Vienna, pronouncing himself guilty of every crime he encounters and thereby drawing attention to it. Symbolically speaking, Mullemann's entire body soaks up all the guilt in his environment. The more his body breaks out and needs to be "covered" with layers and layers of gauze, the more he becomes obsessed with "uncovering" guilt, since this relieves his symptoms. Both Arieh and Dani's identities have increasingly become absorbed by the identities of other people: their continual metamorphoses have turned them into signifiers that are constantly changing and have no base. Unlike Arieh, Dani becomes a freak celebrity in the guilt-ridden German-speaking world, acknowledging guilt and exposing it everywhere. He is even invited to be on a German TV show, and finally moves beyond the confines of the German-speaking world to other big European cities and even to other continents (Rabinovici 1997: 174–75), tracking down the guilty, making them confess, and receiving medals of recognition everywhere.

At this point, Rabinovici has also long left Kafka's *Metamorphosis* behind. Another important intertext from North American popular culture has emerged in the form of Woody Allen's film, *Zelig* (1983), where *kafkaesque* metamorphoses are displayed through Woody Allen's vision (see Bruce 1998: 173–203). Like Mullemann, Zelig is a "human chameleon," taking on the personal and physical characteristics of individuals whom he encounters. Zelig becomes famous, too. The public is described as Zelig-crazy: everyone talks about him, there is a new "Doin' the Chameleon" dance, there are photos of him for sale, and Hollywood even makes a film about him in 1935, called *The Changing Man*. The film is explicit on how the public exploits him, because Zelig "sells": "There were not only Leonard Zelig pens and lucky charms but clocks and toys. There were Leonard Zelig watches and books and a famous Leonard Zelig doll. There were aprons, chameleon-shaped earmuffs, and a popular Leonard Zelig game." In *The Search for M.*, Mullemann now becomes Arieh's (i.e., 'Lion' King Arthur's) modern complement, a cowboy in arms from American popular culture, "a Zorro in white. Women sent him love letters. . . . Fathers sent their sons gauze masks for their birthdays. A rollercoaster in the amusement park hired barkers in gauze costumes to proclaim and extol its thrills" (Rabinovici 1997: 174–75). He also becomes Arieh's nightmare, when he sees "Mullemania everywhere" (Rabinovici 1997: 181). Furthermore, Mullemann's travels around the world with Kommissar Karl Siebert remind us of the Hunger Artist's travels with his impresario. However, Woody Allen uses Kafka's "Hunger Artist" as well, and his Zelig goes on tours also and is exhibited everywhere, until he really cannot take it any longer and disappears. After yet another trial, he finally returns 'home' to the one person how truly loved him, his first doctor, Eudora Fletcher, who kept searching for Zelig and always wanted to cure him.

Similarly, Mullemann is allowed a way out. His mother recounts that at this stage of his life, he is so overworked that he completely ignores his appearance: Mullemann is "all bundled up in those bandages which hardly ever get changed. They finally get so shabby hanging down behind him that he has to trudge along with them in tow" (Rabinovici 1997: 177). This description echoes Gregor Samsa's toward the end of his life: he is covered with dust and "fluff and hair and remnants of food trailed with him, caught on his back and along his sides . . ." (Kafka 1971: 130). But Mullemann does not die like Gregor Samsa. On one of his trips to Berlin, where he is working closely with the Berlin police force, suddenly Mullemann disappears to start a new life, presumably to find his way back to Sina Mohn, who, like Zelig's Eudora Fletcher, almost cured him in the short time he was with her, and who also searched for M. and wanted him back (Rabinovici 1997: 163).

The Search for M. places Jewish identity problems into a larger multicultural context and draws on several cultural traditions (past and present), combining, for instance, the first German sound film M with Kafka and Woody Allen. However, unlike many of the Canadian works, the overall context of Rabinovici's novel is almost exclusively male. Jeffrey Peck rightly criticizes "the dominant and rather exclusive masculinization of Jewish discourses in Germany, among critics as well as literary writers" (Peck 1999). We hear nothing about Arieh's mother, who is twenty-five years younger than his father (Rabinovici 1997: 61), except that her parents' paintings were stolen and Arieh's father helped her retrieve them and married her. Also, no information is given about Arieh's grandmother who, it turns out, lived in the same city but never met her son or grandson, because Arieh's father had changed his name. The Turkish woman Gülgün is developed a little more in order to explain the circumstances behind the murder; as is Sina Mohn, the one woman who understands and cares for Mullemann and to whom he might be returning. But even with Sina Mohn, someone who should be an important character, we only learn that she is an art historian, cares about degenerate art, and is able to acknowledge racism in her own family (Rabinovici 1997: 142). It would have been interesting to hear more.

Rabinovici's *The Search for* M., then, crosses many cultural boundaries, but does not question the gender status quo. Of the Canadian Jewish writers, Klein is very traditional in his search for Truth and the gender issue does not enter here. Cohen rewrites—in a postmodern fashion—the (male) Jesuit narrative about the life of a Native/Christian female martyr and saint, and presents a self-indulgent, postmodern (male) "New Jew," "the founder of Magic Canada, Magic French Québec, and Magic Canada. . . . New Jews—the two of us, queer, militant, invisible, part of a possible new tribe" (Cohen 1966: 161), in an ironic fashion. The German male writers do not yet have this ironic distance to the male Jew. The three Canadian women writers all use Kafka to express their female transatlantic solitudes: Robin's neo-nomadic postmodern narrative seeks admittance to the Castle on the hill; Eisler searches for reconciliation after the holocaust; and Goliger's first and second generation attempt to construct a Jewish identity after the holocaust. In terms of subject matter, Goliger's 'novel' comes closest to Rabinovici's *The Search for* M., but she complements Rabinovici by giving a voice to all female characters. Nonetheless, with its confusing multiple identities, its shifting expressionistic scenes, and its mixed cross-cultural signifiers, *The Search for* M. is the most original postmodern novel by a Jewish writer to come out of Austria yet.

Notes

1. For an overview of Canadian Jewish fiction, see Greenstein 2004: xi–l. I would like to thank Sonja Hedgepeth and Michael Greenstein for their advice and suggestions for this essay.

2. The Austrian born Canadian writer Henry Kreisel (1922–1991) frequently evokes Kafka himself. In one of the short stories in *The Almost Meeting*, a protagonist by the name of Drimmer (dreamer) returns to his village after the holocaust. The surreal setting reminds us of the desolate, dreamlike, foggy landscape when Kafka's K first enters the village of *The Castle* and also echoes the theme of Kafka's short text "The Homecoming" (see Kreisel 1981: 39–77).

3. Jean de Brébeuf recorded these tales in 1636. Cf. <http://www.sceniccaves.com/green/caves-trails.htm> (accessed on 11 January 2008). For the legend of Oscotarach in Cohen, see also the article by Leslie Monkman (Monkman 1974).

4. Cf. Krusche 1979: 659–61 and Neff 1972: 902. See also Fingerhut 1980: 384–403.

5. In talking about Philip Roth, Maxim Biller remarks that, "the American Jewish authors are not restrained by anything and expose whatever people do not want to know or hear about their lives" (Biller 1991: 165–66). Seligmann has been compared with Roth many times; in fact, he has been called the German Philip Roth (Cf. Gilman 1995: 49–54).

6. See Dischereit 2001.

7. Rabinovici 2004. My thanks to Anneliese & Ernst Pöhling for sending me this article.

8. For the literary historical context of this novel see Lorenz 1999: xi–xxxiv.

9. Youngkin 1999: 64. Beyer 1988: 54. Cf. Hofmann 1998: 31.

Works Cited

Allen, Woody. "Zelig." *Three Films of Woody Allen*. *Zelig—Broadway Danny Rose—The Purple Rose of Cairo*. New York: Orion Pictures Corporation, 1987. 2–141.

Biller, Maxim. "Philip Roth: Die Zeit der Ungeheuer ist vorbei." *Die Tempojahre*. München: dtv, 1991. 164–70.

Beyer, Friedemann. *Peter Lorre. Seine Filme—sein Leben*. München: Wilhelm Heyne Verlag, 1988.

Bruce, Iris. "Mysterious Illnesses of Human Commodities in Woody Allen and Franz Kafka." *Studies in Twentieth Century Literature*, 22.1 (Winter, 1998): 173–203.

Cohen, Leonard. *Beautiful Losers*. Toronto/Montreal: McClelland and Stewart, 1966.

———. *Let Us Compare Mythologies*. Toronto/Montreal: McClelland and Stewart, 1956.

———. *Selected Poems 1956–1968*. Toronto/Montreal: McClelland and Stewart, 1964.

Cohen, Matt. *Typing. A life in 26 keys*. East Mississauga: Random House Canada, 2000.

Dischereit, Esther. *Mit Eichmann an der Börse in jüdischen und anderen Angelegenheiten*. Berlin: Ullstein, 2001.

Eisler, Irena. "Chestnuts for Kafka." *not quite mainstream: Canadian Jewish Short Stories*. Ed. Norman Ravvin. Calgary: Red Deer Press, 2001. 202–11.

Fingerhut, Karlheinz. "Drei erwachsene Söhne Kafkas. Zur produktiven Kafka-Rezeption bei Martin Walser, Peter Weiss und Peter Handke." *Wirkendes Wort* 30.6 (Nov./Dec. 1980): 384–403.

Gilman, Sander. *Jews in Today's German Culture*. Bloomington and Indianapolis: Indiana University Press, 1995.

Goliger, Gabriella. *Song of Ascent*. Vancouver: Raincoast Books, 2000.

Greenstein, Michael, ed. *Contemporary Jewish Writing in Canada. An Anthology*. Lincoln and London: University of Nebraska Press, 2004.

———. *Third Solitudes. Tradition and Discontinuity in Jewish-Canadian Literature*. Kingston, Montreal, London: McGill-Queen's University Press, 1989.

Herzog, Todd. "Hybrids and *Mischlinge*: Translating Anglo-American Cultural Theory into German." *The German Quarterly* 70.1 (Winter 1997): 2–3.

———. "New York Is More Fun." *Deutsch-Jüdische Literatur der Neunziger Jahre. Die Generation nach der Shoah*. Eds. Sander Gilman & Hartmut Steinecke. Berlin: Erich Schmidt Verlag, 2002. 204–13.

Hofmann, Felix and Stephen D. Younkin. *Peter Lorre. Portrait des Schauspielers auf der Flucht.* München: belleville Verlag, 1998.

Kafka, Franz. Kafka, *Letters to Milena*. Trans. Philip Boehm. New York: Schocken, 1990.

———. *The Complete Stories*. Ed. Nahum N. Glatzer. New York: Schocken, 1971.

———. *The Castle*. Trans. Mark Harman. New York: Schocken, 1998.

Klein, A.M. "Hemlock and Marijuana. Review of *In the Penal Colony: Stories and Short Pieces by Franz Kafka*" (17 December 1948). *Literary Essays and Reviews*. Ed. by Usher Caplan & M.W. Steinberg. Toronto: University of Toronto Press, 1987. 275–78.

———. "Political Parties in Israel" (28 October 1949). *Beyond Sambation. Selected Essays and Editorials 1928–1955*. Eds. M.W. Steinberg & U. Caplan. Toronto/Buffalo/London: University of Toronto Press, 1982. 371–73.

———. *The Second Scroll*. Toronto: McClelland and Stewart, 1951.

Kreisel, Henry. "The Homecoming." *The Almost Meeting and Other Stories*. Edmonton: NeWest Press, 1981. 39–77.

Krusche, Dietrich. "Beispiele produktiver Aneignung (Walser, Weiss, Jens, Handke)." *Kafka-Handbuch. Band 2: Das Werk und seine Wirkung*. Ed. Hartmut Binder. Stuttgart: Alfred Kröner Verlag, 1979. 656–66.

Lorenz, Dagmar, ed. *Contemporary Jewish Writing in Austria. An Anthology*. Lincoln & London: University of Nebraska Press, 1999.

Monkman, Leslie. "Beautiful Losers: Mohawk Myth and Jesuit Legend." *Journal of Canadian Fiction* (1974). <http://www.webheights.net/speakingcohen/canfic74.htm> (accessed on [date]). 1–6.

Neff, Kurt. "Kafkas Schatten. Eine Dokumentation zur Breitenwirkung." *Kafka-Handbuch. Band 2: Das Werk und seine Wirkung*. Ed. Hartmut Binder. Stuttgart: Alfred Kröner Verlag, 1979. 872–909.

Peck, Jeffrey. "After Bubis' Death. Critiquing the Critics: Brumlik, Broder, and Seligmann." GSA paper 1999. <http://jsis.artsci.washington.edu/programs/europe/wendep/PeckPaper.htm> (accessed on June 28, 2002). 1–5.

Rabinovici, Doron. "Im Griff gefährlicher Vergangenheit." *Westfälische Nachrichten* Nr. 62. Münster Feuilleton RMS 11 (March 13, 2004).

———. *Suche nach M*. Frankfurt: Suhrkamp, 1997.

Robin, Régine. *The Wanderer*. Trans. Phyllis Aronoff. Montreal: Alter Ego Editions, 1997.

Schruff, Helene. *Wechselwirkungen. Deutsch-Jüdische Identität in erzählender Prosa der 'Zweiten Generation.'* Hildesheim/Zürich/New York: Georg Olms Verlag, 2000.

Youngkin, Stephen D., James Bigwood, and Raymond G. Cabana. *The Films of Peter Lorre*. Secaucus, NJ: The Citadel Press, 1982.

Zipes, Jack. "The Contemporary German Fascination for Things Jewish." *Reemerging Jewish Culture in Germany. Life and Literature Since 1989*. Eds. Sander Gilman and Karen Remmler. New York & London: New York University Press, 1994. 15–45.

9

A German-Jewish-American Dialogue?

Literary Encounters between German Jews and Americans in the 1990s

Todd Herzog

In the middle of a dismissive review of Doron Rabinovici's recent novel *Ohnehin* (Nonetheless, 2004), Thomas Rothschild includes a seemingly unmotivated condemnatory digression on the role that books such as Rabinovici's have played in American universities. Noting the unusually large interest in German- and Austrian-Jewish culture among American scholars, he argues that this interest is motivated by self-interest and self-promotion rather than the intrinsic interest of the topic itself:

> There are not only elite universities in the United States, but also lots of mediocre academic institutions that nevertheless follow the principle of "publish or perish" and are consequently continually making themselves heard. One therefore finds regular conferences about Jews in Austrian literature taking place in which the intellectual modesty of the presentations—which consist of simple summaries, biographical details, and excerpts from European reviews—are combined with the immodesty of the presenters, on whom one can count to continually cite their own publications in the footnotes of their papers. Many even manage to bring their entire academic production into their footnotes. (Rothschild 2004)

As a young academician hoping to make a career at a large American university that Rothschild would surely classify as "mediocre," and who has consistently worked on the subject of German- and Austrian-Jewish culture, it is difficult not to take this condemnation personally—however absurd and mean-spirited it might be. Rothschild insists that people like me (and presumably those of you who are reading this book) should turn our attention away from what he views as the "positivistic hooting and hollering" that characterizes American studies of German/Austrian-Jewish literature and toward an exploration of more pressing questions, such as: "why in Vienna, in contrast to German cities, literary works by Jews have in recent years been plentiful, while German-language novels, plays, and poems by migrants (again in comparison with Germany) have been underrepresented" (Rothschild 2004).

This is an interesting question, which I will not pursue here. I intend rather to pose another line of inquiry pointedly raised by Rotschild's review (and echoed in countless other recent feuilletonistic articles in German and Austrian papers): Is there a "special relationship" between North American Germanists and German-Jewish writers? And if there is indeed a special relationship, what is its nature and why does it come under consistent attack from European cultural critics? Clearly, there is something at stake here greater than a relatively small group of American scholars and the equally small number of texts they are writing about. And yes, Mr. Rothchild, I intend to quote European reviews and footnote myself at least once in the course of this article.

The past decade has witnessed an unexpected reemergence of Jewish literary culture in Germany, Austria, and Switzerland. One particularly interesting aspect of this new generation of German-Jewish writers is that they have increasingly turned, not to pre-Holocaust German-Jewish traditions, but rather quite vocally and explicitly to Jewish American authors as a model for their own work. Not only Jewish American authors, but also the space of America itself has consequently played a notable role in this literature.

The past decade has also witnessed a remarkable amount of interest among North American scholars in this new German-Jewish literature. Conferences, special issues of journals, and volumes such as this devoted to the topic of post-*Wende* German-Jewish culture are regular fixtures on the North American German Studies landscape. Clearly, there has developed an interesting relationship between German-Jewish literature and America. In this chapter, I want to explore this relationship and the increasing tensions that it has produced. In order to understand what is going on here, I will first examine the image of America in contemporary German-Jewish literature, then I will turn to its reception in North America.

The Image of America in Contemporary German-Jewish Literature

America as a space has played a notable role in recent German-Jewish literature. In Daniel Ganzfried's *Der Absender* (The Sender, 1995), the crucial moment of confrontation between father and son takes place atop the Empire State Building in New York City. In Barbara Honigmann's 1991 novel *Eine Liebe aus nichts* (A Love out of Nothing), the unnamed German-Jewish narrator falls in love with a Jewish American man and repeatedly expresses her wish to live on Ellis Island. The characters in Irene Dische's and Maxim Biller's short stories move fluidly between American and German locations, and even identities. The main character in Rafael Seligmann's 1999 novel *Der Milchmann* (The Milkman) desperately seeks an American audience for the film he wants to make. Finally, nearly all of the authors of these stories openly express the influence of Jewish American writers such as Philip Roth and Saul Bellow on their own work.

In Barbara Honigmann's novel *Eine Liebe aus nichts*, the German-Jewish narrator and her Jewish American lover are discussing the possibility of their traveling to the United States, when the narrator expresses her long-held desire not just to visit Ellis Island, but to take up residence there. When he explains to her that one is not allowed to live on Ellis Island and assures her that she would quickly make it through passport control, she protests: "No, no! When I finally make it to Ellis Island I will never leave. Ellis Island is my home" (Honigmann 1991: 57). Ellis Island serves as a space in which the various identities that she is otherwise unable to reconcile elsewhere can be reconciled. This fantasy America is a place of infinite possibilities, a place where one does not have to choose between ethnicities and nationalities. I will return to this text and this fantasy about America shortly.

In an interesting article on the Jewish-American writer Philip Roth, Maxim Biller similarly depicts the United States as presenting possibilities for Jews that simply do not exist in Europe. The main freedom with which they are presented is the possibility to argue among themselves, to offer different versions of what it means to be Jewish after the Holocaust. The result is a type of literature unthinkable in Europe: "They have an extreme type of Jewish literature that would be unthinkable over here, because the burden of the Holocaust and its unmediated effects weigh too heavily on us" (Biller 1991: 165). Jewish-American authors such as Roth, Saul Bellow, and Joseph Heller—who are frequently cited as models for recent German-Jewish writers such as Biller and Rafael Seligmann—are, Biller argues, granted more freedom in their ability to explore the panoply of Jewish life today. Biller expresses Roth's argument thus: "I am an artist; I will not remain silent about something simply because Hitler and Goebbels once caused trouble. . . . Every people has its wax figure museum of heroes, anti-heroes, non-heroes, with good people and bad people. I am responsible for the entire Jewish paopticum" (Biller 1991: 166). Like his fellow Jewish American writers, Roth is thus able to confront the varied and often paradoxical nature of post-Holocaust Jewish life "without sentimentality, without shying away from comic exaggerations and the truest truths" (Biller 1991: 167). But he can do so only because of where he lives and works: "And in that he is helped, as I have already mentioned, by his location. He is an American, not a German." (Biller 1991: 167). Roth himself explores this theme, as Biller notes, in the epilog to his Zuckerman series, *The Prague Orgy*, in which his fictional alter ego, the writer Nathan Zuckerman, emerges from a confrontation with anti-Semitism in Europe as a changed, more subdued figure. In Europe, he finds himself labeled a Jew and no longer seems to have agency in constructing himself as whatever type of Jew he pleases. As in Honigmann's novel, the contrast between America as a space of opportunity for self-construction of identity is sharply contrasted with Europe as a space in which this opportunity is not granted to Jews—writers or otherwise. And, Biller argues, the proximity to the site of the Holocaust is precisely the difference here: the "unmediated effects" that one feels in Europe are safely filtered and mediated through museums and films in the United States.

Proximity to the Holocaust also plays a crucial role in Doron Rabinovici's short story *"Der richtige Riecher"* (The Right Nose, 1994), but Rabinovici here presents a radically different (though related) image of Jewish life in America compared to Jewish life in Central Europe. At the opening of the story, the protagonist, a young Austrian Jew named Amos, comes upon a demonstration and counter-demonstration over past and present racism in Austria. The demonstration turns violent, blows are exchanged, and one of the participants shouts to Amos: "If you don't like it here, then go to Israel—or New York" (Rabinovici 1994: 61). "New York is more fun," an American Jewish professor at Columbia University tells Amos a couple of weeks later (Rabinovici 1994: 62). The professor continually repeats this statement, explaining that in New York Jews come out on top because, as he puts it, "all the narrow-minded, racist Jews in Brooklyn are free to hate the blacks" (Rabinovici 1994: 63). Not in spite of this fact of America's being more fun, but precisely because of it, Amos announces that he would choose Israel over New York. However, this is not the real choice presented in this story. For, as Professor Rubenstein quickly adds, Israel too has its attractions to Jews, especially American Jews who travel to Israel "in order to hate Arabs with better reasons" than they hated blacks in Brooklyn (Rabinovici 1994: 63). Jews both in America and Israel have it good: they exist in large numbers and are able to hate another minority group. Jews in Austria—and, of course, Germany—in contrast, do not have it so good, as Rabinovici details in the continual encounters with both overt and latent anti-Semitism in this story. But precisely this difficult existence makes Austrian and German Jews stronger, tougher: the climactic act of the story comes at its conclusion, when Amos is confronted with the confused anti-Semitic comments of a non-Jewish friend and responds by punching him in the face and breaking his nose. This parallels the physical attack on a foreign counter-demonstrator at the opening of the story and turns Amos into "the family hero" (Rabinovici 1994: 73).

The argument of the story is clear, as Sander Gilman noted: Jews in America may indeed have more fun, but precisely because of this they have become weak, and indeed less "Jewish." When Amos' family invites the family of the Columbia Professor to a Passover Seder, the Americans are described as enjoying the ceremony without really understanding it:

> The Rubensteins were neither traditional nor sentimental, but they nevertheless enjoyed the challah, kreplach soup, gefilte fish, and the rest of the dishes. They didn't understand a word of old Getreider's prayers, but were enthusiastic about the Hebrew songs and the rest of the folklore. (Rabinovici 1994: 62)

The Rubenstein family's relationship to Judaism is primarily culinary: Passover is fun.

The German-Jewish-American writer Jeannette Lander presents a similar scene in her 1976 novel *Die Töchter* (The Daughters), which traces the lives of three European-Jewish sisters who end up in Germany, America, and Israel. While none of the sisters come across as having anything like an "authentic" relationship to Judaism, the American sister certainly has the easiest relationship to her Jewish identity. Jewishness, for her, amounts to a variety of social obligations and opportunities. In one scene, the sister, Minouche, visits a friend who is sitting shiva for her father. This usually solemn event becomes an occasion for a social gathering, as the various guests decide what type of makeup to wear and how to dress. The hosts are even mixing cocktails for the guests. When a friend of Minouche's arrives, he "waves at her as if it were a party," leading her to recall sitting shiva for her own father in her childhood: "ugh! It wasn't like that at all back then in France" (Lander 1996: 79). Katja Behrens adopts a less parodic tone, but takes a similar position in her story, "*Salomo und die anderen*" (Salomo and the Others, 1993), in which a woman imagines a German-Jewish boy named Salomo moving to America: "Her oldest son could be called Sally and be a good American who has forgotten what it is like to be a foreigner in the big melting pot and hardly knows anymore what it is like to be at home nowhere" (Behrens 1993: 46). The language here ("forgotten," "hardly knows anymore") indicates a certain lack in the American Sally as opposed to the German Salomo. In these fantasies about American Jews, they do, indeed, have it better, but they are therefore "inauthentic." Austrian and German Jews, on the other hand, are continually confronted with racism and must negotiate on a daily basis a territory with a terrifying past. As a result, they are seen as tougher and thus more "authentic" Jews.

Contemporary German-Jewish Literature in America

Just as German-Jewish writers have consistently made a claim for themselves as "authentic" Jews in contrast to weak and "inauthentic" American Jews,

American critics have reversed this claim, charging German Jews with inauthenticity. Reviewing an anthology of writings by young German-Jewish writers translated into English, *Jewish Voices—German Words* (edited by Elena Lapin, this 1994 collection remains one of the few sources of new German-Jewish literature in English), Tom Reiss argues in *The Forward* that "with the Jewish place in Germany and Europe shattered," these writers are turned into "righteous, guilt-ridden freaks, defending an untenable connection to a *Heimat* that would only truly accept them as fertilizer" (Reiss 1994). They are, according to Reiss, "trapped without a fatherland, for the great Germany that produced Goethe and Schiller and Einstein and Freud now burns more brightly by far in New York and Tel Aviv than it does in Berlin and Vienna" (Reiss 1994). Now, the assertion that Jews should not live in the so-called "lands of the murderers" is, of course, nothing new. Critics have also frequently expressed the idea that Jewish literature in German is not possible after the Holocaust. However, Reiss seems to go a step further, arguing that *writers* have no place in Germany today—even Goethe and Schiller seem to have been forced into exile by the Nazis. Indeed, Reiss continues,

> [t]he Germans have inherited their language, but they have been denied the spark that once lit the minds who spoke it—created by German rubbing against Jews, Jew against German—that ultimately left one group to inherit history's greatest shame, the other its greatest accomplishment. They have inherited the library, but the books went to cousins across the seas. (Reiss 1994)

Not only are these German-Jewish writers not authentic Jews, according to Reiss, they are not even authentic writers! While Gertrud Koch has complained that recent German-Jewish writers have not taken up the mantel of the great tradition of pre-War German-Jewish writers, and while Thomas Nolden has countered that they face enough obstacles and inflated expectations that they cannot be expected to be casting themselves in the tradition of Heine and Kafka, Reiss makes a different argument: it is not a question of desire or ability—they have no rights to this tradition. Those rights, he explicitly argues, have been inherited by American Jews and Israeli Jews. Not only are "authentic" Jews to be found only outside of Germany, so too are "authentic" German-Jewish writers to be found only outside of Germany—it is Philip Roth or Amos Oz who somehow seem to lay claim to the rights to Heine, Schnitzler, and Kafka, not Maxim Biller or Esther Dischereit. The only writer in the anthology who escapes Reiss's attack is Henryk Broder, whom Reiss however strips of his German passport and his part-time residence in Berlin by proclaiming him "a literary provocateur who sends his salvos to the German press from his exile in Israel" (Reiss 1994). The German-Jewish literary tradition, according to Reiss, ended in 1933. The last chapter has been written. The sequel is set in New York or Tel Aviv.

Though Reiss's review is extreme, it is representative of the limited popular reception in America of contemporary German-Jewish literature. Rather than the position of "bearers of memory" or gadflies who force a remembrance of the past and a confrontation with history that these writers are commonly—and often unwillingly—thrust into in the German reception of their works, American critics have described contemporary German-Jewish literary culture as consisting of "Germans who cannot face their history and Jews who cannot face theirs" ("Growing Up Jewish" 1994). The signs of a seeming reemergence of a vibrant German-Jewish culture have not been taken as such in reviews of these works in translation. German-Jewish culture is dead; as one critic put it: "Listening carefully to these German-speaking writers struggling so mightily with their Jewishness in these often startling essays and tormented fiction and poetry, one cannot help but agree that for most Jews, Germany is now just a huge cemetery" (Miron 1994).

In contrast to the pessimistic, dismissive, and often patronizing assessment of contemporary German-Jewish culture in the English-language popular press, the academic reception of this literature in the United States has been relatively widespread and largely enthusiastic. One of the first assessments of post-*Wende* German-Jewish life and literature was the anthology co-edited by Sander Gilman and Karen Remmler titled *Reemerging Jewish Culture in Germany* (1994). As the title already makes clear, this collection of essays offers a much more positive valuation of the present and future of German-Jewish culture. The diverse voices represented in this collection—both of Germans and non-Germans, fiction writers and scholars—as the editors note, "by no means converge to a consensus about the possibility of a vital Jewish culture in Germany. Rather they begin a dialogue among scholars and writers" (Gilman and Remmler 1994: 11). However, the general thrust of the book—as precisely the lively disagreements among the various essays demonstrate—is that a noteworthy German-Jewish culture *is* developing in post-*Wende* Germany. Interestingly, the North American based critics, such as Jack Zipes, Marion Kaplan, Jeffrey Peck, and Susan Neiman, as well as Remmler and Gilman, tend to adopt a more optimistic—Neiman even uses the term "utopian" (Gilman and Remmler 1994: 265)—stance toward the potential for a vibrant Jewish culture in Germany than do the German-based contributors, such as Katharina Ochse and Rafael Seligmann.

Without attempting to elide the differences among American academic critics of contemporary German-Jewish literature and culture, I think that it can be largely classified within two broad categories: cosmopolitanism and cultural hybridity, on the one hand, and gender studies, on the other. In the German reception, these categories are much less pronounced; the emphasis tends to be more on Jewish identity, and especially confrontations with the Holocaust.

The reception of German-Jewish literature from within the discourse of post-colonial criticism continues the optimistic—even, I would argue, utopian—trend of American academic discourse on this subject. US-based critics have repeatedly read the texts of German Jews as examples of the achievement of a cosmopolitan, hybrid identity. I mentioned earlier that Barbara Honigmann's novel *Eine liebe aus nichts* posits the United States (specifically Ellis Island) as a utopian space in which a complex hybrid identity is possible. The German-American German-ist Guy Stern has written that Honigmann's novel occupies this space, claim-ing that it creates "continuity out of fragmentation" and that "symbolically and structurally exile extends into homecoming—both for the father and daughter" (Stern 1994: 330, 331). Leslie Adelson writes in an essay of the "curious (but for Jews traditional) paradox of finding one's grounding precisely in that foreignness" (Adelson 1990: 117). And theorists such as Homi Bhabha have attempted to revalue the figure of the "wandering Jew" as a positive figure. For Bhabha, the Jew is the essence of cosmopolitanism: "Jewishness stands for a form of historical and racial *in-betweenness*" (Bhabha 1995: 14). But does Honigmann's novel—or the other writings of the Third Generation of German Jews—ever achieve a positive Jewish hybridity, a continuity out of fragmentation, a *"Heimat in der Fremde?"*[1] The narrator in *Eine liebe aus nichts* never manages to foster a true connection—either with her romantic partners, or with the cities in which she lives. As she walks through the streets of Paris, she has the feeling of never having arrived: "I sat there or walked around just like on Ellis Island, an immigrant, an emigrant, a flaneuse" (Honigmann 1991: 20). Ellis Island becomes a metaphor for her entire existence. She identifies with the nineteenth-century immigrants to the United States: "Now he sits on Ellis Island, that damn island; he has made a break with his whole life behind him and has not yet set foot in America" (Honigmann 1991: 14). Honigmann's narrator attempts to reconcile her German and Jewish identities in what initially seemed like a space of infinite possibilities, the fantasy America represented by Ellis Island. However, as her friend tells her, Ellis Island "hasn't existed for a long time" (Honigmann 1991: 57). The hybrid finds herself in an impossible position, stuck on an unlivable "damn island" that is neither the old *Heimat* nor the new *Heimat*, and which in fact does not even exist any longer. Honigmann's hybrids, like those in other recent German-Jewish fiction such as Esther Dischereit's *Joëmis Tisch* (Joëmi's Table, 1988), Irene Dische's *"Eine Jüdin für Chales Allen"* ("A Jewess for Charles Allen," 1988) and Maxim Biller's *"Ver-rat"* ("Betrayal," 1990), never achieve the home in homelessness that Ameri-can academic critics have ascribed to them; rather, they remain, as the father in *Eine liebe aus nichts* repeatedly exclaims, "always and everywhere an alien enemy" (Honigmann 1991: 63).

Although American academic critics throughout the 1990s tended to cham-pion this new literature, there seems to be a recent increase in contentiousness, as is evident in the title of a paper Jeffrey Peck presented as part of a conference commemorating the tenth anniversary of the *Wende*: "Critiquing the Critics: Brumlik, Broder, and Seligmann." Continuing the tendency to assign importance to gender identity, Peck asserts that "Jewish male voices such as Broder, Selig-mann, and Brumlik may also have to bear critiques—about gender, such as their own masculinized self-presentations or others—that they are not used to hear-ing" (Peck 1999). Peck also quickly establishes who is in the best position to offer such critiques—academics based outside of Germany: "it remains for critics like myself to address in detail the dominant and rather exclusive masculinization of Jewish discourses in Germany, among critics as well as literary writers" (Peck 1999). What Peck, who is one of the most astute critics of German-Jewish cul-ture on either side of the Atlantic, realizes and communicates here, of course, is that certain criticisms are possible from a position outside of Germany that are simply not possible in Germany.

There are moments in Peck's paper that convey a sense of adversarial critique that is often missing from criticism on the subject. Henryk Broder comes un-der especially intense criticism. Referring to Broder's well-known essay on the concept of *Heimat*, he comments that "unfortunately Broder's more systematic analyses become by the end of the essay a case of pure emotional *Yiddishkeit*, a perspective that while it has its own ethnographic flare, does not do justice to the complexity of identity formation, even for a journalist, rather than an academic" (Peck 1999). Peck is quite aware of the important role that North American academics play in the reception of these authors and criticizes Broder for "his disdain and arrogance towards the entire Jewish scholarly establishment in Ger-man Studies that supports his travel . . . to conferences organized by academics such as myself" (Peck 1999).

In return, Rafael Seligmann's novel *Der Milchmann*, published the same year Peck presented his lecture, takes an equally contentious stance toward critics of recent German-Jewish culture. His anti-hero Jakob Weinberg announces his avoidance of Holocaust literature: "Nobody had to tell him what had happened in the past—neither an Italian chemist, nor a Viennese literary scholar from America, and least of all know-it-all Israelis who were still green behind the ears" (Seligmann 1999: 50). Elsewhere, Weinberg asserts that "a Jewish Germanist is like a vegetarian lion: an unviable being" (Seligmann 1999: 95). But it is not only the Germanists and foreign critics who come under attack in Seligmann's novel. Weinberg also voices his strong opinions on German- and Austrian-Jewish writ-ers such as Jurek Becker and Robert Schindel, whose books he pronounces as full of "weaklings" "nogoodniks" (Seligmann 1999: 26, 276–77). Weinberg seems, in contrast, to prefer a more aggressive, confrontational writer such as Seligmann himself. Once again, the question of who is a more and less "authentic" Jew seems to be at issue here and is bound up with the question of tough Jews and weak Jews. Am I being too narcissistic when I read these passages as answers to North American critics, who have greeted Schindel and Becker, just like Honig-mann and Dischereit, with a more positive reception than we have greeted Selig-mann? Perhaps Weinberg's position could be characterized thus: weak vegetarian lions valorize weak conciliatory Jews, while tough, authentic, uncompromising writers such as Seligmann get shuffled aside?

There has, of course, long been talk of a "German-Jewish dialogue." In this article, I have endeavored to point to an emerging "German-Jewish-American dialogue." In this dialogue, as in the German-Jewish dialogue, distance and distanciation also play an important role. The results of this distance are at once a certain romanticization (of America as a space of infinite possibilities, of German-Jewish culture as an example of a successful cosmopolitanism) and a sometimes nasty struggle over who holds the copyrights to the German-Jewish cultural tradition (who has the right to write about what). I am looking forward to the next installment of this still young and increasingly animated discussion. Perhaps, as in Maxim Biller's characterization of Philip Roth's work, this messiness and contentiousness are signs of an increasingly vibrant, healthy—and dare I say normal—Jewish culture in today's Germany and its role in the American academy.

Notes

1. For more on this question, see Herzog 1997.

Works Cited

Adelson, Leslie. "There's No Place Like Home: Jeannette Lander and Ronnith Neumann's Utopian Quests for Jewish Identity in the Contemporary West German Context." *New German Critique* 50 (Spring/Summer 1990): 113–34.

Behrens, Katja. "Salomo und die anderen." In *Salomo und die anderen: Jüdische Geschichten*. Frankfurt: Fischer, 1993. 43–53.

Bhabha, Homi K. "Unpacking My Library Again." *Journal of the Midwest Modern Language Association* 28:1 (Spring 1995).

Biller, Maxim. "Philip Roth: Die Zeit der Ungeheuer ist vorbei." *Die Tempojahre*. München: dtv, 1991. 164–70.

Biller, Maxim. "Verrat." *Wenn ich einmal reich und tot bin*. München: dtv, 1990. 160–69.

Dische, Irene. *Fromme Lügen*. München: dtv, 1988.

Dischereit, Esther. *Joëmis Tisch. Eine jüdische Geschichte*. Frankfurt a.M.: Suhrkamp, 1988.

Gilman, Sander L. and Karen Remmler, eds. *Reemerging Jewish Culture in Germany: Life and Literature Since 1989*. New York and London: New York University Press, 1994.

"Growing up Jewish in postwar Germany." *Boston Jewish Advocate* (10 June 1994).

Herzog, Todd. "Hybrids and *Mischlinge*: Translating Anglo-American Cultural Theory into German." *German Quarterly* 70.1 (Winter 1997): 1–17.

Honigmann, Barbara. *Eine liebe aus nichts*. Berlin: Rowohlt, 1991.

Lander, Jeanette. *Die Töchter*. Berlin: Aufbau Taschenbuch Verlag, 1996.

Miron, Susan. "In Enemy Territory." *Congress Monthly (American Jewish Congress)* (June 1994).

Neiman, Susan. "In Defense of Ambiguity." In *Reemerging Jewish Culture in Germany*. Ed. Sander L. Gilman and Karen Remmler. New York and London: New York University Press, 1994.

Peck, Jeffrey. "After Bubis' Death. Critiquing the Critics" (1999). Available at <http://jsis.artsci. washington.edu/programs/europe/wendep/PeckPaper.htm> (accessed on June 28, 2002).

Rabinovici, Doron. "Der richtige Riecher." *Papirnik*. Frankfurt a.M.: Suhrkamp, 1994. 60–73.

Reiss, Tom. "Airy Empire of Dreams," *The Forward* (13 May 1994).

Rothschild, Thomas. "Wiener Besonderheit." *Freitag* 14 (26 March 2004).

Seligmann, Rafael. *Der Milchmann*. München: Deutscher Taschenbuch Verlag, 1999.

Stern, Guy. "Barbara Honigmann: A Preliminary Assessment." *Insiders and Outsiders: Jewish and Gentile Culture in Germany since 1989*. Ed. Dagmar Lorenz. Detroit: Wayne State UP, 1994. 329–46.

Part IV

JEWISH WRITERS IN GERMANY AND AUSTRIA

10

"ATTEMPTS TO READ THE WORLD"

An Interview with Writer Barbara Honigmann

Bettina Brandt

Introduction

Barbara Honigmann was born in 1949, the year in which the former German Democratic Republic was founded. Her parents, both Jews who were atheists and identified as Socialists, had returned from exile in England to settle in East Berlin. Honigmann studied theater at the Berlin Humboldt University and worked for three years in theater production in Brandenburg and Berlin. In 1975, she became a freelance artist and writer. Her early writings were scripts, mostly one-act plays, some of which were later revised for radio.

In 1984, the author moved with her husband and her two sons to Strasbourg, France, where she still lives—a city that provided her with the third largest Jewish community in France and that reflected her own desire to regain her Jewish heritage. While simultaneously at a clear distance and a close proximity to Germany, Honigmann scrutinizes the ambiguities of Jewish identity in the former GDR, life in her chosen exile in France, and her relationship to Germany and the Germans. The French might call her writings *autofiction*, a bricolage of fictionalized autobiography into which she also incorporated the experiences of her parents.

In an essay entitled "Von meinem Urgroßvater, meinem Großvater, meinem Vater und mir" ("On my great-grandfather, my grandfather, my father and me"),

Barbara Honigmann discusses her family's increasing cultural alienation. Her great-grandfather, David Honigmann, was not only the secretary-general of the Silesian railway but also a writer, who battled for the emancipation of the Jews in Prussia his entire life. Her grandfather Georg Gabriel Honigmann, a professor of homeopathy and medical history at the university of Gießen, broke his ties to Judaism and had already assimilated. Finally, her father, Georg Friedrich Wolfgang Honigmann, worked as a journalist for the *Vossische Zeitung* in Berlin before being driven into exile by the National Socialists. When he returned after the war, he joined "that political movement that promised 'equality and fraternity,' liberty was not discussed as much. The movement that claimed not to know any race but only class divisions and that wanted to simply abolish 'The Jewish Question' as such; Communism" (Honigmann 1999: 44).

Barbara Honigmann describes her own relationship to Germany and the German language as follows:

> When I came to that other country, even if it was only three blocks beyond the border, I also began to write—or shall we say, 'really' to write, like my great-grandfather, my grandfather and my father. I wrote, of course, in German, like them, and published with German presses. That was, then, already a return and I had scarcely left. But perhaps writing was also something like homesickness and an assurance that we really did belong together, Germany and I, that we, as they say, could not get away from each other, especially not now, after everything that had happened. (Honigmann 1999: 46)

Honigmann has published three novels: *Eine Liebe aus Nichts* (a love made out of nothing, 1991), *Soharas Reise* (Zohara's Journey, 1996), and *Alles, alles Liebe* (All my love, 2000). Her collections of short stories include *Roman von einem Kinde* (Novel from a Child, 1986), *Am Sonntag spielt der Rabbi Fußball* (Sundays the Rabbi plays soccer, 1998), *Damals, dann und danach* (At that time, then and afterward, 1999), and *Ein Kapitel aus meinem Leben* (A Chapter of My Life, 2004). Her work has been translated into various languages, including French, Dutch, and Italian. *A Love Made Out of Nothing* and *Zohara's Journey* (David R. Godine Publishers) were recently published in English.

A recipient of the coveted *New York Stipend* of the *Literaturfonds*, Barbara Honigmann spent the late fall of 2003 as writer-in-residence at New York University's Deutsches Haus where this interview took place, in German, in late December.

In it the author discusses the background of her epistolary novel *Alles, alles Liebe* for which she won the *Kleist Prize* in 2000. The short novel, a stylistic and compositional delight, introduces us to a group of GDR bohemians trying to come to terms with the inconsistencies of love and life in the 1970s. The theater has a central place in their lives; the novel's main character is a dramaturge and, like the author herself, a child of Jewish emigrants who belong to the founding and political elite of the GDR. The novel portrays the marginalization of Jewish artists and intellectuals against the stifling provincial atmosphere of the GDR.

Interview

In the 1970s, you worked as a dramaturge at the Volksbühne and at the Deutsches Theater. What made you decide to leave the theater behind?

The theater in the GDR was really quite excellent, but I finally realized that it just was not my world. I like being with people, but because I am such a social person, I easily lose myself in a group, and cannot find my independent artistic form. I also tend to avoid conflict. In theater, however, people thrive on conflict and competition. Theater production is a very dynamic group process; many people participate in the creation of a play. I was, also, psychologically speaking, not able to cope with that group mechanism.

I knew that I had an artistic impulse and that I wanted to express myself, although I didn't yet know exactly how. I realized quickly that if I was indeed going to express my artistic impulse, I had to do it on my own. So, I stopped working in the theater and wrote a few plays. I always had a literary interest in the theater rather than a fascination with the limelight. Successful theater people get euphoric every time the lights are turned on. Even the people who work behind the scenes love this atmosphere. Their hearts beat faster when they smell the theater. That was not my situation.

My first play was an adaptation of one of the lesser known fairytales of the brothers Grimm called *Das singende springende Löweneckerchen*. It is a beautiful tale with similarities to *La Belle et la Bête*. I was pregnant at the time, which, in retrospect, is of course funny considering that the first script I wrote was a fairy tale! It's a piece that marks the transition from my work as a dramaturge to my later prose writings; a dramaturge could have adapted this tale for the stage. At that time, I was still living in the GDR and a theater publishing company, the Henschelverlag, was enthusiastic about the play and added the title to their program. It was frequently performed in the GDR. I would say that this had much less to do with the quality of the play itself, but rather that it provided theaters with a niche. It was written in a different tone of voice, not in the tone of socialist realism, and while it was poetic, it was not critical of the system. It could be and was staged, so to speak, next to, and parallel to the official theater program.

When did all of this take place?

I wrote it in 1976 (I always remember that exactly because my son was born in '76), the play was published and premiered in Zwickau in 1977. It was for me mostly a monetary success that allowed me to survive financially until I left the

GDR. They even turned it into a record of fairytales for children. Today, even after so many years, I still encounter people in their mid-thirties who come up to me saying, "I grew up with the *Singende springende Löweneckerchen!*" These GDR performances were excellent productions, with first-rate actors. It really was a stroke of luck.

Your novels, short stories, and also your paintings have provoked
strong autobiographically inspired interpretations. How do
you react to these kinds of readings of your work?

Autobiographically inspired readings might have some value but, most often, they are blind to what is really important in a text or painting. After all, every artistic expression is somehow autobiographical; for certain writers it might just be a little more obvious than in others. But every artistic expression is intensely personal; it has to be that way because it comes out of the personality of the artist. What is interesting in art, however, is what exceeds that, what goes beyond it. It's quite dreadful that readers always want to return to that autobiographical moment, which is the most uninteresting of them all.

How do you explain this urge to retransform art and literature
back into the specific details of a writer's life?

I have asked myself that question and I addressed it in my *Poetikvorlesungen* because it irritates me too. First of all, there is always a certain voyeuristic interest in the reader or the viewer. I am familiar with that and I even share that interest. When I read something that leaves an impression on me, or when I see a great painting, I also want to know who the artist was, whether he had a wife, and whether he cheated on her and with whom. This voyeuristic impulse is also partly produced by the writer or the painter who exposes him or herself, which makes it all even more complex. The one who is doing the exposing, in a way, doesn't have the right to complain later when people are indeed looking.

The second reason is related, but is perhaps a slightly more positive impulse; we have never been able to fully understand how artistic creation functions, where exactly it comes from and where it resides. Indeed, we can't understand that process and there is nobody to explain it, so we look into the autobiography or the biography of an artist hoping to find "the secret," the secret of creation.

There is an interesting story about Henri Bergson. He went to great lengths to legally establish that, after his death, his private letters could not be published. About a year ago, his correspondence was finally published in France in four volumes anyway. I read a review about these letters in *Le Monde* in which the author argued that Bergson's correspondence was utterly conventional and uninteresting. Though I have not read Bergson's correspondence, I easily believe that this is true! Bergson knew that what he intended to get out into the world had been said in his published writings already. His correspondence concerned his social life that was uninteresting to him as well. When they then edit and publish the correspondence anyway, people should not be surprised at the quality of what they get to read. This relentless poking into the author's life can actually harm the work.

A writer like myself, who does indeed circle very much around her own experiences, and the experiences of her parents, can't really complain when people come up to her to ask if this writing is autobiographical. But again it remains pointless nevertheless. What touches us in a literary work is not whether something is true or not.

How would you describe Jewish life in the GDR?

It was insignificant. It really almost didn't exist. The Jewish community had perhaps two hundred members and eighty percent of those were sixty or older. A few years before we left the GDR, there was a worldwide "return to the roots" movement and this wave, in a modest way, also reached us. There were a few people, including my husband and myself, who were interested in learning more about Judaism. We knew so very little!

The Jewish community in East Berlin then started to organize what you would normally call a "youth group," though the group included people from several generations. We would meet once a month to listen to a talk or to attend an event. The majority of those who attended these meetings shunned religion, they were somehow afraid to get in touch with the religion itself, but a few of us were eager. So we formed a small group, with four people only, and we would meet at each other's place to read and discuss religious texts. These four people left the GDR very soon afterward; my husband and I moved to France, the other two to Israel. You cannot easily revive Jewish religion with just four people.

In your acceptance speech of the Kleist Prize in 2000, you describe your life
in Strasbourg as a life in a double bind.[1] Years ago, you still expressed the hope
that this double bind might eventually form a whole, become, as you say, a
"Grossfamilie" (an extended family), but nowadays you stress the impossibility
of bringing these two parts together because everything in this relationship is
askew or "schief." Your speech, really a eulogy for Kleist, also has the wonderful
title, "Das Schiefe, das Ungraziöse, das Unmögliche, das Unstimmige"
(The Skewed, The Ungracious, the Impossible, the Disharmonious). Could
we then perhaps interpret "das Schiefe" as a positive category as well?

Kleist wrote a play called *Der zerbrochene Krug* (The Broken Jar). We should ask ourselves why Kleist chose exactly this title for this comedy that is really quite brilliant and actually funny. People double up with laughter ("*da lacht man sich ja wirklich schief*"), but at the center of the play, there is, nevertheless, something that has been broken. The woman goes to court with her jar, but the jar is broken, broken forever. They can give you money or *Wiedergutmachung* all they want, but the jar remains broken anyway. This must have been one of Kleist's points, underneath it all.

"Positive" is only right in the sense in which I ended my speech. It just simply is this way. Not all things do, and not all things will or can, fit together. I have to accept this situation as is. When all the pieces are broken, when we can barely pick up the fragments to put them next to each other, then you have to accept that and stop trying to put them together, to make them go together. There just are things that don't happen to fit together anymore, just like the pieces of the broken jar.

Kleist was an important author in the GDR and many of us, or at least some of us, recognized ourselves in his confrontation with the status quo without being able to fully separate from it either. I really love Kleist; now that is not very original, to love his writings (laughter), he isn't a "secret tip."

I worked on a production of *Amphytrion* at the *Brandenburger Theater* as an assistant dramaturge. Now, who has the truth in *Amphytrion?* It remains unresolved. What Kleist, this difficult, non-conformist poet exposed, this state of non-resolution, he himself, of course, in the end couldn't bear. I, however, read it as something that one has to endure. This has been my own personal experience. Not that I want to put myself on the same level as Kleist by any means. (Laughter).

The design of my life has been pulling me into two different directions. These two directions do not converge; on the contrary, they diverge. I have stopped asking myself whether that is good or bad, it just is the way it is. Some moments I think this is okay and other moments I think it's quite awful.

My impulse to be closer to religious Judaism or to at least move into that direction, but simultaneously, somehow, to move into literature are two movements that socially, at least, totally diverge, and intellectually, perhaps as well. Perhaps at the very end, again, there might be a resemblance, because both, when looked at from a certain distance, are attempts to read the world. If you do not limit religious Judaism to a certain kind of obsessive *practice*, the circling around the text is, in its best form, I would say, indeed an attempt to read the world. The reader asks himself and the text what is happening, what has happened and how to make sense of it all. At that point perhaps, as a reading practice, they ultimately come together. Religious Judaism, however, looks, of course, quite different in its worldly appearance and has a lot to do with orthodoxy. It manifests itself in a certain way of living that contrasts sharply to an artist's life. It can fit somehow on the intellectual level, where it can perhaps in the distant horizon come together in reading. In daily life, on the other hand, they diverge a lot.

Over the last couple of years, I have increasingly dedicated myself to religious studies. First I studied religious texts with my girlfriends, but none of us knew very much and we wore ourselves out—we exhausted ourselves with the text. Then I found a "maître," well perhaps I should not really call him a " maître," he is younger than I am. We sit with him and work through the prophets and the rabbinical texts (*Maharal*) from the sixteenth century; sometimes we read a chapter from the Torah. He is somebody who knows a tremendous amount, who has studied a lot. He is quite an unusual teacher; he is very orthodox but he does not dress entirely the way you might expect. In this textual appropriation, in this attempt to knock the text around, to try to penetrate into the text, I find a lot of inspiration. I don't mean to imply that this guided reading directly inspires me to write, but it gives me, how shall I call it, perhaps a certain kind of rootedness, a certain knowledge that these things do touch each other, namely precisely in the attempt to read the world. However paradoxical and however difficult that might be.

I also live in a Jewish community, and that is explicitly my choice. But that community also carries, somewhat, all those features that are shared by communities everywhere; it is a little dull, a little petit-bourgeois, a little mediocre, a little narrow-minded, simply the way groups are that absolutely want to be a group. That is sometimes pretty dreadful. But then I tell myself that it also teaches me a lesson, a lesson in modesty. There, in my community, I am not at all the writer. That's not interesting to them at all. It's good to learn this lesson in modesty, but nevertheless to continue to write and to not care what people think.

We just talked about how the German and the Jewish part of your life do not fit, do not really come together, but rather stand next to each other. I could imagine that this particular type of juxtaposition could have resulted in a radical, in an experimental kind of voice. But in your writing that's not at all the case.

That's right, I am not experimental at all! I am, in some ways, probably very conventional. I don't really believe in the experimental a whole lot. I guess, I still have a somewhat naïve understanding of literature, where the writer should tell a story and where the message, some kind of a message anyway, should come across. It is, of course, delightful to play with words or colors but, in the end, it's just play, though that is of course an important part of art.

You mentioned the word naïve earlier. It made me think about how you play with the role of the child, perhaps even with the childish, in some of your texts.

That's a tricky topic. One the one hand, I am, of course, *not* naïve; I know German literature well and I know what has been written and I have read a lot of it. The impulse to simply want to tell a story, I don't know whether we should call that "naïve" or not, is just there, and I believe it is something that any writer who takes himself or herself seriously shares. They actually want to get rid of a story or a message; they want to get it out into the open. This writing goes hand in hand with a certain kind of artistic effort, which is, of course, also not simply naïve in the way cave dwellers perhaps were naïve or children are. But it could be perceived as naïve to simply want to tell a story. If there is a childlike aspect in my writing, then only in one respect—that I set out into the world to tell a certain story, to rid myself of stories so to speak.

You have called France, "the land of freedom," and you describe yourself in France as an observer and a guest. Why do you see yourself as a guest in France?

Well, I am quite simply not French. I am German, German without a doubt, and there is nothing to be done about that either. I am *profondément* not a French woman. I emigrated to France when I was thirty-four years old. I did not grow up in France; there is nothing that I take automatically for granted there. It all quite interests me, and, by now, I also know a fair amount about the country, but I am also still in the process of discovering France and French culture. I don't know Germany all that well either of course, for instance, I really don't know every-thing about Germany at all. But somehow, beginning with the German language and because I grew up there, there is a certain kind of matter-of-factness within me, that I do not have in France. Even after twenty long years in France, I can still be amazed about "how" and "why" things are done a certain French way and I can find certain situations odd or just funny (laughter).

How does the French disinterest toward foreigners, about which you write in "Damals, dann und danach" and about which you say that it is hard to take, express itself in your life?

Well, first of all, the French are *fundamentally* not interested in the non-French. Everything that is not *authentically* French is somehow uninteresting to them. That's laughable, of course, but nevertheless true. They really keep to themselves. I have only been in New York City for about three weeks, but it seems different here. After the first week, my neighbor came by to introduce himself. When I told him that my husband would be joining me soon, he sug-gested that we all should have dinner. After twenty years in Strasbourg, not a single neighbor has had dinner or even just a tea with me. We pass each other in the building and say *bonjour* and that's it.

This, of course, also has its advantages. It means, for instance, that unlike say the Germans, they don't give a running commentary about everything you do. They keep at a distance. I also cherish this built-in distance because, as a result, nobody tries to tell you what to do, there are also fewer regulations than in Germany and they do not pretend to know everything better all the time. But it also means that, in a certain way, they really do stay indifferent. Especially if you don't share a political cause, then personal relations can be limited indeed. Up until a few years ago, I wouldn't have expressed it like this because these are all, in a way, clichés, just generalities and generalities tend not to hold water, but now I am starting to think, somehow they are *true* after all (laughter), something about them seems true.

You describe your neighborhood in Strasbourg as a "quartier populaire," as a place where people from many different national backgrounds are living together. Is there any kind of social interaction between these various groups or have they also already adopted this approach of staying at a distance?

Well, those who have newly arrived in the neighborhood are mostly Arabs. Over the last couple of years, the situation has become more and more tense. The conflict has come to a head; Arabs are actually attacking Jewish schools and school busses, they have desecrated Jewish cemeteries all over France on a regular basis. The situation is really quite critical. This is also a perfect example of how the integration of Arabs in France has failed. This is, of course, not only the fault of the Arabs. The aggressors themselves are idiots, that much is obvious. But they live in those *H.L.Ms*, in those isolated badly built high-rises that you call the projects, almost exclusively amongst themselves. At sixteen, they drop out of school, and then they become unemployed. In the projects, there are no movie theaters; there is really nothing for them to do at all. For all kinds of different historical and world political reasons, they then let their built-up frustrations out on the Jews, on the Jews in France.

The French, they just observe the situation, they don't really know how to react and, above all, they don't take a clear stand. Even the French government made public statements in which it condemned these desecrations only after a long, embarrassing delay. Quite bluntly, the French model of integration has totally and completely failed. The French do not yet dare to admit this openly, but it must have slowly become painstakingly clear to them as well.

You describe the GDR in your novels as provincial and as quite unattractive.

Yes, I still think that is an accurate description.

What is your explanation for "Ostalgie," for the nostalgia for the GDR?

Human beings, plainly and simply, like to fool themselves. They don't like to look at their own situation critically. People in general and, between you and me, Germans in particular, like to always think of themselves as victims. I still remember the stories that my mother told me. You know, she came to the GDR from England, which like Germany, was, of course, bombed as well, where they survived hard times as well. When my mother arrived in Germany after the war, she just could not believe that the Germans were moaning, complaining, and lamenting all of the time, all day long. They almost succeeded in making you believe that *they* were the victims, even the only victims of the war and that nobody else suffered at all. What my mother told me, others also described, and, it seems to me to depict the postwar situation in Germany accurately. That's how it must have been then, and, you know, that is how it is again today.

I fundamentally don't buy the argument that there was a *Führer* and that all citizens, all regular people were just victims. It wasn't like that during the Nazis and it wasn't like that during the GDR either. I know I am quite harsh in my judgment here. The people, and some more so than others, supported, or at least tolerated the system. Many were part of the system, adjusted to it, were at peace with it, profited from it, and established themselves in it quite comfortably. Then, when the system fell apart, a strong earthquake hit and a massive shock followed. People lost their orientation. Earlier, everything had been comfortable and cozy. Life in a prison also has its cozy aspects; you always get your food, you never have to think about anything, and you don't have to make any decisions. That was, somewhat, the way life was in the GDR as well. So now they are trying to hold on to a time or to a product, to things that were known and familiar then. Historical change brings with it big shocks and many people find it difficult to adapt; they simply are not up for the task.

When you were working as a dramaturge in East German theaters,
did you at all cross paths with someone like Emine Sevgi Özdamar who
was involved in that theater scene as well, who worked with Besson
and Marquardt, probably more or less around the same time?

Emine must have been there either shortly before, or shortly after me. I know that her latest novel, which I really would like to read (*Seltsame Sterne starren zur Erde*, 2003), is largely based on those theater experiences. She too was at the *Volksbühne* and must have worked with the same people. But no, our paths did not cross there.

But you were also with Besson at the Volksbühne, right?

Yes, when I was at the *Volksbühne*, Besson was still managing director. I saw him there, but I was working with other people. I lucked out and got an important internship with Karge/Langhoff when they were producing *Die Räuber*. That was probably around 1970. I was still a student and it was simply wonderful to see the whole production process from close up. Later, I worked with Fritz Marquardt, who wanted to produce Kleist's *Penthesilea* at the *Volksbühne*. Heiner Müller was asked to adapt the play, which, in the end, was never performed, at least not at the *Volksbühne*. I addressed the circumstances of this "non-production" in my acceptance speech of the Kleist prize. That was still during the Besson period. We were hanging around a lot and I saw all the comings and goings. I was working as a dramaturge for Marquardt. Karge, Langhoff, and Besson, they were all hanging around. Heiner Müller was around a lot as well. In the theater scene, there is actually a lot of sitting around, which is something that irritates me to no end. Everybody is always drinking a lot a well. It was the local underground scene. It was not, of course, literally "underground" because theater was being produced and plays were being performed on stage, but there was most certainly a subversive climate.

Just after finishing my studies I worked as dramaturge in Brandenburg with Thomas Valentin, the son of Maxim Valentin. Together we produced a Russian play called *Tarelkins Tod* by Alexander Suchovo-Kobylin. But that didn't work out either.

In my last year at the theater, I worked at the *Deutsches Theater* with (Adolf) Dresen, who was working on Kleist's *Prince Friedrich of Homburg*. Dresen died recently, but working with him was a delight; truly inspiring, creative, and productive.

There was nothing boring about East German theater. It really had something to offer and there was a lot more happening in theater than in any other part of the cultural business. It really all goes back to Brecht. It's his legacy; he created a space, a space also for the future that was less assailable than any other cultural sphere. People came from far and away to see a Lorca play or a Besson production.

Even today, when I go to the theater in France (and I don't like to go very often anymore) the plays are utterly predictable, especially when you are, like me, in a certain way, a product of the Brechtian tradition. Peter Brook or Ariane Mnouchkine are wonderful exceptions, of course, but the regular French theater is a bore. It's so very seventeenth century. You can truly feel that they did not have a Brecht. No matter what you think about Brecht, he really aired out the theater, he just swept through it. He changed the theater forever and for that we can't thank him enough!

Notes

1. The quote from the Kleist Prize speech is as follows: "Ein Leben, das ich mir inzwischen in einer wenigen komfortablen Situation eingerichtet habe, in einer doppelten Bindung nämlich: an die deutsche Sprache und Kultur, in die ich hineingeboren wurde, einerseits, und an das Judentum, in das ich ebenfalls hineingeboren wurde, andererseits. Ich versuche dieses 'Doppelleben' anzunehmen, trotz der Komplikationen und Einschränkungen, die es mit sich bringt, und trotz

der Versuchung zum Extrem, die es in sich birgt, denn die einfachere Lösung wäre allemal eine eindeutige Hin-oder Abwendung" (Honigmann 2001).

Works Cited

Adelson, Leslie. "There's No Place Like Home: Jeannette Lander and Ronnith Neumann's Utopian Quests for Jewish Identity in the Contemporary West German Context." *New German Critique* 50 (Spring/Summer 1990): 113–34.

Chedin, Renate. "Nationalität und Identität: Identität und Sprache bei Lea Fleischmann, Jane E. Gilbert und Barbara Honigmann." O'Dochartaigh, Pol, ed., *Jews in German Literature since 1945: German-Jewish Literature?* Amsterdam, Netherlands: Rodopi, 2000. 139–51.

Fachinger, Petra. "Rewriting Home: The Border Writing of Barbara Honigmann and Renan Demirkan." *Rewriting Germany from the Margines.* "Other" German Literature of the 1980s and 1990s. Montreal and Kingston: McGill-Queen's University Press, 2001.

Fries, Marilyn Sibley. "Text as Locus, Inscription as Identity: On Barbara Honigmann's *Roman von einem Kinde.*" *Studies in Twentieth Century Literature.* Summer, 14(2) (1990): 175–93.

Fiero, Petra. "Identitätsfindung und Verhältnis zur deutschen Sprache bei Chaim Noll und Barbara Honigmann." *GDR-Bulletin.* Spring, 24 (1997): 59–66.

Günther, Petra. "Einfaches Erzählen? Barbara Honigmanns 'Doppeltes Grab'." O'Dochartaigh, Pol, ed., *Jews in German Literature since 1945: German-Jewish Literature?* Amsterdam, Netherlands: Rodopi, 2000. 123–37.

Guenther, Christina. "Exile and Construction of Identity in Barbara Honigmann's Trilogy of Diaspora." *Comparative Literature Studies*, vol. 40. no. 2 (2003).

Harig, Ludwig. "Aufbruch in ein neues Leben. Der Weg der Schriftstellerin Barbara Honigmann." *Neue Deutsche Literatur. Zeitschrift für Deutschsprachige Literatur*, 47, no.1 (523), (1999 Jan-Feb): 154–60.

Herzog, Todd. "Hybrids and Mischlinge: Translating Anglo-American Cultural Theory into German." *German-Quarterly* 70, no.1 (1997 Winter): 1–17.

Honigmann, Barbara. *Das singende springende Löweneckerchen.* Berlin: Henschelverlag, 1977.
———. *Die Schöpfung.* Frankfurt am Main: Verlag der Autoren, 1977.
———. *Don Juan.* Frankfurt am Main: Verlag der Autoren, n.d.
———. *Der Schneider von Ulm.* Frankfurt am Main: Verlag der Autoren, n.d.
———. *Roman von einem Kinde.* Sechs Erzählungen. Darmstadt: Luchterhand, 1986.
———. *Eine Liebe aus nichts.* Berlin: Rowohlt, 1991.
———. *Soharas Reise.* Berlin: Rowohlt, 1996.
———. *Am Sonntag spielt der Rabbi Fußball.* Heidelberg: Wunderhorn, 1998.
———. *Damals, dann und danach.* München: Carl Hanser, 1999.
———. *Alles, Alles Liebe.* München: Carl Hanser, 2000.
———. "Eine 'ganz kleine Literatur' des Anvertrauens." *Sinn und Form Beiträge zur Literatur*, no. 6 (2000).
———. "On My Great-Grandfather, My Grandfather, My Father, and Me." Trans. Meghan W. Barnes. *World Literature Today: A Literary Quarterly of the University of Oklahoma (WLT).* 69, no. 3 (1995 Summer): 513–16.
———. "Das Schiefe, das Ungraziöse, das Unmögliche, das Unstimmige. Rede zur Verleihung des Kleist-Preises. "*Sinn und Form. Beiträge zur Literatur.* 53, no. 1, (2001): 31–40.
———. *A Love Made out of Nothing* and *Zohara's Journey.* Boston: David. R. Godine Publishers, 2003.

Lermen, Birgit. In der 'Fremde der Heimat.' Die Schriftstellerin Barbara Honigmann.

In Helga Abret and Ilse Nagelschmidt (Hrsg.), *Zwischen Distanz und Nähe.*
Eine Autorinnengeneration in den achtziger Jahren. Frankfurt a.M: Peter Lang, 1998, S. 107–25.

Peck, Jeffrey, M. "Telling Tales of Exile, (Re)writing Jewish Histories: Barbara Honigmann and Her Novel, *Soharas Reise.*" *German Studies Review* 24. no.3 (2001 Oct): 557–69.

Steinecke, Hartmut. "Schriftsteller sind, was sie schreiben": Barbara Honigmann.
In Dieter Borchmeyer (Hrsg.), *Signaturen der Gegenwartsliteratur. Festschrift für Walter Hinderer.* Würzburg: Königshausen & Neumann, 1999, S. 89–97.

Stern, Guy. "Barbara Honigmann: A Preliminary Assessment" In Dagmar C.G. Lorenz, ed., *Insiders and Outsiders: Jewish and Gentile Culture in Germany and Austria since 1989.* Detroit: Wayne State UP, 1994. 329–46.

BEHIND THE TRÄNENPALAST

Esther Dischereit

She was in a hurry—getting from *Bahnhof Friedrichstraße* to *Schiffbauerdamm*. "Parallel" is what Ann's voice had stressed. Parallel to what she could not remember now. "It's very simple, really very simple, you can't miss it." She felt exposed in this part of the city. Ten years after reunification that hadn't changed. The splashing water in the canal was cloudy, almost black. She would have to keep going.

The neighborhood looked abandoned, the streetcar station far away. *Tränenpalast* and the flight of her girlfriend, the flight of . . . the border guards . . . that's a story . . . that you can now rent the *Tränenpalast*, recreate the GDR . . . for a company outing in original costume . . . or for a rock concert.

Pedestrians were still hurrying by just a minute ago. Nobody walks here. A dark solemn evening. The place is supposed to be called *Scheune*? Shouldn't people be heading toward it? Some people turned a corner, stood still next to her. Have tickets for the Cabaret here. "Do you want them cheaper?" She did not want tickets and hurried along uttering a "*Danke schön.*" Finally, she found the house called *Scheune* where she was meeting Ann.

Ann, whose hours had been filled with spinning leaves stirred up by the wind, with long threads of jellyfish, with birds taking off and landing. Ann had taught dance for children. She had taken her own daughter there often, and had sometimes stayed. Earlier, Ann had danced with a well-known group and then had stopped. Now she choreographed and gave lessons.

The daughter had gone to these lessons a couple of times. It was impossible to tell whether she actually liked going.

She started setting the table, put the plates down, cut the bread open with the long knife and filled a carafe with some water. When she finally sat down, her daughter asked for a different drink. A drop was stuck to the chocolate mug. It was spreading. The child did not like what was on the table. She set a red bowl down. The stain had not become bigger.

"The woman was also wearing a star." With a knife she stabbed a hard lump of butter, it dropped on the tablecloth. She scraped it off the linen. "What do you mean by "star," she said. Her breath was superficial and quick. "Well—you know, a star." She dug the knife into the butter. "What did the star look like?" "You know." The daughter drank her hot chocolate and left.

She went along with the child to the next lesson. Ann wore long dance pants. Her naked feet looked pretty. "Are you Jews?" Ann asked. Last time she was wearing a t-shirt that she had brought back from a trip to Israel once, Ann said, with a giant Star of David on it and the child had said that she also had such a star, at home. A giant Star of David on it . . . Ann had brought a second t-shirt along. Whether the child would like to have it . . . Her daughter remained silent.

During the lesson she went out to the nearest café. She ordered a hot chocolate with Amaretto. Then she went back to pick up the child.

Some time later Ann gave birth. She named the boy Mino, Mino, after a mountain in the land of Canaan, and argued with the registrar about the name. When her daughter had been born she had also argued with the official. For four weeks the child had remained nameless.

Her daughter did not want the star-shirt gift. She gave the newly born Mino her green wool cap. After that they lost sight of each other.

Her legs are dressed in flared pants. Somebody is giving her the finger. "Fuck your knee." He says, "That's a Jew expression." Then he draws a swastika on the cheek of the girl from the bench. "First one side . . ." The pen pushes into her soft skin, "then the other side." "And finally," he says, "finally," and turns toward her, "I will shave the Jew Star on your head. And then"—pause—"And then . . . who is running away? The Jew kid."

Someone is bouncing a ball in the playground. He loses the ball. Loose gravel is scattered around. The player slips. The ball jumps into the bushes. She reads through the telephone class list. Someone picks up the phone. Listens, they don't know each other. He apologizes on behalf of his son. The son will also apologize. "If the Nazis were strong again, and if there were a lot of them again," the girl talks in a steady voice, "then I would have told everyone that I am. I would have already admitted it, you understand?"

The next day she talks to R.R. who tells her that she is not allowed to eat meat if she is a real Jew. "I am a Jew by birth," she says. She sees the girl from the bench. The swastika has been wiped off from her cheek.

Eventually, she found the entrance to the theater. The people from Akko were supposed to play. The people from Akko are well-known. They put on experimental plays, plays that went on for several days and had something to do with the Holocaust. It is still early, windy, coats in the checkroom. She would rather go inside, not wait here. There is a German shepherd on a leash sitting at the entrance. Perhaps she should leave. She is not going to see a play that begins with a German shepherd on a leash at the entrance. The ticket cost 58 DM. Actually someone was supposed to meet her here. She stays in front of the entrance, does not go in. A group therapy experiment for Aryans—. . . She would not . . .

Young women are coming in; their fresh faces are slightly red from the onset of the cold evening. Strands of hair are coming undone from their hairdos. The coats, the gloves . . . they are going to the auditorium. Are coming back, want to talk to the owner. Which owner? The owner of the dog. The woman at the coat check says: "He'll be here in a few minutes." She is sure of that. Asks if she can help. The women wait. Carrying a long-stem yellow rose the man enters the building. His coat gapes open. The woman from the coat check takes his hat. "It is about the dog," says the young woman, "about the dog." "One moment, please," says the man. He asks for the press tickets and inquires whether the ticket person had seen these names. Other nights you can dance tango here. That is his great success. Now he takes a step toward the young woman. "You wanted to talk to me . . ." The actor is supposed to take the rose from him. "You can't keep a dog on such a tight leash," "To leave him home isn't a solution either, don't you think?" The theater bell rings.

12

GERMANS ARE LEAST WILLING TO FORGIVE THOSE WHO FORGIVE THEM

A Case Study of Myself

Jeannette Lander[1]

I hesitated when I was asked to participate here. "Jewish Identity and Jewish Writing in German after 1980," was going to be the topic. Further down in the program description I read the following statement: "After 1945 a Jewish Literature in Germany seemed possible only as labor of mourning. Only in the 1980s, after a period of silence, could a new Jewish literature evolve in the German-speaking countries." I asked myself whether this description applied to me, whether my writing fell under this statement. Three of my novels, as well as a volume of stories, all with Jewish themes, were published in this German-speaking environment of ours during the seventies—that is to say in a *period of silence*. One more novel, one in which Jewishness plays only a peripheral role, came out in 1980. Perhaps I had purposefully pushed the Jewishness aside since my Jewish literature, as this thesis shows, was not perceived as such. "Boundaries crossing Boundaries"—I wanted to see if I could cross this limit.

"Jewish Identity and Jewish Writing" is supposed to mean that what one carries inside, what one drags along, what one can't leave behind is Jewish identity. Is that right? Is this Jewishness within me an inner border, one which restricts me, holds my spirit captive, clouds my vision, regardless of where and when I write—in the United States, Germany or in Sri Lanka, before or after 1980. And regardless of the topic?

I personally don't experience it like that, I experience my spirit as free, my vision as clear, but perhaps I am wrong. Maybe I am making a mistake when I claim that I am crossing boundaries completely without luggage, and can freely buy what the foreign has to offer. When I assume that I am open-minded, impartial, intellectually able to judge factually, and artistically able to abstract from myself in my work.

I will look into this because the presence of inner boundaries that I deny would explain some of what has happened to me in my literary life in Germany.

In my case, the luggage would be doubly heavy because, besides a Jewish identity, I also have an American identity on my back. That is to say: I see as a wide-eyed American but can—with Jewish *Witz*—interpret what I see in my favor.

When I came to Germany in 1950—I was eighteen—I was wide-eyed, naive, and it worked in my favor—I understood this with my Jewish instinct—to see what I saw in a *positive* light. More than a decade later I described my arrival in the novel *On Strange Ground*:

> The simple geranium was the first flower that had caught Yvonne's eye when she arrived from the States, Yvonne, eighteen years old. Pregnant. Children leading children.
>
> Coming from the airport. In the flower boxes of the bombed-out tenement houses five years after the war. In the flower boxes of the half bombed out. Red geraniums in the only flower box on the only balcony of the whole ruin, the one flower box that was still there. Otherwise just hollow windows in a hollowed-out facade.
>
> Because she had collected scrap in America, scrap metal for those bombs, carried to school through the dusty-sunny streets of a small Southern town, Yvonne, schoolgirl, patriotic-proud, had collected and carried it. And it was not that long ago.
>
> Geranium ruins. Ruins period. Streets full of ruins through which the bus with the funny snout front rattles along with Yvonne. Yvonne, who is pregnant and should not be rattled, is not frightened of ruins for which she collected and carried bomb-hate-scrap-metal, to hit German geranium houses from which the blond tattooed SS had collected and carried off her people, through the streets, the same streets, and he holds her hand, blond, in the snout-nosed bus, Friedrich-blond.
>
> Ruins that bombs have made look like this. "Bomb" until now had been a word carried by her mouth like the scrap metal carried by her arm. Every Friday the plain-and-frank teacher announced the number of bombs that could be produced from the scrap metal that had been collected by this class.
>
> A gold paper star was attached on the oversized class list on the wall, every Friday, next to her name; a gold paper star for extraordinary patriotism not merely a blue one for ordinary patriotism. Thus Yvonne collected. It had to be a gold one so that it resembled the yellow one. All that was missing from the gold star was

the other point. For those wearing the yellow star Yvonne collected scrap, for her people, in Germany, in Berlin, in these streets.

"Germany" just a word, even though her small, round Yiddish father, sitting in his deep armchair, read aloud from the Yiddish newspaper, the names of the streets, the squares that he once knew in the old country, night after night, more and more tired all the time, like the Rabbi read out loud the names of the families that had been carried off; though his cheeks shuddered, his shoulders sank as he read out loud the street names where the bombs fell, Germany was just a word.

A word like enemy. No death' s head windows, no geranium ruins, no people in Germany. "Thinkers but no people." We, the ones Yvonne passes in her rattling bus, and they don't even notice it. Pay no attention to the snouty bus and the death's head windows, people who plant respectable geraniums, for whom America is just a word, a word like airlift.

But bomb is more than a word. For Friedrich as well, whose hand she is holding and who is holding hers. Who had been a sniper, lying in the trenches and protecting the camps in which people wearing the yellow star were forced to stand naked in front of those who wore the uniform that he wore, monstrously carrying on, in black boots, stiffly moving his legs forward in parade step, those who ordered that the ovens should be fired up.

These are people. Like everywhere. Like Friedrich next to her. Her husband. People who did not want it. Who did not know it. And did not believe. Not.

This novel, my second, received positive reviews in Germany, but did not sell well. It has not been translated into English. Nevertheless it is, like my first novel, taught in numerous seminars, and is the topic of Master theses and dissertations in the US as well. Until now, I had not really given these differing receptions much thought. But it is a pattern. That is why I dare to put forward an explanation.

My novels are all based on an attitude of trying to understanding. I am searching for the reasons behind the phenomena. I want to understand why things are the way they are. My characters are always searching. Like Yvonne. They want to understand.

Presumably, this attitude of mine has something to do with the humanism of the Jewish religious philosophy. It also has something to do with my American heritage. To be understanding, to not carry a grudge, to forgive—positive characteristics as far as I am concerned. On the other hand, this attitude implies that there is a guilt that needs to be forgiven. Someone who represses guilt and compensates for it also avoids those who forgive him. He does not forgive that he is forgiven and thereby reminded of his guilt again. If anything, he thinks he should be cursed, punished, confronted.

I should have insulted the public like Peter Handke. Or shown allegorically how they wallow in their own mud a la Heiner Müller. Or even better, not in an allegorical or in any other figurative way, but naturalistically, which is an increasingly successful formula on German stages; the characters naked, covered in blood, playing with their excrement, as Elfriede Jelinek prefers in her plays.

Germans, so it seems, want to be humiliated, tortured, otherwise they can't get worked up. It is not by chance that German writers, including our new Nobel laureate, prefer the language of excrement in their love scenes. This kind of thing pleases literary critics in this country. It is precisely in the revolting and the disgusting that they seem to find the possibility of aesthetic transcendence. A love scene is something difficult to handle. It easily slips into a wine-and-candlelight sentimental style. Or becomes clinical—and written in French, on top of it—like in Thomas Mann's *Magic Mountain*. He had to turn to French because of the lack of erotic vocabulary in German. In German, we fall into a rather obscene vocabulary when we want to represent the act of love. Try it! It is an eye- and ear-opening experiment.

In my first novel, *A summer in the Week of Itke K.*, which unfolds in the summer of 1945 in Atlanta, Georgia, I avoid this problem. Itke, the main character and narrator is fourteen years old. Her parents, Jewish immigrants from Poland, run a local grocery store in a predominantly African American neighborhood. The apartment is located above the store. In this scene Itke's mother comes into the bedroom and pulls down the blinds:

> The shades, which would have offered a view of Tessie's house. Fat black Tessie who sold moonshine liquor under the table. The shades facing the back yard where the honeysuckle covered the wall of Kovsky's Krom, climbed up towards the windowsill of my bedroom, which it had just reached in my fourteenth summer, and in the hottest of all hot May and June nights smothered the air around my bed, sickly sweet with the smell of honeysuckle. In the back yard hidden, under the wooden staircase maybe, between the staircase and the stilts perhaps, or possibly in the corner between the store wall and the staircase, where the additional room that had been built on stilts created a "roof" and cast a shadow, perhaps that is where the lovers meet, late on Saturday nights. Mamma's shades were no match against the whispering voices, against the groans, against his increasingly short commands.
>
> I could imitate them, could reproduce them exactly the next morning in front of the mirror, but I could not find them amongst the clarinet voices of the blacks in the store. Every Saturday night I listened for them. In vain. Simmering chimeras. In the Deep South the heat starts on May fourteenth.

In this first novel, I experimented with language, played with form, but in the end it is a political novel, just like all my other works. Oddly enough, German literature critics missed this point. I drew a parallel between Itke's sudden eruption into sexual maturity and the sudden uprising of rebellious black youths immediately after World War II. I represented the solidarity that existed at the time between the two minorities, Black and Jewish, in the American South.

In one of the novel's scenes, the narrator imagines what takes place on a rainy day in the tiny packed store of her parents as if it were a ballet. Tatte, her father, is the maestro. Young Sam, who works for Tatte, is the lead dancer. The other clients belong to the *corps de ballet*. In this scene Tatte takes a telephone order:

The maestro grabbed the hellohellohellosaying receiver from the basket of turnips and excitedly continued his conducting. Immediately, the lead stood behind him on the tip of his toes, watched over his shoulder to read the strange scorebook and leapt excitedly from shelf to shelf, gathering the ordered items. To the right of the divine dancer stood Ty Jones and Wilmateen in a relaxed beautiful flirting pose. Aunt Bell and Tessie formed the aesthetic counter part on the left of the masterfully leaping dancer. The violins were playing from all around the door. The rain thundered in the background. The maestro was selling by phone in the Monday harmony of Kovsky's Krom.

All at once a white man ducked in through the door. With an umbrella. And a hat. With a paper file filled with dense typing. With a look and a pause for Tatte, who suddenly was no longer conducting, merely taking a phone order. With a belly and a receding gaze at Sam, who suddenly was no longer dancing but rather just placing the can of fried beans on the counter table. With a starched collar and a step back by Tessie and Aunt Bell who suddenly turned away, not just from him but from the whole scene.

With wide, respectable pants and a glance up and down at Wilmateen, at which Ty Jones raised his quills like a porcupine.

When Tatte put the conducting-pencil back behind his ear, the curtains of the ballet performance of Itke's imagination had long since fallen. The man stood on the deserted dance stage and said: "Mr. Kovsky?" and the emptiness around him echoed: ovsky, sky, i.

"Jo" said Tatte.

"Do you know a certain Ty Jones?" ones, one o?

"Neen," said Tatte. Said it immediately and spontaneously and without hesitating and without turning right or left and without wrinkling his forehead. "No." Sam did not make a face. Tessie did not say that Tatte should not lie, that nobody was worth lying for. Ty Jones did not hide, did not shyly look out of the corner next to Wilmateen. Wilmateen gave no sign to be a part of it. Mamma did not start shaking. Aunt Bell did not put on her defiant face. I did not take note of the collapse of Tatte's principles in order to confront him with it at the right moment later. We do not know any Ty Jones, Mister.

"You don't know Ty Jones?"

"No," said Tatte, "Un Eich kenn ich ochet nicht." You I don't know either.

"Rudy Brown, SuperSalesIncorporated. You see I am looking for . . . how odd, your name and address are written down here. This Jones gave you as a recommendation when he bought a radio.

"So?" said Tatte. "Jo, dos ist seltsam." Strange isn't it.

"But we don't have an address for him. He was in the midst of moving. He was going to give us the new address. He hasn't made any payments yet."

"A schlimazel," said Tatte.

"No. Indeed. I mean." Yes, he has to make the first payment within three months if he wants to keep the appliance. I need to get the appliance back, ack, ck.

"So."

"Yesterday time ran out." Ou, u , t.

"Nu, mir ist er nicht bekannt." Well, I don't know him.

"Maybe his name isn't really Jones," said Ty Jones.

"Well, that is the name he gave. I assume he showed some type of I.D. Yes, it says here that he used an envelope with his address on it as I.D."

"Well, then it must be right," said Ty Jones. "I just figured that Jones is a name, you know, that you say even when your name is Smith."

"That Company there must be hot to get rid of their radios. Let you take them away and don't really ask where to." said Tessie.

"Who covers the cost, you?" asked Wilmateen.

"Me?" laughed the representative. His laugh sounded hollow low ow.

"No, no. The salesman who sold the appliance."

"Nice job," said Sam.

"Abi es soll nicht der Company varlieren ka Geld! Asa Company, as groiße." "God forbid, the Company should lose its money. Such a big Company." Even Mamma said.

"Then why you showing up here and no salesman?" asked Wilmateen.

"He's the fucking company-blood-hound," said Ty.

"Nice job," said Sam.

"No, he eats well," said Ty.

"But the company eats better," said Wilmateen.

"Leave him alone, it aint none a his fault," said Aunt Bell.

"Skunks have to make a living too," said Tessie.

"Äfscher wollt es gewe'en besser, Ihr wollt gegangen." "Perhaps, it would be better if you left now," said Tatte.

He moved into the no-man's-land around the Company Man, seemed short in front of his height, seemed more wrinkled in front of his smoothness, filled with garlic breath that no-man's-land between the scotch-and-soda-face and the turnips-and-fatback-belly, sent a garlic phalanx into battle: "Mir kennen alle nicht asa Mann, weleche ihr sucht. Ich gloib tacke, es wollt gewe'en besser, ihr wollt jetzt gegangen." "We don't know this man your looking for. I really do think it would be better if you left now."

"Yeah, you sure as hell have other folks to search for 'round here," Ty said at the border of the no-man's-land. Sam crossed the border, quickly snuck up close to the white man, light and fast next to his ear, although the guy was backing away, Sam covered his mouth and whispered loudly: "Wanna buy a nice switchblade? Cheap. Excellent. Look!" and in a flash the thing came out of his pocket and, in half a move, was in the Company-Man's face. His hand slid quickly and automatically to the polished, black, hip belt that shone from under his jacket—but Ty already was holding his one arm and Sam the other and Ty said:

"It's not all just fat underneath there."

And they brought him to the door.

And Sam said: "Äfscher es wollt gewe'en besser, ihr wollt gegangen." "Perhaps it would be better if you left now." They pushed the man out and shut the door behind him, and Tatte was ash gray, and Mamma shaky after all. The man stood outside in the rain and yelled something, which in the downpour was hard to understand. But it surely was what Tatte was saying now: "The police he will call," and right now Tatte has no use for the police. Maybe he will lose his business license.

Sam paraded up and down with the hat and the umbrella of the Company Man. Chase that rat; got a brand new hat, and a fine umbrella; Sam's such a fine black fella; chase that rat.

In this passage, I'm saying something about race discrimination in the US, and about solidarity amongst minorities. But with whom does the German reader identify? With the African-Americans? With the smalltime crook Ty Jones? With the knife-wielding half-pint Sam? With fat Tessie who sells moonshine? Or maybe perhaps with Tatte, the Yiddish-speaking Jew?

At the time, I could smile at the passage, but now I recognize it as wry Jewish humor or as down-home American humor. It is with the duped representative of the white race, standing outside in the rain, no hat and no umbrella, who is only doing his job after all, that the respectable German-speaking reader is more likely to identify.

In the novel *On Strange Ground*, where I denounce the bigotry in certain circles of American Jews, I must also have hit a false note. In that novel the main character, Yvonne—a Jewish American who over the years has become thoroughly European—is visiting her family in the United States. In one of the scenes, her own family and their most intimate friends reproach Yvonne for having betrayed herself and her people because she is a Jew living in Germany. She has abandoned her people, they reproach her:

I have not abandoned you, said Yvonne. I have not abandoned you, no matter where I live and among whom. For thousands of years we have been living among strangers and never lost ourselves. You have lost yourselves. You have abandoned yourselves now that you have a country, that you call your "property," Better for you to have remained moneychangers, now that you have become haters. Better to be moneychangers than soldiers. Better usurers than conquerors.

What a foreboding fragment. This novel was published in 1971. But already with the premise I hit the wrong note for readers in Germany. Because not only Jews in America have some deep-seated emotional reaction against Jews living in Germany. As becomes more and more clear, a large portion of the German population also have something vague and instinctive against it.

Something similar happened to my novel *The Daughters*, which partially takes place in Israel. I already examined the victim-perpetrator question in that novel, which appeared a quarter of a century ago. A dispute between two brothers brings out the problem. The younger one, Benjamin, who sympathizes with the Palestinians, is against violence. The older brother says:

I am fed up with you crying doves, Benjamin. Afterwards you will erect a new monument: *Jad Vashem II* with a flame. "Shed no innocent blood.

Better to march into the sea, as you did then into the gas chambers. You, Benjamin, you and those who think as you do!"

"And why did we march into the gas chambers?"

"Oh, come on, what are you asking?"

"It is a serious question."

"The story can't be unfamiliar to even you with your tender age, dear Benjamin. At the very latest with the Eichmann trial you must have had the opportunity to familiarize yourself with it. Or don't you understand the nature of dictatorship. Don't you know what terror is?"

"That's not an answer, it is the avoidance of personal responsibility."

"I don't understand."

"Yes, why did we march into the gas chamber? Don't tell me we had no choice. I don't want to hear we had no choice. There is something not right. I tell you, we have learned nothing from it until we know, why we went into the gas chambers. It is also not enough to know that they wanted to murder us. It is not enough to know why they wanted to kill us. No economic, sociological, political, nor any psychological examination of their actions is sufficient. That's what they should do. That is what they need to do. We have to give an accounting of our own actions. We have to come to terms with our own past, not theirs, but our own. It is besides the point to judge Eichmann. What we need to know is why we stripped ourselves naked before him, obeyed his command to dig our own grave, lined up at the edge in front of his shiny boots, let him shoot us to the crack of his whip—quietly and neatly, so that no sound reached the outside.

What kind of people are we that we could do this? What made us into people like that? We, who praised ourselves because we educated ourselves and lived our lives according to the high ideals of humanism. What kind of people are we educating now? We can't know that until we know what kind of a people we are to have educated our fathers, because they are the ones, our fathers, who let themselves be wiped out like flies. I want to know why we marched into the gas chambers. Don't tell me we had no choice. You can choose whether you get shot in the chest or in the back. Otherwise it will just continue with this "no choice". I am sick of it. Now we also have no choice. Now the Arab world forces us to be strong, forces us to put on boots, to take up the whip, forces us to raze their villages, to destroy them. There is something not right. We are always the victims. We are always compelled. First to die. Then to kill. Always we have no choice, and we will never have one, until we find out why we didn't have one before.

And we will never find out. Because we don't want to know. We are afraid actually, we could gain insight about us, knowledge whose logical conclusion would be that we have to change ourselves. It is more comfortable, to remain as we are, to condemn the others for their inhuman treatment, and to condemn others yet again because they compel us to treat them inhumanly and always the same old song about having no choice. The melody is so pleasing to our ears. A lullaby. A lament, a lullaby lament."

This passage, I think, is more relevant than ever. Yet again, this scene as well as the whole novel received no attention, even though it was published by Suhrkamp, who also carried Walser.

Why? Because I did not insult, I did not attack anyone directly? Because Benjamin wants to understand, both the perpetrators and the victims. And this attitude is unforgivable to people who deep inside understand all coming to terms with history as a memorial and a caesura.

I have learned that I have learned nothing that would change my mind. And even in my more recent books, *Leftovers. A Brief Erotics of the Kitchen*, I adopt this disgustingly humanistic tone. In this novel, I describe in pure and simple autobiographical terms my first passage from New York to Rotterdam, eleven days on the Dutch ship "Veendam" followed by my arrival.

As pleasant and exciting as this passage had been for me, a young girl without experience of the world from the mostly rural state of Georgia, what I initially encountered in Europe was just as unexpected and frightening. The world from which I had come was still intact. To be sure, the willingness to engage in violence, which defines it today, was already latent in my childhood. I had merely never been confronted with it. And although I had heard and seen the newspapers and radio reports, the weekly newsreels in the movies, the stories from soldiers and veterans of the war in Europe, I can say that war and the consequences of war had never before penetrated my image of the world. No radio report, no newsreel could have conveyed to me the reality into which I entered as I left the ship in Rotterdam. The city lay in ruins and ashes. Five years after the war had ended—five years are for a nineteen-year old a considerable length of time, a quarter of her life—and I believed that I could still see smoke rising out of those ruins as I walked past them alone and lost across boards that covered the broken asphalt in the bombed out streets. I could smell death. I could hear the screams. I thought there would never be life here again, life as it had been, normal life as I had lived it totally unconcerned and unaware not eleven days before. And the small daily worries, that had kept me and the people which I had left behind in America, so busy, seemed to be not just banal but outrageous in the face of this suffering.

It cannot be a coincidence that not far from the spot where the harbor bus brought us I saw a red neon sign with the letters "Hotel Atlanta." I did not ask what it cost to stay overnight. That evening I did not leave the hotel again. Once inside I was back on the world of the ocean steamer. In the hotel restaurant we ate on elegant dishes with gold trim as if the war had never happened. The heavy, old silver utensils were overly large in my hands. The waiter laid in my lap a damask serviette embroidered with the hotel emblem. Without hesitating he spoke to me in English quietly and graciously, yes, even deferentially. It occurred to me that I belonged to the nation that had been in part responsible for the liberation of Holland. I was very disoriented.

No less so in Berlin. What was I here? An enemy? A liberator? An occupier? It took me a long time to accept that it was in part American bomber pilots who had wrought the destruction that I saw before me. It took me a very long time to stop asking with each new acquaintance, how the person in question had acted under Hitler, how he had stood then and how he stood now regarding the extermination of the Jews. Nevertheless, I could not sort my feelings according to good and bad, according to victims and perpetrators, according to guilt and retribution. I was an American woman, a Jew, the wife of a German, who had been a private in Hitler's Wehrmacht, I was soon going to be the mother of his child. I had naively, as well as despairingly, wished that these designations would simply fall away, designations which divide people up into groups that out of some supposed loyalty stand opposed to each other as enemies, hating and killing, destroying all the human beauty in the world by smashing it evilly and senselessly to the ground.

Note

1. Translated by Bettina Brandt and Daniel Purdy. Daniel Purdy is Associate Professor of German at Penn State University. His publications include *The Tyranny of Elegance: Consumer Cosmopolitanism in the Era of Goethe* (Johns Hopkins UP, 1998) and *The Rise of Fashion* (Minnesota, 2005).

13

MISCHMASCH OR MÉLANGE

Doron Rabinovici[1]

It's a photograph of a school class taken in the year nineteen hundred seventy-six. I am not, or to be more precise, was not the boy clad in lederhosen standing in front of the pencil sharpener. My mother, who had escaped extermination, would have never put me in this traditional Alpine costume. I was also not the chubby boy whom my beloved grade school teacher had just asked a question and who, as the photograph shows, is looking rather timidly at the book in front her. I remember that already on the first day of kindergarten my Austrian peers all seemed a little too plump, docile and stiff to me. They somehow looked like bread dumplings; round, white bloated pasty figures.

On our first day in Vienna, my brother and I immediately ran out of the house immediately. Without believing our parents or their warnings. We wanted to go find playmates because we, two Israeli brothers, were used to doing it like that. In Tel-Aviv we had been able to romp around with our friends in front of our house and to frighten all the cats in the courtyard. But in the Taubstummengasse and in the Favoritenstraße of the 1960s we just stood there, mute and at a complete loss: no children our age anywhere to be seen, instead adults only, some of them with dogs on leashes. Cars were roaring by.

The apartment had excited me. Its rooms soared higher than anything I, little Sabre, had ever seen. The corridor to the outside seemed uncannily long and, for a long time, uncanny. Here, if you wanted to leave your house, you had to move through long corridors, past the mezzanine and the first floor, push open the swinging doors, only to arrive at the doors of a gate which even grown ups could not move. Small doors had been cut into the wood of these huge house gates, but to slip through them you still needed a key.

I was not a Jew in Austria, instead I became a curious Maccabee in the Donau City and a Jekke in Tel-Aviv, a Southerner amongst the Alpine residents and a model Viennese child in the Oriental native country, where he alienated and delighted his relatives with his "Bitteschön" and "Dankeschön," with his "toda raba" and "bewakascha." My parents believed that next year, or at the latest, the year after that, we would go back to Israel: they promised each other. This intention was repeated as many times as the departure was postponed, to the next year, or the year after that.

I am the boy at the far right. We were an all boys class and I was the only one who thought that this division was rigidly Austrian, behind the times, and who really liked to play with the girls next door. The guy on the picture, who once was me, is turned away from the others somehow and looks at the teacher only from over his shoulder.

Behind the teacher is her box with all the letters: the shrine for the beginning reader, a box of magic tricks. I had moved to Austria before the age of three. Nobody understood me in the foreign city. A little boy was walking with his mother through Vienna, insulting some men in Hebrew: "You dumb ass, I am so little and can already talk, and you are so big and can't understand me." The boy wanted to learn German as quickly as possible, wanted to speak it better than the locals.

I put the language to use, and it was not so much what I said, but rather who I was that made my words contradict the silence that dominated Austria during the Sixties. The East-European Jewish survivors had not raised their Israeli son to stand still and stay quiet. I was supposed to appropriate the foreign without losing what was mine in the process. My name was a sign. No sooner had I uttered it, we had enough material for a two-hour discussion.

Out of the two-sided necessity of not belonging I made a double virtue. I learned things about which Israeli children knew nothing, and I knew a world about which the Viennese classmates had no inkling. The little boy, who I was, found himself in the role of the mishmash. I was a changeling of different countries and continents, who was turned into a remnant of a centuries-old homelessness and a keepsake of a new migration.

Note

1. Translated by Bettina Brandt and Daniel Purdy. Daniel Purdy is Associate Professor of German at Penn State University. His publications include *The Tyranny of Elegance: Consumer Cosmopolitanism in the Era of Goethe* (Johns Hopkins UP, 1998) and *The Rise of Fashion* (Minnesota, 2005).

CONTRIBUTORS

Richard Bodek is Professor of History at the College of Charleston. He is the author of *Proletarian Performance in Weimar Berlin* (Camden House, 1997). At present, he is working on a manuscript tentatively entitled, *Berlin 1932: City on the Verge of a Nervous Breakdown.*

Bettina Brandt grew up in the Netherlands and in Belgium. She received master's degrees in French and German from the University of Utrecht and a PhD in Comparative Literature from Harvard University. Brandt taught at M.I.T. and Columbia University before joining Montclair State University as an Assistant Professor of German. She has published on Romanticism, contemporary German literature, women and the avant-garde, German comedy, theater, and translation. She is currently finishing a book about Herta Müller, Emine Sevgi Özdamar, and Yoko Tawada, tentatively entitled *Cutting Out: The Aesthetics of the Avant-Garde and the Literature of Migration in German after 1989.*

Iris Bruce is an Associate Professor of German and Comparative Literature at McMaster University in Hamilton, Ontario, Canada. She is the author of *Kafka and Cultural Zionism. Dates in Palestine* (University of Wisconsin Press 2007) and has published many articles on Kafka and Yiddish literature, Jewish folklore, Zionism, and Kafka in popular culture.

Esther Dischereit is a poet, novelist, essayist, and stage and radio dramatist. Her works include *Joëmis Tisch* (Joëmi's Table, 1988), *Merryn* (1992), *Als mir mein Golem öffnete* (When My Golem Opened the Door, 1997), and *Mit Eichmann an der Börse* (With Eichmann at the Stock Exchange, 2001). She has won stipends from the Hessian Ministry for Science and Art, the Stiftung Preussische See-handlung in Berlin, the Berlin Senate, and the Erwin-Strassmann-Stiftung.

Roland Dollinger holds a PhD from Princeton University. He is an Associate Professor of German and German Literature at Sarah Lawrence College and is author of *Totalität und Totalitarismus: Das Exilwerk Alfred Döblins* (Königshausen & Neumann 1997), and co-editor of *Philosophia Naturalis* (Königshausen & Neumann 2001), *Unus Mundus* (Peter Lang 1992), and *A Companion to the Works of Alfred Döblin* (Camden House 2004). He has published essays on Goethe, Romanticism, Döblin, and Şenocak.

Petra Fachinger is an Associate Professor of German at Queen's University. She holds a PhD in comparative literature from the University of British Columbia. She is the author of *Rewriting Germany from the Margins: "Other" German Litera-ture of the 1980s and 1990s* (McGill-Queens UP 2001), as well as several articles on transnational literature in English and in German. She is co-editor of the *Seminar* Special Issue, "Poland in Postwar German Literature and Culture."

Margy Gerber received her PhD from Stanford University and is Professor Emer-itus of German at Bowling Green State University. She was primary organizer of the annual interdisciplinary New Hampshire Symposium on the German Demo-cratic Republic (1977–1990) and the New Hampshire Symposium (1991–2000) and a seven-time Director of Bowling Green's Academic Year Abroad in Salz-burg program between 1976 and 1996. She is author of numerous articles on East German and German-Jewish topics.

Cathy S. Gelbin received her PhD in German Studies from Cornell University. She is an Associate Professor in German Studies at the University of Manchester, UK. She specializes in German-Jewish culture, Holocaust studies, gender, and film. Her publications include: *An Indelible Seal: Race, Hybridity and Identity in Elisabeth Langgässer's Writings* (Blaue Eule 2001), *Archiv der Erinnerung: Inter-views mit Überlebenden der Shoah* (co-ed., Verlag für Berlin-Brandenburg 1998), and *AufBrüche: Kulturelle Produktionen von Migrantinnen, Schwarzen und jüdischen Frauen in Deutschland* (co-ed., Ulrike Helmer Verlag 1999). She has written on postwar Jewish authors and artists such as Esther Dischereit and Tanya Ury, and is currently preparing a cultural history of the Golem trope in nineteenth and twentieth-century German culture.

Hillary Hope Herzog is an Assistant Professor in German Studies at the Uni-versity of Kentucky. She has written articles on a wide range of topics, including Arthur Schnitzler, Austrian-Jewish culture, and Irmgaard Keun. She is currently working on a book about Jewish Vienna from the end of the nineteenth to the beginning of the twenty-first century.

Todd Herzog is an Associate Professor of German Studies at the University of Cincinnati. He is editor of *A New Germany in a New Europe* (Routledge 2001, with Sander Gilman) and author of *Crime Stories* (Berghahn Books forthcoming). He is currently working on a filmography of German cinema 1895–1945 (Caboose Books forthcoming).

Jeannette Lander describes herself as a "German author of Jewish-American-Polish origins." She was born in New York City, grew up in Atlanta, and currently lives in Berlin. She is author of numerous poems, essays, novels, and monographs in Yiddish, English, and German. Her works include *Ein Sommer in der Woche der Itke K.* (A Summer in the Week of Itke K. 1971), *Die Töchter* (The Daughters 1976), *Jahrhundert der Herren* (Century of Gentlemen 1993), *Überbleibsel: Eine kleine Erotik der Küche* (Leftovers: A Little Erotic Tale from the Kitchen 1995), and *Eine unterbrochene Reise* (An Interrupted Journey 1996).

Benjamin Lapp received his PhD from the University of California, Berkeley. He is currently an Associate Professor of History at Montclair State University. His is author of *Revolution from the Right: Politics, Class and the Rise of Nazism in Saxony, 1919–1933* (Humanities Press/Brill 1997). He is now pursuing a research project on Holocaust survivors in the United States.

Dagmar C. G. Lorenz is Professor of Germanic Studies and Director of Jewish Studies at the University of Illinois, Chicago. Her book publications include *Keepers of the Motherland: German Texts by Jewish Women Writers* (Nebraska UP 1997) and *Verfolgung bis zum Massenmord. Diskurse zum Holocaust in deutscher Sprache* (Peter Lang 1992). She is a former editor of *German Quarterly* and has edited and co-edited five books, including companion volumes on Canetti and Schnitzler.

Doron Rabinovici was born in Tel Aviv and has lived in Vienna since 1964. He is an author, essayist, and historian. He has won numerous prizes for his writings, which include *Papirnik* (1994), *Suche nach M* (The Search for M, 1997), *Instanzen der Ohnmacht* (Agencies of Powerlessness, 1997), *Credo und Credit* (2001), and *Ohnehin* (Anyway, 2004).

Index